IN GOOD RELATION

IN GOOD RELATION

History, Gender, and Kinship in Indigenous Feminisms

EDITED BY SARAH NICKEL
AND AMANDA FEHR

UNIVERSITY OF MANITOBA PRESS

In Good Relation: History, Gender, and Kinship in Indigenous Feminisms

28 27 26 25 24 3 4 5 6 7

University of Manitoba Press
Winnipeg, Manitoba, Canada
Treaty 1 Territory
uofmpress.ca

Cataloguing data available from Library and Archives Canada
ISBN 978-0-88755-851-1 (PAPER)
ISBN 978-0-88755-853-5 (PDF)
ISBN 978-0-88755-852-8 (EPUB)
ISBN 978-0-88755-879-5 (BOUND)

Cover image: Tenille Campbell
Cover design by Naoli Bray
Interior design by Karen Armstrong

Printed in Canada

The University of Manitoba Press acknowledges the financial support for its publication program provided by the Government of Canada through the Canada Book Fund, the Canada Council for the Arts, the Manitoba Department of Sport, Culture, and Heritage, the Manitoba Arts Council, and the Manitoba Book Publishing Tax Credit.

Funded by the Government of Canada | Canadä

Contents

Introduction

SARAH NICKEL[1]

On 15 March 2016, Indigenous scholars Kim TallBear (Sisseton Wahpeton Oyate), Kim Anderson (Cree/Métis), and Audra Simpson (Mohawk) arrived in Saskatoon for a discussion playfully named the "Indigenous Feminism Power Panel." In a packed room at Station 20 West (a Community Enterprise Centre on Saskatoon's west side), scholars, community members, artists, and others came to hear these women talk about their identities and experiences as Indigenous feminists. Considering the long history of Indigenous feminism and the strong canon of Indigenous feminist literature that has emerged over the past thirty years, many were surprised when the women spoke cautiously and reluctantly about their identities as Indigenous feminists. After all, had they not been invited to speak on an Indigenous feminism panel? Responding to this mood, Anderson wryly noted, "I guess we were all outed as being Indigenous feminists on this panel."[2] It was clear, then, that such political identities were not straightforward. The reticence among the speakers epitomized a number of common trends within Indigenous feminisms, including a general anxiety around the term itself, a desire to explain one's "journey to feminism" (if that is, in fact, a final destination), and the tendency for outsiders to ascribe identities to individuals they themselves might not always embrace.[3]

In her comments, TallBear, a Canada Research Chair in Indigenous Peoples, Technoscience, and Environment at the University of Alberta, insisted she didn't come to Indigenous feminism the "typical way" through engagements with Indigenous women, but rather through her understandings of feminist ideals in science. Wanting to bring marginalized voices together to dismantle hierarchies and "be in good relation" with one another, TallBear insisted: "Indigenous thinkers need to be at the table with feminists, we need to be at the table with disability scholars, and we need to be at the table with Queer theorists because we have very similar critiques of power. So that's how I became a feminist. It wasn't because of Indigenous women . . . [and] I don't think there is only one road to Indigenous feminism."[4] This final point was certainly true for Anderson, an associate professor of Indigenous studies at Wilfrid Laurier University, who spoke of her journey toward motherhood as crystallizing her identity as an Indigenous feminist. Yet this identification first came from others who viewed her work on Indigenous women and motherhood as feminist. "I didn't know I was an Indigenous feminist," she admitted, but Indigenous feminism helped her to see the gendered fault lines in Indigenous communities and gave her the language and tools to address them.[5]

Simpson, a professor of anthropology at Columbia University, had a similar experience as a young woman and used feminist language to describe the gendered landscape around her. Initially involved in the "white feminist movement" in Brooklyn, New York, Simpson quickly became frustrated, believing her fellow students' concerns about abortion and fair wages had nothing to do with Indigenous women's experiences. Indeed, for Simpson—as for many other Indigenous women—white feminist movements simply did not and could not represent Indigenous women's interests and realities, leading many to eschew feminism altogether.[6] When Simpson returned to her home in Kahnawake, however, and saw the impact of Indian Act–based gender discrimination on Mohawk women, she decided to use her "privilege" as a "full blood" in the local Native Women's Association of Canada chapter to seek change. As she reflected on whether or not this made her an Indigenous feminist, Simpson clarified: "I stopped being the other kind of feminist and I just started being a responsible Mohawk."[7] As it had for TallBear, for Simpson, Indigenous feminism became synonymous with "acting in good relation" and "being responsible" to community.

As my co-editor and I listened to these three women grapple with what Indigenous feminism meant to them, we were left wondering how useful Indigenous feminism was for describing the multiple ways in which Indigenous folks act in good relation. A term that had seemed boundless and full of potential when we first conceptualized this collection now appeared limiting, dated, and flat. Although TallBear, Simpson, and Anderson should not be viewed here as the representatives of Indigenous feminisms, this event and the conversations that emerged from it offer several useful entry points for discussion. We wondered if we should be embracing broader views, such as Simpson's and TallBear's conceptions of good relations and responsibility, or perhaps Indigenous gender and queer theories, which seemed to make more room for experiences beyond those of cis-gendered heterosexual women. Yet upon closer reflection on the multiple approaches to and expressions of Indigenous feminism reflected in the literature, lived experiences, and submissions for this collection, we realized the continued possibilities and relevance of this concept—not as an isolated area of scholarship but as a way to connect previously separated conversations.

Put simply, Indigenous feminisms reflect and capture the multiple ways in which gender and race, and therefore the systems of power related to these (sexism, racism, and colonialism) shape Indigenous peoples' lives.[8] Indigenous feminisms have the potential to expose and destabilize patriarchal gender roles and the structures that sustain and promote continued Indigenous dispossession and disempowerment through colonialism. Understanding the unique ways Indigenous peoples experience gender and colonial bias provides the foundation for most discussions of Indigenous feminism and it therefore remains a beneficial lens and set of experiences that can challenge assumptions about colonialism, sexism, identity, the gender binary, normative sexualities, and time and space. It can also complicate and complement other concepts such as Indigenous queer theory and Indigenous masculinities, which are often siloed into their respective scholarly corners. We see this collection as building on a strong foundation of Indigenous feminist work (intentioned or not) to tear down these interpretive barriers. We envision increased dialogue between gender theories and a framework with which we can consider how Indigenous feminisms can contribute to the conversations and lived experiences of queer and gender theories, and how these in turn can make us think differently about Indigenous feminisms.

Scholarly Genealogies

The field of Indigenous feminism has grown considerably in the past thirty years, and a number of scholars have traced this development in previously published works.[9] Recently, Joyce Green (Ktunaxa and Cree-Scots Métis) reflected on the state of the field in the second edition of her iconic collection *Making Space for Indigenous Feminism* (2017), noting that in the past ten years there has been "a significant body of writing relevant to Indigenous feminism, and within some Indigenous and non-Indigenous political organizations there is some recognition that gendered analysis is critical for political legitimacy and for sound policy and strategy."[10] Yet Green and others remain acutely aware that "sexism, misogyny, and racism continue to afflict Indigenous women, and serious engagement with these factors is not yet consistent or routine in either Indigenous or settler governments and communities."[11] Even academic Indigenous feminists are not safe from reprisals.[12]

Thus Green and others, including Joanne Barker (Lanape), Cheryl Suzack (Anishinaabe), Mishuauna Goeman (Seneca), and Jennifer Nez Denetdale (Diné), have incisively convinced readers of the longevity, challenges, and continued need for Indigenous feminist theory and action through their detailed explorations of academic and activist genealogies.[13] And I will not reproduce these efforts here. Instead, I will provide a generalized sweep of the state of the field in order to orient the reader to the work in this collection and its contribution to ongoing conversations. There are several discernible genealogies of Indigenous feminism, taken up by academics, community members, poets, activists, and others (some intentionally feminist and others not), and these can be understood through several trends. Thirty-five years ago, Beatrice Medicine (Standing Rock Sioux) and Patricia Albers produced one of the first academic works to privilege Indigenous women's lives, and while it was not framed explicitly as Indigenous feminist analysis, it aligned with the basic principles of Indigenous feminisms.[14]

The 1986 book *The Sacred Hoop: Recovering the Feminine in American Indian Traditions*, by Paula Gunn Allen (Laguna Pueblo), stands out as one of the first Indigenous feminist texts and is often cited as a seminal work for the field.[15] The novels and poetry of Leslie Marmon Silko (Laguna Pueblo) similarly emphasized the resilience and empowerment of Indigenous women, particularly those of the Laguna Pueblo tribe, drawing readers' attention to the impacts of settler colonialism on Indigenous women.[16] Likewise, in using poems, music, literature, and performance to emphasize the resilience and empowerment of Indigenous women, individuals such as Beth Brant (Tyendinaga Mohawk), Maria Campbell (Cree-Métis), Buffy Saint-Marie (Cree), Louise Bernice Halfe (Cree), and Pauline Johnson (Mohawk) are widely considered to be contributors to Indigenous feminisms. Practising what Maile Arvin (Kanaka Maoli), Eve Tuck (Unangax), and Angie Morrill (Klamath) label "Indigenous feminist theories," which make room for individuals to challenge gendered colonial oppression without openly identifying as Indigenous feminists, these authors (and others) highlight the longevity and flexibility of Indigenous feminisms.[17]

Twenty years ago, celebrated author and critic Lee Maracle (Stó:lō), speaking about Indigenous women's relationship to white feminism, explained: "I am not interested in gaining entry to the doors of the 'white women's movement.' I would look just a little ridiculous sitting in their living rooms saying 'we this and we that.'"[18] Maracle and others, including Allen, challenged the centrality of white feminisms and argued for different expressions of feminism that aligned with Indigenous realities and theories, and from this, the concept and experiences of Indigenous feminisms gained currency.[19] This is not to say there haven't been moments of cooperation and feminist solidarity, however. In addition to community events such as yearly memorial marches for Missing and Murdered Indigenous Women and Girls (MMIWG), solidarity has included the events organized in 1973 by the Status of Women Council, after Jeanette Lavell lost her bid to have her status reinstated after marrying a non-Indigenous man;[20] cooperation in the 1990s, when the Native Women's Association of Canada (NWAC) and National Action Committee on the Status of Women organized around the Charlottetown Accord;[21] and further cooperation in 2016, when the Canadian Feminist Alliance for International Action, together with NWAC, made a submission to the United Nations Committee for the Elimination of Discrimination against Women.[22]

And yet, some have overtly insisted that feminism simply is not needed in Indigenous communities, and others reject the term itself as a European construction.[23] Indeed, Green offers a robust discussion of the challenges to Indigenous feminism and feminists in the introduction to the second edition of *Making Space*, where she explores issues of tradition and authenticity, and the fraught relationship between Indigenous sovereignty and feminism. Green maintains that "too many Indigenous women have been silenced or had their social and political roles minimized by invocations of appropriate tradition relative to women's voices and choices."[24] Joanne Barker's recent collection *Critically Sovereign* takes up these challenges as well, with authors "demonstrate[ing] the concerns within critical Indigenous gender, sexuality, and feminist studies over how critical sovereignty and self-determination are to Indigenous peoples . . . [while addressing] the politics of gender, sexuality, and feminism within how that sovereignty and self-determination is imagined, represented, and exercised." Barker insists, simply: "It is not enough to claim you are sovereign as Indigenous, you must be accountable to the kinds of Indigeneity the sovereignty you claim asserts."[25] Despite historical and continued resistance, strong scholarly conversations have produced a robust field of inquiry that promises to reshape understandings of Indigenous experience.

In the past ten years, there have been two principal trends within Indigenous feminist scholarship: works that explicitly engage with and interrogate Indigenous feminism as a theoretical concept and identity, and those that apply Indigenous feminism as a form of analysis across a number of fields and topics. In the first category, the most well-known studies include two groundbreaking anthologies: Joyce Green's *Making Space for Indigenous Feminism* (2007, 2017); and *Indigenous Women and Feminism: Politics, Activism, Culture* (2010), edited by Cheryl Suzack (Anishinaabe, Indigenous studies and English scholar), Shari Huhndorf (Yup'ik, professor of ethnic studies and women's and gender studies), Jeanne Perrault (English professor), and Jean Barman (historian). The first trend also includes two journals: the *American Quarterly*'s "Forum: Native Feminisms without Apology" (2008), edited by media and cultural studies professor Andrea Smith and anthropologist J. Kēhaulani Kauanui (Kanaka Maoli), and the "Native Feminism" issue of the *Wicazo Sa Review* (2009), edited by gender and American Indian studies scholar Mishuana Goeman and historian Jennifer Nez Denetdale (2009).[26] Within these pages, many of the contributors grapple with the complex and often troubled relationship between Indigenous women and feminism and produce rich theoretical debates that traverse international boundaries and disciplinary conventions. They reflect on their own feminist ideals and practices, expressions of feminism in art and culture, law, politics and activism, and everyday life. Kim Anderson and Bonita Lawrence's collection *Strong Women Stories: Native Vision and Community Survival* (2003) should also be considered here, even though it was not overtly characterized as Indigenous feminism as the other publications were.[27] Framed around Indigenous women's stories, the contributions explore the impact of colonialism and patriarchy on women's lived realities through stories of community and identity, politics and leadership, health, education, and activism.

Across these collections, transnational conversations highlight shared struggles as well as strong divergences in how Indigenous women around the world envision themselves and feminist ideologies. Perhaps most importantly, these collections present definitions of Indigenous feminism their authors take up, critique, and contribute to on their own terms. Scholars concerned with Canadian Indian policy such as Joanne Barker, Dian Million (Tanana Athabascan), Cheryl Suzack, and Audra Simpson, for instance, frame Indigenous feminism in the context of codifying heteropatriarchy through the settler-colonial Indian Act, yet many authors also unapologetically locate feminism as an Indigenous concept.[28] Goeman and Denetdale, for instance, question the deep-seated assumption that "feminism is long held to be in the purview of white rule, according to much literature on Native women and feminism. It is long believed to be a European invention or, much worse, a colonial imposition that sought to destroy tribal ways of life."[29] Likewise challenging notions of feminism's supposed whiteness, Kauanui and Smith, in their "Native Feminism without Apology" forum firmly assert the power of Indigenous feminism to challenge colonialism and sexism.[30]

Alongside (and in some cases within) these collections are a number of articles that mobilize Indigenous feminism or expand Indigenous feminist theory into new areas of analysis, including law, gendered violence, and Indigenous research methodologies. Historian Maile Arvin, critical race and Indigenous studies scholar Eve Tuck, and ethnic studies scholar Angie Morrill further challenge understandings of Indigenous feminism as a recent phenomenon and look to Indigenous women's historical activities to demonstrate how Indigenous feminist theories, as they term them, forward the Indigenous feminist project regardless of the labels women use for their own political identities. The authors similarly situate Indigenous feminism as an explicitly political project, challenging prevailing assumptions that Indigenous women are not political.[31]

Applying Indigenous feminism to the field of law, legal scholars Val Napoleon (Saulteau) and John Borrows (Anishinaabe/Ojibway) and Indigenous studies and gender studies scholar Emily Snyder expose and analyze the ways in which Indigenous laws are gendered, despite claims to the contrary.[32] In their co-authored article "Gender and Violence: Drawing on Indigenous Legal Resources," Snyder, Borrows, and Napoleon eschew interpretations of Indigenous culture as being disconnected from power and Indigenous legal traditions. They offer a "critical gendered approach to Indigenous laws," cautioning against romanticized views of "the 'Indigenous' past as being non-violent and non-sexist" in order to understand and address historical and contemporary gendered violence.[33] This analysis is confirmed within Indigenous feminism, with Green insisting that "Indigenous feminist analysis goes further than other Indigenous libratory [*sic*] critiques in suggesting that not all pre-colonial Indigenous social practices were innocent of oppression, including sex oppression."[34]

Elsewhere, Snyder challenges "gender 'neutral' approaches, which are pervasive in Indigenous legal studies" and "often rely on a universal male subject and express a male-centred version of Indigenous legal theory and laws."[35] To address the erasure of other gendered experiences and combat false claims of gender equality, Snyder proposes an alternative framework—Indigenous feminist legal theory—that "is intersectional, attentive to power, anti-colonial, anti-essentialist, multi-juridical, and embraces a spirit of critique that challenges static notions of tradition, identity, gender, sex, and sexuality."[36] Professor and lawyer Sarah Deer (Muscogee) takes a similar approach to understand sexual violence against Indigenous women. Mobilizing an Indigenous feminist framework, Deer notes how male-dominated traditional and settler legal systems marginalize rape victims, either by forcing Indigenous women to forgive Indigenous men, or by working within a settler legal system premised on victims proving the perpetrator's guilt. Preventing further harms, she argues, requires centring Indigenous women in all legal systems.[37]

Beyond legal considerations, Indigenous feminism is central to discussions of gendered violence, which scholars such as Sherene Razack, Mishuana Goeman, Andrea Smith, and Sarah Hunt explore through concepts of geographical and socio-political space, while others such as Rauna Kuokkanen (Sámi), Robyn Bourgeois (Cree), and Mary Eberts examine through policy and the justice system.[38] Indigenous feminism has also permeated methodological discussions in Indigenous studies specifically. Both Goeman and TallBear have integrated Indigenous feminist theories into their methodological practice—framing Indigenous women's standpoints as essential to conducting ethical and situated work.[39] Goeman takes a broad view of the potential of Indigenous feminist methods to intervene in many fields of inquiry. She insists: "The various methods employed by Indigenous feminist studies asks [*sic*] us all to rethink the structures that make possible great injustices that often have an intersectional gendered undergirding, and they ask us to reconsider moves toward justice that do not reaffirm settler-colonial hierarchies that rely on normative gender, sex, and racial hierarchies."[40]

Indigenous feminisms also inform academic and community conversations on political resistance and sovereignty. Additionally, LGBTQ2 issues are emergent, pushing back against the tendency to view Indigenous feminism as a concept solely concerned with normative genders and sexualities. Joanne Barker's recent collection *Critically Sovereign: Indigenous Gender, Sexuality, and Feminist Studies* (2017) brought together gender, sexuality, and feminism to reflect on Indigenous sovereignty, colonialism, and imperialism, thus offering critical insights into necessity of gendered political analysis.[41] This represents a growing trend of scholarship that highlights women's activities and interventions as political, where they might otherwise be considered "social," thus expanding our understandings of concepts such as sovereignty and politics as inherently gendered processes.[42]

The present collection builds on this foundation. Its title highlights the centrality of Indigenous feminisms as well as the relational conversations (and scholarly genealogies) that brought us to this place. It takes up Green's assertion of the "transformative potential of feminism" for understanding how "racism and sexism fuse when brought to bear on Indigenous women"—and, we would add, on LGBTQ2 individuals as well.[43] It continues to broaden and deepen understandings of what Indigenous feminisms are, and incorporates theories, practices, and bodies outside traditional purviews. It takes up and expands existing definitions of Indigenous feminism, following Sarah Nickel and Emily Snyder's assertion that "Indigenous feminisms examine how gender and conceptions of gender influence the lives of Indigenous peoples, historically and today. Indigenous feminist approaches challenge stereotypes about Indigenous peoples, gender and sexuality . . . and address the many ways that sexuality, gender and gender norms (expectations about how people should act or behave based on perceptions about their gender) shape Indigenous people's lives."[44] This collection, therefore, offers room for questioning, revising, and reinventing Indigenous feminisms and includes pieces that question gender roles, identities, and tradition, explore kinship and sexuality, and centralize self-reflection. The threads of Indigenous feminisms highlighted here are not intended to reflect "the new directions" in Indigenous feminisms, and do not presume to subsume or overtake the work done by past Indigenous feminists, or by those working in Indigenous queer and masculinity studies. Instead, we wish to cultivate cross-fertilizations and dialogue.

To accomplish this, we bring together voices of Indigenous feminisms from junior scholars, community members, artists, and others that may not find representation in academic collections, and this helps us to consider the broad and even contradictory range of ways that diverse peoples engage with Indigenous feminisms today. Through poetry, creative pieces, and more traditional scholarly works, authors prove that Indigenous feminist theories are everywhere and, as such, bridge the false dichotomy between "academy" and "community" that Audra Simpson, Andrea Smith, and Kim TallBear argue is central to "demystifying" theory.[45] Representing and embracing diverse opinions and experiences, this inclusive and non-essentializing collection presents critical interventions into history, politics, and theory by outlining the transformative potential of Indigenous feminisms.

To enable these conversations, differences, and cross-connections to take place, this collection is organized around the notion of "generations." Here, the term is not meant to denote a strict temporal or age-based distinction, but rather alludes to "waves" of Indigenous feminist thought that are becoming distinct from one another while retaining important affinities. Our goal here is to capture how movements, ideas, and experiences grow and change over time and across space. By conceiving of changes in scholarship and experience as generational within an Indigenous context, we can explore change as well as continuity and connection. In order to challenge myopic understandings of Indigenous feminisms, we offer representation from broad geographical areas (Canada, the United States, and Sápmi territory in northern Europe) and disciplinary influences (history, Indigenous studies, social work, sociology, and English), and from diverse contributors with different backgrounds (activists, artists, scholars) and positionalities (gender, race, class, ethnicity, sexuality, age).

If we use the idea of generations to encapsulate both the divergences and connections in our work, then we also see this notion in personal terms. In this sense, the collection is a multi-generational nod to those who came before us and those who walk beside us—to the Indigenous feminist scholars, community members, and others, who in action (if not in identity) embraced the ideals of Indigenous feminism by living, surviving, talking, acting, resisting in their homes and communities, as well as in courtrooms and in community halls.

What Follows

The collection is anchored around three thematic sections. The first, "Broadening Indigenous Feminisms," looks beyond established categories and spaces to consider historical expressions of Indigenous feminism, transnational and regional experiences, as well as violence, representation, and resistance. The opening poem "The Uninvited," by Anishinaabe scholar Jana-Rae Yerxa, introduces the spirit of the collection, which offers space to individuals who feel their work may not be fully represented in current iterations of Indigenous feminism. Indicating the "arrival" of the contributors and insisting it is their "turn to speak" serves as a strong introduction to what follows. Elaine McArthur's poem "Us" then gestures toward many of the themes explored here, including stereotypical representations of Indigenous peoples, colonial violence, cultural survival, and resistance.

In Chapter 1, white settler historian Madeline Knickerbocker demonstrates the historical nature of Indigenous feminism through her analysis of Stó:lō women's roles in late-twentieth-century political activism. Using archival and oral history interviews, Knickerbocker explores the gendered nature of Stó:lō politics through the battle for Coqualeetza, which brought together Stó:lō women as cultural educators and Stó:lō men as formal political actors. Challenging the erasure of Indigenous women as political actors, Knickerbocker situates Stó:lō women firmly within the political dialogues surrounding Indigenous sovereignty and cultural preservation, where they engaged in direct action, storytelling, and preserving Stó:lō culture and community.

If Indigenous feminism can travel in time, as Knickerbocker demonstrates, so too can it move across space. In Chapter 2, Sámi and Norwegian anthropologist Astri Dankertsen challenges us to think about Indigenous feminism beyond the North American context, putting forward the idea of "Sámi feminist moments" to create space for the everyday ways in which Indigenous feminism is manifest. Focusing on the traditional territory of the Sámi peoples, Dankertsen reveals how colonialism's particular expression in Nordic countries has contributed to pervasive mythical stereotyping of Sámi peoples, which demands a culturally appropriate framework as a solution. Indigenous feminism in Sápmi territory, Dankertsen argues, is often subtle and indirect, and we need to understand this unique cultural element in order to fully appreciate the ways in which Sámi peoples perform feminism and resistance.

Representations likewise play a key role in Chapter 3, where Cree/Métis filmmaker and professor of English Tasha Hubbard, along with Joi T. Arcand, Zoey Roy, Darian Lonechild, and Marie Sanderson, explore Indigenous feminist expressions through film. Hubbard, together with her collaborators, focuses on how young Indigenous women in the Canadian prairies challenge stereotypical representations of Indigenous peoples and combat the inherent dangers of being an Indigenous woman in violent settler-colonial spaces. Hubbard uses her short film *7 Minutes* to engage Indigenous women in conversations about Indigenous feminism and resistance. The film, which follows a young female Indigenous nursing student on her walk from campus home, reveals Indigenous women's everyday encounters with the dangerous white male gaze and threats to their safety. Hubbard's multi-layered chapter highlights important conversations among young Indigenous women about their experiences with violence, harmful representations, and most importantly, their continued resistance to these.

Finally, in Chapter 4, historian and Indigenous studies scholar Sarah Nickel (Secwépemc) uses case studies of twentieth-century Indian Homemakers' Clubs in western Canada to explore Indigenous women's complex engagements with the Eurocentric theoretical underpinnings of the clubs, as well as settler involvement in the clubs' operations. Embracing the inherent contradictions of the clubs, which were both sites of settler domesticity and oversight as well as Indigenous women's leadership, reveals the broad variation of Indigenous women's political work.

Taken together, these chapters suggest that Indigenous women have always been political but have had to navigate stereotypes, representations, and gender expectations that equate their roles to apolitical motherhood and community caretaking, restricting politics to spheres defined as male. The authors here show how women, Two-Spirit, and other individuals who have typically been excluded from so-called political activities nevertheless engage in political and feminist work, consciously and strategically as well as subconsciously and accidentally, through everyday relationships, activities like socializing, cultural preservation, homemaking, sewing, and storytelling.

The second thematic section on "Queer and Two-Spirit Identities, and Sexuality" furthers our project of envisioning Indigenous feminism as a flexible and multi-vocal concept with wide-ranging applicability. Here we explore the intersections between Indigenous feminisms and the growing field of Indigenous queer studies. The authors centre lesbian, gay, bisexual, transgender, queer/questioning, and Two-Spirit (LGBTQ2) folks in these conversations. They disrupt depictions of Indigenous cultures and traditions that erase LGBTQ2 identities, and grapple with longstanding questions about how Indigenous peoples addressed and continue to address sovereignty, sexism, health, and sexuality from LGBTQ2 identities and experiences. As Qwo-Li Driskill, Chris Finley, Brian Joseph Gilley, and Scott Lauria Morgensen insist, "Indigenous GLBTQ2 identities are deeply complex. The issue of terminology always pushes at the limits of language."[46] Many of the authors here use the term Two-Spirit—a Pan-Indigenous term adopted in 1990 at an international gathering held in Beausejour, Manitoba—as this serves as both an umbrella term that is broadly applicable as well as one that was internally defined and accepted by Indigenous LGBTQ2 communities. The specific applications of and discussions around these terms are detailed throughout the individual chapters.

Two-Spirit Métis/Sault Ste. Marie Nishnaabe American studies doctoral student Kai Pyle begins the section by bringing Indigenous feminism to critically engage with curriculum deficiencies in Chapter 5. Seeing Indigenous peoples represented in the curriculum according to stereotypical and generalized "traditional" gender roles, Pyle centralizes Two-Spirit perspectives to (re)build healthy and accurate Indigenous gender roles. Situating this issue as one intimately linked to health, Indigenous sovereignty, identity, and self-determination, Pyle calls for changes to be made in communities, organizations, and academia.

In Chapter 6, Aubrey Hanson, a queer Métis professor of Indigenous education, brings a literary Indigenous feminist approach to analyzing the work of Indigenous poet Chrystos. Troubled by the erasure of Two-Spirit Indigenous peoples in Indigenous feminist conversations, Hanson argues for Two-Spirit communities to reclaim this space through the erotic, which she insists is a site of both sovereignty and Indigenous feminisms. Hanson calls for connection and cohesion as a way to bring Indigenous people back into feminist discourse, to redefine it in ways that enable better representation.

Taking the connections between Two-Spirit experiences and sexuality in a different direction, Indigenous studies scholar Chantal Fiola (Michif/Métis) uses an Indigenous feminist lens in Chapter 7 to understand the role that Two-Spirit folks play in the pursuit of mino-bimaadiziwin (a good balanced life). She notes the problematic ways in which so-called traditional gender roles and colonial heteropatriarchy have oppressed Indigenous women and naawenangweyaabeg (the Anishinaabe concept for a person who mends, or keeps others together and from wandering). Fiola draws on the reflections of four naawenangweyaabeg role models to expose the complexities of Indigenous sexuality, highlight the roles and responsibilities of Two-Spirit people, and show how intergenerational relationships and alliances are essential to decolonization and mino-bimaadiziwin.

In Chapter 8, Xicana (Yaqui/Mexica), social work professor Ramona Beltrán, doctoral student Antonia Alvarez (mestiza Pinay), and Two-Spirit Indigenous anti-violence worker Miriam Puga broaden our understandings of Indigenous feminist analysis to include Two-Spirit identity in health education. Focusing on the experiences of Two-Spirit and/or LGBTQ-identified Indigenous youth participating in culture-centred HIV prevention program that uses the Indigenous Youth RiseUp! curriculum, the authors demonstrate how Indigenous feminist and queer approaches to curriculum creation contribute to participants' increased self-esteem, cultural pride, and improved community development. The authors emphasize the positive impact these theoretical frameworks can have on the lived experiences of people accessing health programming.

The third thematic section, "Multi-Generational Feminisms and Kinship," confirms Indigenous feminism as a family affair but highlights the multiple, shifting, and at times deeply uncomfortable and contradictory ways this manifests for many people. As in the previous section, the authors in some chapters challenge the dominance of Indigenous motherhood in discussions of Indigenous feminism and consider how feminism relates to various Indigenous kinship relationships across a mixture of spaces, time periods, and emotional landscapes. Contributors reimagine and complicate ideas of parenthood, tradition, responsibility, and decolonization.

In Chapter 9, sociologist and anthropologist Zoe Todd (Métis/otipemisiw) looks to her great-grandmother as a theorist to help her understand and explore multi-generational Métis feminisms. She draws on the histories, experiences, and stories of her family to challenge stereotypes about political action, Indigenous identity, and tradition to centre narratives of women's resistance and the complexities of place and belonging.

Anishinaabe gender studies scholar Waaseyaa'in Christine Sy also looks to family and kinship in Chapter 10 and challenges ideals of heteronormativity, culture, and tradition with a creative narrative on decolonial Anishinaabe parenting. She offers deep intersectional and multi-generational analyses of Indigenous feminism and parenting as she reproduces conversations with her black-Anishinaabe daughter. Waaseyaa'in discovers divergences between her and her daughter's ideology and experiences of feminism, and highlights these as spaces for dialogue and convergence.

In Chapter 11, Cree-Métis-Salteaux storyteller and curator Lindsay Nixon explores connections and relationships in the Canadian Indigenous art community to understand what applying Indigenous Relational Aesthetics (IRA) through an Indigenous feminist lens can offer to the work of decolonization. Using the 1990 exhibit *Native Love* as a case study, Nixon exposes the rich potential of IRA to enact feminist change in art museums, and the Indigenous and dominant art communities.

Chapter 12 features another cross-generational dialogue: Nêhiýaw historian Omeasoo Wāhpāsiw and her mother, the poet Louise Bernice Halfe, contemplate their complex and shifting identities as Indigenous feminists as well as their broader kinship relationships, experiences with activism, and roles as mothers. Wāhpāsiw envisions an expression of Indigenous feminism that makes space for herself as a Cree intellectual, mother, daughter, and activist, as well as for her young son and other male relatives. Grappling with her identity as a feminist amid kinship relationships that at times serve to maintain patriarchy drives Wāhpāsiw's deep reflection on what Indigenous feminism means—and can mean for her. Closing this section, and indeed the volume, are photographs of artist Anina Major's ceramic figures titled "These Are My Daughters." These artworks offer a visual representation of culture and kinship connections—drawing Major toward the knowledge of her grandmother's artistry and illustrations of culture and home.

Conversations

Taken together, these chapters create a meaningful dialogue about the nature and definition of Indigenous feminisms across a number of themes, methodologies, and disciplines. Many of the essays engage with kinship and relationships in both complementary and contradictory ways that epitomize the flexibility of Indigenous feminisms. For some, including Sy, Wāhpāsiw and Halfe, and Major, motherhood and womanhood are central and meaningful (though challenging) components for Indigenous feminism, while Pyle, Todd, and Hanson insist these categories are limiting and have the potential to exclude other gendered bodies and sets of experiences. For Sy, motherhood is deeply intersectional and bound up in multiple genealogies and relationships that make up our families. For Wāhpāsiw and Halfe, motherhood is mediated through complex family gendered relationships and power dynamics that are rarely discussed openly, if at all. They are also rife with assumptions about family responsibility, which often falls disproportionately on mothers. Fiola believes in the centrality and importance of motherhood but cautions against constructing this in limiting ways (including placing the importance of motherhood over other experiences and realities) that exclude other gendered bodies. Knickerbocker and Nickel demonstrate the ways in which Indigenous women's gendered roles (including motherhood) can be used as strategic political resistance. Overall, we are left with a sense of both the power and privilege of motherhood, as well as the ways in which it is bound up in colonial heteropatriarchy, which assumes women's bodies dictate their social roles and capabilities, thus ignoring gendered bodies that exist outside these normative demands. We also see the ways that Indigenous peoples resist these expectations and how Indigenous feminism can provide the tools to do so.

Another significant thread throughout the collection is the concept of relational responsibility. Through their discussions of education and curriculum—particularly as it relates to Two-Spirit folks—Beltrán, Alvarez, and Puga, and Pyle highlight the need for appropriate education in terms of accountability to community and to those within community who are often excluded. Fiola, Sy, and Major remind us of ancestral and kinship responsibilities and suggest that cross-generational influence and learning is not unidirectional—moving from older generations to younger—but multidirectional, and Hubbard informs us that we can learn as much from ourselves as we can from each other. Wāhpāsiw's and Halfe's engagement with Indigenous feminism embodies this dialogue in that Wāhpāsiw's understandings of and experiences with Indigenous feminism diverge significantly from those of her mother. Wāhpāsiw also challenges these categories to create new possibilities for her son Kopit, whom she sees as integral to Indigenous feminist ideals. This multi-generational conversation demands an iteration of Indigenous feminism that makes sense for these diverse realities and positions.

Representation is also central to many of the chapters in this collection. Hubbard, Dankertsen, Pyle, and Fiola address mythical, "authentic," stereotypical, and "traditional" representations of Indigenous peoples, suggesting that figures such as Sámi goddesses, Indian princesses, warriors, and hypersexualized Indigenous women do not reflect Indigenous realities but promote violence, shame, and damaging misconceptions. Gender stereotyping and assumptions about gender roles were also prevalent in twentieth-century Indigenous communities, as demonstrated by Knickerbocker and Nickel, and Indigenous women engaged in significant labour to combat political erasure as well as erasure from collective historical memory. Indeed, Indigenous peoples have always resisted the violence (Dankertsen, Hubbard, and Hanson), gendered erasure (Todd, Knickerbocker, Nickel, Pyle, Sy, and Beltrán), and misrepresentations meted out as "punishment" for transgressing gender identity boundaries, or cultural and sexual expectations, or even for simply daring to exist in white spaces (Nixon, Hubbard, Major, McArthur, and Yerxa). This collective resistance, as Dankertsen and Fiola remind us, is critical for building capacity among Indigenous peoples, but it must also leave space for unique cultural needs and individual self-identification so as not to produce Indigenous feminist moments that homogenize and flatten Indigenous experiences. These conversations of resistance, survival, and Indigenous feminisms are never far from discussions of Indigenous sovereignty, nationhood, and individual autonomy. All are intertwined and necessary for ensuring the well-being of all Indigenous folks.

Indigenous feminisms, represented in the following spaces of refusal and reclamation, are where we can reject heteronormativity, colonialism, and patriarchy, and reclaim space for LGBTQ2 peoples and Indigenous feminist actions that do not necessarily find representation elsewhere. Indigenous feminisms move across time and space, and as the contributors to this book demonstrate, are articulated and performed in people's everyday lives. There is also a desire for connection and cohesion through a concept or theory or experience that is inclusive.

New Areas for Exploration

In addition to expanding understandings of Indigenous feminisms, this collection offers new perspectives on a series of underexplored research areas and subjects. Beltrán, Alvarez, and Puga's piece points to a need for Indigenous LGBTQ2-identified people to be better represented in Indigenous feminist health literature. There is a strong and growing body of work on sterilization and on nutritional and medical experimentation, but LGBTQ2 experiences are largely excluded.[47] Discussions of kinship in this collection also point to new areas of interest, including kinship relationships and belonging through adoption, relationships not defined as family, and making space for those who lack connection to kin for a variety of reasons. Wāhpāsiw's reference to "creat[ing] a whole new family everywhere I go" points to kinship relationships that are built through friendship, proximity, and shared experiences. There is a tendency to view women as integral to the family and community, but these roles and relationships are often strictly defined as maternal and family roles. This leaves little room for friendships, professional relationships, and other roles that Indigenous feminists practise in everyday life. What about those for whom Indigenous feminism is decidedly not about motherhood, kinship, tradition, or community? How can their voices be heard within this space? More work in this arena needs to be done.

Historical representations of Indigenous feminisms also need further exploration. Knickerbocker and Nickel locate Indigenous feminist practices in 1970s Stó:lō territory and the Homemakers' Clubs of Canada's West, and Todd looks to her grandmother as a source of feminist inspiration, yet we still know little about how historical events, identities, and activities can be understood as historical Indigenous feminisms. We need more work that codes Indigenous women's work in particular, as political, activist, and feminist, regardless of the time in which it took place. This will highlight the long roots of Indigenous feminism we know to exist in Indigenous communities.

At the Station 20 West "Indigenous Feminism Power Panel," Kim TallBear, Audra Simpson, and Kim Anderson engaged in deep reflection about the role Indigenous feminisms played in shaping their identities, research, and lives. The contributors here have taken on Indigenous feminisms as a call to action—a way, as TallBear eloquently stated, to act in good relation. Embodying this principle, this collection is a political act of Indigenous feminist survivance. It builds on and reproduces multi-generational dialogue and relationships, and it challenges the very notion of academic scholarship and identity, bringing together individuals from different countries, backgrounds, career paths, and knowledge bases, to have meaningful conversations.

NOTES

1 These introductory thoughts were the culmination of many interesting and productive conversations with Amanda Fehr, Erica Violet Lee, and Emily Snyder. I would also like to thank Eryk Martin, who read and commented on a full draft of this piece, and whose insightful comments made me think more deeply about these issues.

2 TallBear, Anderson, and Simpson, "Indigenous Feminism Power Panel."

3 Arvin, Tuck, and Morrill, "Decolonizing Feminism."

4 Kim TallBear, at TallBear, Anderson, and Simpson, "Indigenous Feminism Power Panel."

5 Kim Anderson, at TallBear, Anderson, and Simpson, "Indigenous Feminism Power Panel."

6 Lee Maracle's *I Am Woman* details her experiences with and apprehensions around feminism, and links these specifically to the notion that Indigenous women must first be concerned with Indigenous rights and racism, not sexism. See also Ross, "From the 'F' Word to Indigenous/Feminisms."

7 Audra Simpson, at TallBear, Anderson, and Simpson, "Indigenous Feminism Power Panel."

8 For further definitions of Indigenous feminism, see Green, *Making Space for Indigenous Feminism*, 1st and 2nd eds. (2007, 2017); Suzack et al., *Indigenous Women and Feminism*; Arvin, Tuck, and Morrill, "Decolonizing Feminism"; Nickel and Snyder, "Indigenous Feminisms in Canada."

9 Green, *Making Space for Indigenous Feminism*, 1st and 2nd eds.; Suzack et. al., *Indigenous Women and Feminism*; Arvin, Tuck, and Morrill, "Decolonizing Feminism"; Barker, *Critically Sovereign*; Goeman, *Mark My Words*; Hunt, "Representing Colonial Violence."

10 Green, *Making Space for Indigenous Feminism*, 2nd ed., 1.

11 Green, 3.

12 Green, 3–9.

13 Suzack et al., *Indigenous Women and Feminism*; Goeman, *Mark My Words*; Goeman and Denetdale, "Native Feminisms," 10; Goeman, "Indigenous Interventions and Feminist Methods."

14 Medicine and Albers, *The Hidden Half.*

15 Allen, *The Sacred Hoop*; Barker, *Critically Sovereign*, 19.

16 Silko, *Laguna Women*; Silko, *Almanac of the Dead*; Silko, *Storyteller*.

17 Arvin, Tuck, and Morrill, "Decolonizing Feminism," 11.

18 Maracle, *I Am Woman*, 18.

19 Allen, *The Sacred Hoop*; Ross, "From the 'F' Word to Indigenous/Feminisms"; Anderson and Lawrence, *Strong Women Stories*; Krouse and Howard, *Keeping the Campfires Going*; Joyce Green, "Taking Account of Aboriginal Feminisms," in

Making Space for Indigenous Feminism, 1st ed., 20–47; St. Denis, "Feminism Is for Everybody."

20 Nickel, *Assembling Unity*, 157–58. See also Nickel, "'A Genuine Revolution.'"

21 Green, introduction to *Making Space for Indigenous Feminism*, 2nd ed., 8.

22 Green, 3.

23 See Green, *Making Space for Indigenous Feminism*, 1st and 2nd eds., especially Emma Larocque's contributions in both; Suzack et al., *Indigenous Women and Feminism.*

24 Green, *Making Space for Indigenous Feminism*, 2nd ed., 15.

25 Barker, introduction to *Critically Sovereign*, 34–35.

26 Smith and Kauanui, "Forum: Native Feminisms without Apology"; Goeman and Denetdale, "Native Feminisms."

27 Anderson and Lawrence, *Strong Women Stories.* See especially chapters 6, 11, and 15.

28 Barker, "Gender, Sovereignty, Rights"; Simpson, "From White into Red"; Million, "Felt Theory"; Suzack, "Emotion before the Law."

29 Goeman and Denetdale, "Native Feminisms," 10.

30 Smith and Kauanui, "Native Feminisms Engage American Indian Studies."

31 Arvin, Tuck, and Morrill, "Decolonizing Feminism."

32 Snyder, Napoleon, and Borrows, "Gender and Violence"; Snyder, "Indigenous Feminist Legal Theory"; Napoleon, "Aboriginal Discourse."

33 Snyder, Napoleon, and Borrows, "Gender and Violence," 596.

34 Green, *Making Space for Indigenous Feminism*, 2nd ed., 12.

35 Snyder, "Indigenous Feminist Legal Theory," 366.

36 Snyder, 401.

37 Deer, "Decolonizing Rape Law."

38 Razack, *Race, Space, and the Law*; Goeman, *Mark My Words*; Hunt, "Representing Colonial Violence"; Smith, *Conquest*; Hunt, "Witnessing the Colonialscape"; Eberts, "Being an Indigenous Woman Is a 'High-Risk Lifestyle'"; Kuokkanen, "Politics of Gendered Violence in Indigenous Communities"; Bourgeois, "Perpetual State of Violence."

39 TallBear, "Standing with and Speaking as Faith"; Goeman, "Indigenous Interventions and Feminist Methods."

40 Goeman, "Indigenous Interventions and Feminist Methods," 192.

41 Barker, *Critically Sovereign.*

42 See also Nickel, "'I Am Not a Women's Libber Although Sometimes I Sound Like One'"; Nickel, "Sewing the Threads of Resilience"; Blaney, "Aboriginal Women's Action Network"; Blaney and Gray, "'Empowerment, Revolution and Real Change.'"

43 Green, *Making Space for Indigenous Feminism*, 2nd ed., 12.

44 Nickel and Snyder, "Indigenous Feminisms in Canada."

45 Simpson and Smith, introduction to *Theorizing Native Studies*; TallBear, "Standing with and Speaking as Faith."

46 Driskill, Finley, et al., introduction to *Queer Indigenous Studies*, 3.

47 Torpy, "Native American Women and Coerced Sterilizations"; Stote, "The Coercive Sterilization of Aboriginal Women in Canada"; Stote, *An Act of Genocide*; Mosby, "Administering Colonial Science."

Part I
Broadening Indigenous Feminisms

The Uninvited

by Jana-Rae Yerxa

Be like the beauty and brightness of the sun
emerge without permission
because fierce is never invited.

Tap on darkness's shoulder
to say "I am here, it is my turn"
while lighting up the sky.

Us

by Elaine McArthur

In homes, churches
on park benches in cities small towns, on reserves and on the road
we are dirty clothes battling ghosts in the liquor store doorway
with a hand out for your change

Painted faces
high heels mini skirts
a backseat tumble
for a twenty dollar fumble we are in school
reading our way out working everyday praying that sons and
daughters stay out of gangs and out of your car

Beaded pieces adorning our bodies in modest length dress being led by
the beat of a drum yet we are living in fear
that we might be the next high cheek boned missing

CHAPTER 1

Making Matriarchs at Coqualeetza: Stó:lō Women's Politics and Histories across Generations

MADELINE ROSE KNICKERBOCKER[1]

On the morning of 3 May 1976, a group of Stó:lō protestors arrived at Coqualeetza and occupied a two-storey brick building on the site that the Canadian Armed Forces (CAF) used as overflow housing for their adjacent base in Chilliwack, BC.[2] Originally known as Kw'eqwá:líth'á, Coqualeetza is an important Stó:lō cultural site that settlers appropriated in the nineteenth century.[3] For decades, Stó:lō people had been pushing for the initiation of a land claims process for return of the site, owned by the federal government and managed by the Department of Public Works. Additionally, as Stó:lō cultural education programs expanded rapidly in the 1970s, Stó:lō educators saw the Coqualeetza site as the obvious place to establish a permanent community space for their work. By 1976, Stó:lō efforts to reclaim the land had become entwined with the potential use of the space for cultural education, and the occupation that began that day was the final escalation of years of activist efforts.

The roughly forty occupiers—Stó:lō and other Indigenous people of all ages—were mainly women; they arrived midmorning with supplies and gear, prepared for an occupation of several days. Their first actions were to gather in a circle and declare that the occupation would be non-violent and drug- and alcohol-free. In response to this peaceful demonstration, soldiers stationed at the nearby CAF base moved onto the site, conducting drills and positioning snipers on nearby buildings. In the early evening, the army, now supported by the Royal Canadian Mounted Police (RCMP), ordered the occupiers to exit or prepare to be removed and arrested. Defying this ultimatum, the occupiers barricaded themselves inside the building and began singing and drumming together, declaring "This is our land!" At 6:30 p.m., soldiers attempted to enter the building by force and were met with resistance from the activists inside, but eventually gained entry after breaking through a glass door. The incursion provoked the departure of some occupiers, while about twenty-three stayed. Armed forces personnel physically removed activists: some were on their feet as flanking soldiers pushed them out; others who refused to walk were forcibly hauled out by officers. The occupation ended as the army segregated the seventeen remaining protestors by gender, ordered them onto army trucks, and drove them down to the police station, under arrest.[4]

The Coqualeetza occupation is a significant moment in late twentieth-century Stó:lō histories of culture and politics. In this chapter, I focus specifically on what the occupation and the protests leading up to it reveal about the gendered dynamics of Stó:lō politics during the 1970s. While Coqualeetza's position as a cultural site caught up in a political battle encapsulates the interconnectedness of heritage and sovereignty in Stó:lō politics, employing such a lens in isolation frames the activism at Coqualeetza entirely within the context of Stó:lō–settler conflicts over land and knowledge. Considering the significant number of women involved, their leadership of the occupation, and their role as cultural educators, exploring the gender dynamics at play between Stó:lō people during the occupation is necessary, and reveals a more complex understanding of the protest's significance. Incorporating gender analysis into Stó:lō-centred narratives of the Coqualeetza occupation still highlights the strength of Stó:lō political agitation against the settler state, while simultaneously affirming the power and necessity of Stó:lō women's work as cultural curators and political leaders in communities that, to variable extents and because of historical context, were influenced by settler-colonial patriarchy.

This essay has four parts. First, I briefly trace the ways this work relates to academic literature on Indigenous feminism broadly, and Stó:lō women in particular, situating these arguments in relation to that scholarship. From there, I move on to discuss Stó:lō oral traditions relating both to gender roles and to Coqualeetza, showing the long histories of Stó:lō women's power as political actors and cultural curators at that site specifically. This mirrors what we see in Zoe Todd's discussion of her great-grandmother's powerful, if largely unacknowledged, political role in Chapter 9, as well as in Sarah Nickel's exploration of Indigenous women's activism through Homemakers' Clubs and sewing in Chapter 4. This foundation established, I shift to considering both changes and continuities in Stó:lō territorial sovereignty and gender dynamics during the late nineteenth century's settler-colonial land appropriations and imposition of heteropatriarchy. Finally, I analyze Stó:lō cultural sovereignty in the 1970s, examining the politicization of cultural education work at Coqualeetza in a moment when Stó:lō political leadership was almost exclusively a male occupation, while Stó:lō cultural education was often led by matriarchs and women. Analyzing the Coqualeetza occupation from a gender perspective in this way rejects and corrects the historiographic absence of Stó:lō women from scholarship about their own communities. Moreover, considering Stó:lō women's cultural and political work in the late twentieth century in relation to the long histories of Stó:lō women's leadership reveals the intergenerational nature of women's power—a revelation that has implications for understanding and framing Stó:lō feminist action in the past, present, and future.

Indigenous Feminism, Stó:lō Women, and Historical Research

Indigenous feminist literature is central to these arguments, especially to the field's debate around Indigenous feminism itself. In conversations with her research partners, Indigenous women from across Canada of different ages, Grace Ouellette learned that they were generally ambivalent about feminism, unsure of what it meant, and held starkly divergent positions on whether feminism had value for them.[5] Within the academy, Indigenous scholars are asking these same questions as well. Kim Anderson, Joyce Green, Shari Huhndorf, and Cheryl Suzack point to the problematic history of white women's goals and voices overshadowing the concerns and problems of Indigenous women and women of colour. Further, this obfuscation of Indigenous women's needs becomes doubly oppressive when, within Indigenous communities, white feminism's lack of relevance can be used to dismiss Indigenous women's concerns or refute the existence of Indigenous feminism at all.[6] In particular, this essay is a response to Green's semi-sarcastic comment that "[it] is as though some authority has decided that Aboriginal women cannot be culturally authentic, or traditional, or acceptable, if they are feminist."[7] While Green's statement is certainly tongue-in-cheek, it represents the nearly ubiquitous notion that Indigenous women cannot be feminist—an idea this chapter seeks to counter. An analysis of Stó:lō women's histories at Coqualeetza can help refute any such claims, as in this instance, women's actions are connected to Stó:lō historical traditions relating to women's roles at the site specifically. Though ascribing the label "feminist" to historical actors is an admittedly fraught endeavour, the Coqualeetza occupation reveals how Stó:lō women's politics and actions are linked to Stó:lō traditions of gender roles and women's power.

Scholarship on Stó:lō histories is likewise foundational to this chapter. That said, historical literature authored by settlers has not yet discussed Stó:lō women's histories in any significant way, despite Stó:lō principles that women merit respect and have important social roles as matriarchs, leaders, and knowledge keepers.[8] Additionally, though Stó:lō authors and academics have written on a wide variety of topics, these works have only rarely centred gender or women.[9] Settler anthropologists have spent more time than historians have on women's traditional roles; however, these discussions represent historic settler views of gender, which are not compatible with either Stó:lō gender norms or current academic and activist understandings of gender.[10] Only recent efforts have begun to seriously grapple with Stó:lō gender and women's histories, but there is as yet no discussion of the possibilities of Stó:lō feminisms.[11]

While my aim is to contribute to the existing discussions on Indigenous feminism and Stó:lō studies, this chapter is also heavily influenced by recent work in Indigenous research methodologies. I am a white settler working within a Eurocentric discipline that has a legacy of marginalizing, erasing, and otherwise doing harm to Indigenous peoples. As Indigenous scholars have argued, settler involvement in research relating to Indigenous communities must be approached carefully so that not only does it do no harm but in fact benefits the communities involved.[12] I have attempted to do my best to follow the practices laid out by Indigenous scholars and Stó:lō Elders and community members to ensure that this research has positive effects for the people who work with me on it.[13] Adopting decolonial and anti-oppressive methods, prioritizing Indigenous voices, ensuring interview partners are aware of their rights to free and prior informed consent, and maintaining reciprocal relationships with the Stó:lō people and families who have engaged with me in the research is crucial for me to maintain my academic integrity and my personal ethics as a queer woman and intersectional feminist. In terms of the research itself, this means that I approach my sources—for this chapter, these include Stó:lō oral tradition, archival documents from Stó:lō and settler sources, Stó:lō and settler newspaper accounts, and oral histories from recent interviews with Stó:lō individuals—as all equally legitimate historical sources, which, as distinct media, must each be read differently and evaluated on their own merits in a way that is not predetermined by their form. In the case of oral tradition and oral histories, I follow protocols that Stó:lō people have taught to me, for example by ensuring the retelling is verbatim to the original narrative, because telling a story incorrectly or incompletely violates storytelling practices. Especially because I am an outsider to Stó:lō communities, I take care to separate my analysis from the retelling, and I follow up with storytellers and interview partners to ensure that this analysis does not harm the tradition or history they shared with me. I have not been in the situation where a Stó:lō interview partner has objected to my analysis; if that were to happen, a commitment to prioritizing Stó:lō voices would mean careful listening to those perspectives, unpacking and probable readjusting of my analysis, and a transparent discussion, perhaps even within the publication, regarding the divergence in outlooks.[14] I also try to be aware, as other academics are, of both the personal and historiographic politics inherent in oral history interviews, where who we are as complex individuals, what we say as narrators, interviewers, and actors, and the record we create together can have real implications for contemporary Indigenous communities and scholarship.[15]

Kw'eqwá:líth'á Sx̱wō̱x̱wiyá:m

Within Stó:lō oral traditions there is abundant evidence pointing to the historical significance of women and the power of women's roles. Sx̱wōx̱wiyá:m, oral traditions, explain Stó:lō myth-age history, a period beginning prior to but extending into the era of lived human existence; sqwélqwel relate oral histories of a particular family, individual, or event. In some ways, sx̱wōx̱wiyá:m function on a separate plane that is x̱á:x̱a (sacred, taboo), though spiritual actors can cross dimensions and their actions have reverberations in the human realm as well. Moreover, though sx̱wōx̱wiyá:m relate histories that occurred eons ago, they are also very much part of contemporary Stó:lō outlooks.[16] Women feature prominently in Stó:lō sx̱wōx̱wiyá:m.[17] For example, X̱ex̱á:ls, the Transformer, appears sometimes as three brother bears and one sister bear, showing that even one of the most potent figures in Stó:lō spirituality has a female aspect.[18] Additionally, there are many important place names in S'ólh Téméxw (Stó:lō territories), such as Lhílheqey (Mount Cheam) and Kw'eqwá:líth'á (Coqualeetza), for instance, which relate to the histories of women.[19] Moreover, sx̱wōx̱wiyá:m about women such as the wife of T'xwelátse and female beings like the giantess Th'owx̱iya offer important lessons about "learning to live together in a good way" and respecting Elders' instructions, respectively.[20] These sx̱wōx̱wiyá:m and others reveal the diverse and powerful roles that women played in Stó:lō communities.

The Kw'eqwá:líth'á sx̱wōx̱wiyá:m is an example that delineates acceptable behaviour along gendered lines while simultaneously emphasizing the positions of respect due to Stó:lō women. The sx̱wōx̱wiyá:m takes place at Kw'eqwá:líth'á, a place in Stó:lō territory where what is now known as the Coqualeetza stream joins Luckakuck Creek. It explains that during a famine, a group of men and their sons left their wives and daughters at home while they went to look for salmon. They caught some but decided to eat them instead of taking them back to share with the women at home. One of the boys disapproved of this and used bark to bind some salmon eggs to his leg before returning to tell his mother about the men's actions. On his arrival and revelation of the eggs, the boy's mother and the other women were angry to hear about their husbands' selfishness. The women began to beat their husbands' beds with sticks, which in Stó:lō spiritual traditions represents an attempt to harm them. The women then took their husbands' blankets, paint, and feathers and caught up to the men at Kw'eqwá:líth'á, where they beat their husbands' blankets and invoked X̱ex̱á:ls to punish their husbands. Realizing what was happening, one of the men quickly began painting the others as particular birds to hide them, but X̱ex̱á:ls granted the women's wishes and transformed all the men into those birds, who then flew off and did not return to their homes.[21]

From written word alone, it is difficult to know what this story would have meant to Stó:lō people in the past. Anthropologist Charles Hill-Tout made the earliest recorded version of this sx̱wō̱x̱wiyá:m in 1902, composing the narrative based on conversations with three Ts'elxwéyeqw Th'ewá:lí men, all from the same family of converted Methodists: Captain John, Commodore, and David Selaketen.[22] Hill-Tout's small number of all-male interview partners, combined with his own sexist outlook, clouds his retelling of the story; for instance, Hill-Tout refers to the women as "angry wives," a type of casual misogyny no doubt common among settler men in the early 1900s.[23] In addition, Hill-Tout makes it clear that he did not fully understand elements of the story yet chose not to investigate further: speaking of the women beating their husbands' blankets, he writes, "The action has apparently some occult import, the nature of which I could not gather."[24] Without this clarification or the insights of Stó:lō women regarding Hill-Tout's retelling, we must understand this version of the narrative to be incomplete. Unfortunately, subsequent anthropologists also only collected transcriptions of this story from men, so it is difficult to assess its significance and meaning for Stó:lō women living in the early twentieth century.[25]

However, when we place this story more fully into a Stó:lō context and read it from a woman-centric perspective, there are many meanings that can be made from this sx̱wō̱x̱wiyá:m. When I have heard Stó:lō knowledge keepers, both men and women, tell the Kw'eqwá:líth'á sx̱wō̱x̱wiyá:m in the past few years, they have closed by emphasizing the importance of sharing and being honest. This perspective is somewhat more neutral than my own, but it informs my analysis of the narrative nevertheless. I see this sxwōxwiyá:m as simultaneously a story of male privilege, a narrative of women's power, and a tale about serious consequences for serious offences. The men's deeds are condemned three times: first by the child, then by the women, and ultimately by Xexá:ls. They have committed a serious transgression against their wives, and we know from other sxwōxwiyá:m that misdeeds, especially against marital partners, are not tolerated.[26] The women are rightly angered and take out their fury in a culturally significant way by beating their husbands' blankets. The fact that "Kw'eqwá:líth'á" translates as "beating blankets" emphasizes the women's agency in this story and centres their rejection of their husbands' transgression as the most important element of the narrative. Moreover, the transformation of the men into the birds they were attempting to disguise themselves as is a common way for Xexá:ls to punish wrong-doers. Xexá:ls, who is not a solely masculine entity, puts a chaotic world to rights in part through transforming people who have committed offences into elements of the natural landscape within S'ólh Téméxw. These transformations are simultaneously punishments of the transgressors and living reminders to other Stó:lō about the need to live in harmony with one another. In addition to other layers of significance that this story may have for Stó:lō people, it also clearly indicates women's strong social and spiritual power and the significance of treating one's spouse and family well.[27] Kw'eqwá:líth'á is thus an important site in terms of Stó:lō women's history, and these themes serve as foundations for Stó:lō women's feminist actions at the site millennia later.

Stó:lō Gender Dynamics, Settler Colonialism, and Patriarchy

Although women's power is definitively demonstrated in sxwōxwiyá:m such as the one about Kw'eqwá:líth'á, this does not signify that historically speaking, there was gender equality within Stó:lō communities. Scholars have so far mainly written about class divisions in Stó:lō histories, arguing that Stó:lō communities were mainly constituted as three classes: smelá:lh, the upper class; s'téxem, a kind of lower-middle class; and skw'iyéth, a slave or serf-like class. Exceptional smelá:lh men led their communities and maintained control over family histories, spiritual knowledge, and resource sites, while those whose actions were considered disgraceful would descend the social ladder.[28] However, while we know much about the systems of class in Stó:lō societies, more research is necessary to fully appreciate the roles and status of Stó:lō women within their communities. According to Stó:lō people today, while women were rarely chiefs, they did have roles in guiding their communities as matriarchs. Though it is not often the focus of study, it can be deduced from the literature that women, especially those within the smelá:lh, had opportunities to hold some social power, but it is likewise clear that these avenues were separate from those that men could pursue. I agree with Carlson's hypothesis that female smelá:lh would have had more in common with male smelá:lh than with female s'téxem,[29] though I would add that these women likely also held more social prestige than male s'téxem. Gender is a crucial area of future research to better understand the complicated ways gender and class intersected in Stó:lō history.

In S'ólh Téméxw, as elsewhere, colonialism changed much. While we cannot assume that colonialism defines Indigenous peoples and their histories, we do still have to acknowledge the significant material changes that come with exposure to disease, genocidal violence, and the rapid loss of land.[30] S<u>x</u>wō<u>x</u>wiyá:m and settler accounts alike explain the devastation that smallpox and other European disease wrought on Stó:lō and other Salish communities beginning in the late eighteenth century.[31] Tensions between Xwélmexw (Halkomelem-speaking Indigenous peoples, including Stó:lō) and Xwelítem ("the hungry ones")—settlers—began as soon as the latter began setting up permanent settlements; for instance, the mysterious fire at Fort Langley in 1827 can be understood as Xwélmexw resistance to Xwelítem appropriations.[32] Xwelítem "discovery" of gold in S'ólh Téméxw in 1858 rapidly expanded the movement of settlers into Stó:lō territories, bringing not only intensive resource extraction but also heightened violence that reached a flashpoint during the Fraser Canyon War. While the Gold Rush drew high numbers of mostly single white men to the area, many were transient workers who left after the rush became a trickle; however, the Fraser Valley's arable land attracted settler families beginning in the 1860s, who came to stay.

Reacting to the rapid influx of settlers, Governor James Douglas literally "reserved" tracts of land for Xwélmexw, with the idea that treaties would come soon after. In 1864, land surveyor William McColl arrived in S'ólh Téméxw and worked with Stó:lō to identify and mark off fourteen reserves amounting to 39,400 acres, which amounted to approximately forty-five acres for each of the 885 Stó:lō in the area surveyed.[33] Subsequent colonial officials abandoned the promise of treaties, and in 1868, Joseph Trutch, the Chief Commissioner of Land and Works, had reserves in S'ólh Téméxw reduced by over 90 percent, down to only 3,430 acres, or less than ten acres per Stó:lō family.[34] S'ólh Téméxw also became bisected by new roads, and important sites like the lake at

Semá:th (Sumas) were drained for more farmland. These massive land appropriations were accompanied by colonial legislation that prohibited Indigenous fishing and potlatching, and compelled children to attend residential schools. Stó:lō fought all of these incursions and became experts in navigating colonial legal frameworks, yet the material losses had tremendous consequences for Stó:lō communities.

This period also saw the appropriation of the Kw'eqwá:líth'á site, the history of which to some extent serves as a microcosm for the tensions existing between Stó:lō and settlers ever since. In the nineteenth century, the area was a shared space for all Stó:lō and commonly used by many bands, especially for fishing. However, since no single community lived there, McColl did not designate it a reserve in his 1864 survey, leaving it open to settler-colonial land appropriation. Five years later, on 16 April 1869, the Crown granted the "asset" of 150 acres to Ann McColl, the widow of the surveyor who had laid out the reserves five years previously.[35] Over the next two and a half decades, McColl in turn sold parts of the property to other settlers, A.C. Wells and Horatio Webb. In 1882, the Methodist missionaries Charles and Sarah Tate established the Coqualeetza Mission Home nearby and began teaching students and proselytizing Stó:lō people. In 1891, the home burned down, and the following year the missionaries acquired 33.9 acres from the parcel originally granted to McColl, opening a new three-storey residential school, the Coqualeetza Industrial Institute, there the following year. The residential school continued to operate there after the United Church sold the Coqualeetza grounds back to the federal government in 1929. On 26 November 1935, the state also opened a tuberculosis preventorium at the site, and after the residential school closed in 1940 its buildings were incorporated into the preventorium, which became the Coqualeetza Indian Hospital in 1941. With the end of segregated health care for Indigenous peoples in 1968 and the decline in tuberculosis, the hospital closed in 1969 though the site remained the property of the Department of National Health and Welfare. In 1974, the Department of Indian Affairs (DIA) proposed to the Treasury Board that the site be transferred to them, with the idea that DIA could lease and eventually sell the site to the Coqualeetza centre. Instead, however, the Treasury Board transferred the site to the Department of Public Works, which began leasing part of what they now considered a surplus Crown asset to the Department of National Defence for use as military offices and barracks, with the remainder of the site going unused.[36] Coqualeetza is thus a complicated space for Stó:lō, representing not only the history related through the Kw'eqwá:líth'á sx̱wō̱x̱wiyá:m, but also the theft of their traditional lands, the growing significance of Christianity in S'ólh Téméxw, the abuses of the residential school area, the stigmatization and pathologization of their communities by settler medical experts, and the bristling presence of settler armed forces in their territories.

Of course, in addition to these material changes, Stó:lō also had to contend with colonialism's accompanying ideologies of patriarchy and heterosexism. While recognizing that pre-contact traditions of gender equality were part of certain Indigenous communities' epistemological outlooks during early contact and colonization, settler men's preference to engage with Indigenous men and their inability to recognize Indigenous women's authority "reordered gender relations to subordinate women."[37] As settlers increasingly showed their patriarchal bias, Stó:lō likely felt pressure to conform to patriarchy because, as Brendan Hokowhitu explains, colonialism compels Indigenous masculinities to adopt patriarchal and heteronormative traits of "dominant invader masculinity."[38] Unfortunately, the existing gender divisions within Stó:lō communities, in which men and women both held different forms of power, could easily be reframed as a strict hierarchy under colonial patriarchy. As settler colonialism became increasingly entrenched, this outlook on gender roles and male superiority bled over and grew in influence within many Indigenous nations.[39] This pattern holds true in Stó:lō history, as women were excluded from at least official positions of power in new settler-colonial systems; however, it seems women retained some social authority within Stó:lō-specific contexts. As Mark Point explains, "You have to remember that under the Indian Act, the old system that Indian Affairs had in place where the chiefs were elected . . . all the chiefs in the old days were all men, always men, and women, their place was in the home, raising the family and being obedient and subservient to their husbands. But that was only the system that Indian Affairs put in place. The old system that was here before contact, European contact, was that women ran things. We were a matrilineal society. Our chiefs, our leaders were determined by women."[40] In Stó:lō territory, the imposition of settler patriarchy continued to limit Stó:lō women's ability to take up official leadership positions for more than a century. By the early 1900s, and certainly by the postwar period, Stó:lō women who were active in their communities as educators, knowledge keepers, and mothers engaged in work we might today see as political or as oppositional to the colonial state, although in general it was not framed as such. Well into the second half of the twentieth century, Stó:lō men occupied nearly all positions of official political leadership in their communities, especially in terms of hereditary and elected chieftainship. However, by the 1970s, Stó:lō women began to not only take on political leadership positions in their bands but also to politicize their cultural and community-based work. This merging of community-centred cultural curation and women's growing political power was central to the push to regain control of the Coqualeetza site.

Coqualeetza, Gender, and Stó:lō Cultural Sovereignty in the 1970s

Throughout the late 1960s and early 1970s, Stó:lō communities increasingly engaged in collective cultural sharing at the Coqualeetza site, and women were central to these efforts. At this time, much of the site was empty, enabling Stó:lō to use it as a community space for these activities, although Coqualeetza remained the property of the Department of Public Works, which leased some buildings on the site to the Department of National Defence. Stó:lō women ran the Salish Weavers Guild, which became well-known even among settlers during this era and operated out of a small building at the Coqualeetza site.[41] The Coqualeetza Elders Group, which formed in 1970 and used the "Big House"—the former home of the principal of the residential school—as the site for their meetings, had forty-four members, thirty of whom were women.[42] During this period, Stó:lō women were the main curators of the expanding series of cultural education programs at Coqualeetza.

Not so in the political realm, where Stó:lō chiefs both elected and hereditary were predominantly men. Stó:lō political leaders at the time sought, as their ancestors had done before them,[43] to protect their connection to S'ólh Téméxw, a challenge that by then looked like seeking the return of appropriated Stó:lō lands, including Coqualeetza, which was still owned by the federal government. In November 1969, the inaugural meeting of what became the Union of BC Indian Chiefs (UBCIC), a pan-tribal organization of Indigenous leaders from across the province, was held in Kamloops, BC. At this meeting, Stó:lō delegates came to entertain the idea of a cultural education centre; participants discussed how establishing such a centre at the site was a viable strategy for promoting both community-based cultural education and for pursuing the land claim to the site.[44] The return of the Coqualeetza site would both rectify a colonial error around land appropriation and provide the necessary space for the expansion of cultural activities at Coqualeetza. Stó:lō chiefs from the Skowkale band, the community geographically closest to Coqualeetza, saw the value in such an entwined strategy and pushed this idea further in 1970. Skowkale leaders passed a resolution stating that since the site was no longer being used as a hospital, and "whereas it has been intimated that this property would be turned back to the Indians for their use," they thereby requested that the federal government "make every consideration to turning over this property to the original owners Skulkayn Band as Indian reserve" for use as an educational complex.[45] There was no federal response to the 1970 Skowkale band council resolution, and the site remained property of the state. However, Stó:lō chiefs stayed committed to the potential political use of a Coqualeetza cultural centre in the years to come.

The creation of the Coqualeetza centre was thus founded through dual political (male) and cultural (female) goals. Male Stó:lō political leaders who hoped that the establishment of the cultural centre would serve their political ends involved themselves in the creation and directorship of the centre. The year of 1973 marks the establishment of the Coqualeetza Cultural Education Training Centre, which I will refer to as simply the Coqualeetza centre.[46] In its first year, there were four women and five men on the board; in 1974, there were three and eight, respectively; and the following year, there were four and five once again. These figures show that the organization generally welcomed women on its directorial team in its founding years, though men maintained a majority at its outset. However, in this cultural venture as in the others previous, women held central positions: Mary Lou Andrew, a Stó:lō woman from Seabird Island band, was the chair of the centre at this time, for instance.[47] In addition to space for the Elders Group, the centre provided a series of dynamic programs to Stó:lō on topics such as Halq'eméylem language, arts and crafts, dance, and Stó:lō history, as well as business and technical vocational courses. As its programs expanded, the centre continued to need additional space for things like a reference library, a language laboratory, and a carving shed.[48] The Coqualeetza centre's position as a cultural space with a political purpose identifies it as a community-driven endeavour, directed by male politicians but fuelled by the work of women staffers.

While the Coqualeetza centre more than fulfilled its potential as a site for cultural education, its establishment did not result in the political response Stó:lō politicians sought. The federal government continued to avoid Stó:lō requests to open negotiations into a land claim for the site, and the Department of Public Works, then owners of the land, began charging the organization rent and utilities for its use of the buildings at Coqualeetza.[49] Naturally, this circumstance was frustrating for many Stó:lō people: the government was forcing them to pay to use land they had never given up, to which they had always laid claim, to which they had a longstanding connection through sx̱wō̱xwiyá:m, and which had a significant contemporary use. Coqualeetza staff and Stó:lō chiefs renewed their efforts, working together to petition Indian Affairs for control of the site. Of particular note here is the strong working relationships between Mary Lou Andrew, Chief Archie Charles (both from the Seabird Island band), and Chief Bill Mussell, who frequently attended UBCIC meetings together. They, along with other Stó:lō chiefs, repeatedly contacted Indian Affairs over the next several years to initiate a land claims process for the Coqualeetza site, to no avail.[50] Judd Buchanan, who became Minister of Indian Affairs in August 1974, was remarkably resistant to the idea of meeting with Stó:lō chiefs or Coqualeetza staff to discuss the land claim, and he more or less ignored their letters, telegrams, and phone calls for the next year and a half.[51] Andrew was tenacious, however, continuing to write to numerous Canadian members of Parliament (MPs) to request their support for Coqualeetza's cause in early 1976. At least four Canadian MPs wrote to Buchanan after hearing from Andrew about Coqualeetza's situation, advising him to formally respond to Stó:lō claims over the Coqualeetza site.[52] Buchanan seems to have ignored the counsel of these MPs, just as he continued to ignore Stó:lō requests. Despite the fact that in Stó:lō communities, cultural education had become coded as women's work and politics were largely the realm of men, Andrew's ability to move through this division demonstrates not only her commitment to the dual goals of the Coqualeetza site but also the increasing permeability of gendered social roles during this period.

While there was a degree of plasticity for some individuals working against the settler state for Stó:lō cultural sovereignty, to some extent gender hierarchy remained between Stó:lō individuals. No anecdote offers a better representation of this complex picture than one from the spring of 1976. Realizing that their efforts to make meaningful contact with Indian Affairs had resulted in no progress for a year and a half, Andrew and Charles decided to organize a sit-in at the site and invited Buchanan to join them. On 18 March 1976, over 100 Stó:lō gathered at the site to participate in the protest. The sit-in was a "peaceful demonstration" with drumming and dancing.[53] Buchanan's response to his invitation was to send Cy Fairholm from the Office of Native Title to meet with Stó:lō at the sit-in. The meeting was unproductive because Fairholm seemed, to Stó:lō people in attendance, to be unacquainted with the issues at stake or the history of their land claim.[54] As the afternoon's discussions drew to an unsurprisingly unsuccessful close, Andrew produced a cheque for $1,187. This was the amount of rent that, according to the federal government, the Coqualeetza centre owed the Department of Public Works for leasing buildings on the site. Instead of presenting the cheque to Fairholm, however, she gave it to Chief Charles, declaring that since Coqualeetza was Stó:lō land, it was to Stó:lō political leadership, not the Canadian state, that the cultural centre was beholden.[55] This symbolic gesture reveals that while Stó:lō were united against the state in their efforts to regain the Coqualeetza site, there remained a fundamental hierarchy within Stó:lō cultural sovereignty efforts, where male politicians held more power and prestige than did female educational staff. It also affirms the politicization of cultural education, while Andrew's acumen in this moment again shows her capacity to embrace that political role, moving beyond the common gender divisions within Stó:lō activism at the time.

After the unsuccessful negotiations in March, Stó:lō cultural workers and political leaders began to plan the 3 May 1976 occupation described in detail at the outset of this chapter. Oral history interviews with Stó:lō activists from 2002 and 2014 reveal the significance of gender dynamics both during the occupation and in the way activists remembered the protest. During the event, women led and actively participated in the day's work. Indeed, of the twenty people charged with trespassing, thirteen were women—a clear majority.[56] Stó:lō oral history interview partners remember that the occupation was supported by a significant number of both women and Elders. During a 2002 conversation with Melissa McDowell, Mark Point, a Skowkale band member, confirmed the assertion of Larry Commodore (a Th'ewá:lí band member) that women were a significant force during the occupation, stating that "there were more women inside than there were men inside, yeah. I don't know. There weren't many men who would stand up and be counted . . . I think the women were more aware that we had to have a change, that we had to take action to do something for ourselves. Because they, of anybody in our communities, knew of the conditions, knew of the changes that were needed to bring about the changes in the quality of lives."[57] Counterintuitively, this recognition of women's significance in the occupation coexists with a privileging of male narratives of the event. McDowell reports that in 2002 when she asked community members whom to speak to about the Coqualeetza occupation, most people directed her to Stó:lō men.[58] Moreover, the Stó:lō men who spoke with McDowell told her that the people who organized the occupation were the chiefs, particularly Archie Charles, along with the Coqualeetza board of directors.[59] Such a framing positions the mostly male chiefs as the central figures, with the board, including the chair Mary Lou Andrew and other women, in a supporting role.

There is another moment in the oral history narratives that demonstrates both women's power at the occupation and male omission of women's centrality in the events. In his conversation with McDowell, Commodore mentions that when it started to become clear that the soldiers were going to enter the building, Skowkale chief Bob Hall helped the group accept that what they should do now was prepare to passively resist. However, in 2014, when I spoke to Commodore and Marian Bisaillon, a non-Stó:lō Indigenous woman who was Commodore's partner during the 1970s and who worked at the Coqualeetza centre, Bisaillon noted that when she became uncomfortable with the rising tensions in the building and the lengths to which occupiers were going to keep the soldiers out, she reminded Hall of the occupation's commitment to non-violence. Bisaillon explained, "Things started getting a little bit crazy, and I went up to Bob, and I said, this is supposed to be a peaceful demonstration, and he's like, 'Oh, yeah, you're right! You're right!' and then . . . because we knew we couldn't hold [the military] back, right, so we kind of all went back into the room and we kind of just all went into a circle and sat down and were like, okay, we're ready to go."[60] Bisaillon's reported ability to guide Hall in that moment reveals the complexity of not only gender at the site but also insider/outsider politics and the social hierarchies of Stó:lō communities. As a non-Stó:lō woman with a Stó:lō spouse,[61] connected to occupation through her position as a Coqualeetza staff member, Bisaillon's positionality in relation to the site was considerably more complicated than Hall's, and this could have limited her social capacity and ability to influence him. And yet, Hall apparently followed her advice, indicating that political leaders valued the cultural educators, and that men took women's perspectives seriously during the occupation.

It is intriguing that even though Commodore has always affirmed that women were more prevalent than men during the occupation, in 2002 he did not share the significant detail that Bisaillon, his partner, had been responsible for guiding Hall during a climactic moment of the occupation. This is not to critique Commodore, Hall, or the other men interviewed, for there are any number of reasons why they did not mention this fact, especially considering that oral history interviews tend to focus on an individual discussing their own lived experiences. However, it is important to note that Bisaillon's actions in facilitating the final moments of the occupation did not emerge until she told me about them during our interview in 2014, indicating that the work of women, particularly Coqualeetza staffers, during the occupation is not part of the common Stó:lō narrative of the event, which predominantly centres male actors. Despite Stó:lō men positioning chiefs as the central figures in the occupation, it is clear from other archival and oral history evidence, including those men's own assertions, that women played significant roles as leaders and participants in the occupation. Greater recognition of this fact is needed both within Stó:lō communities and within the scholarship, for it speaks to the power of Indigenous women's activism, to the real drawbacks that come from excluding Indigenous women from formal political positions, and to the ways that not only the settler-colonial state but sometimes also Indigenous men overlook Indigenous women's voices and agency.

One vignette from after the occupation ended epitomizes the never-ending resistance of Stó:lō women to the settler state. When the occupiers were placed in the RCMP holding cells, women were separated into one part of the building and men into another. Bisaillon recalled: "I just remember standing in the cell, and then the women started singing. So there were all of us in there, singing our little hearts out. . . . We sang and sang." Commodore reflected that he and the other men were able to hear the women's songs from their own cells and that this was an uplifting, strengthening moment: "There were four of us in jail, four men in jail: Kat Pennier, Bob Hall, and Vaughn Jones. Four of us in jail, four men in jail, and then there was a bunch of women in the women's cell too that were arrested and they were singing Indian songs, beating on the bars or whatever. We could hear them where we were at. They were just pounding and singing Indian songs and it was pretty, it was a pretty good feeling, resistance. Even though we were in jail, we're still resisting."[62] These memories again emphasize the crucial role Stó:lō women played in the occupation and thereafter, and their commitment to resisting the settler-colonial state alongside Stó:lō men.

While the occupation itself was a climactic moment in Stó:lō politics, its denouement was considerably more placid, though it too speaks to gender dynamics at Coqualeetza. The charges against the occupiers were dropped. Stó:lō chiefs and Coqualeetza staff continued to pressure the government for the return of the land, and the grievance with the Department of Public Works over the rent continued. Since the Coqualeetza centre was being funded by the federal Cultural Education Centres initiative, government officials diverted the cumulative amount of the rent owed to the Department of Public Works from the money that they had earmarked for Coqualeetza's programming. So for the last quarter of 1976, instead of funds of $36,273, the Coqualeetza centre received only $4,915 to run all of their courses and workshops.[63] Eventually, the Department of National Defence vacated the site, tacitly returning it to Stó:lō people—though even in December 1976, they were already planning to do this.[64] From 1976 onwards, Stó:lō political councils as well as the Coqualeetza centre continued to operate from the site, which is now the bustling headquarters for Stó:lō Nation's various offices and programs. However, the Coqualeetza site continues to be in a complicated position because the Crown still holds title to the site, which remains a "surplus asset." Regardless of the site's legal status, many Stó:lō individuals credit their current control of it to the Coqualeetza occupation.[65]

While it is clear that women's leadership and participation were integral to both the cultural and political work that went into the organizing and protest at the Coqualeetza centre, the impact of the occupation on Stó:lō women's political capital is somewhat more ambiguous. For instance, examining the shifting gender makeup of the Coqualeetza centre's board of directors may speak to the ongoing gendered nature of leadership roles in Stó:lō communities. While the gender makeup of the Coqualeetza centre's board of directors had been fairly equal leading up to the occupation, in the years immediately after, men began to significantly outnumber women on the board. In 1977, the board was made up of three women and five men, but thereafter women's involvement declined abruptly, until 1981 when there was one woman on a seven-person board of directors. The lower numbers of women's involvement coincide with the rising numbers of male chiefs joining the board: Chief John George Sr. joined in 1978, Chief Sam Douglas joined in 1979, Chief Steven Point joined in 1980, and Chiefs Ron John and Frank Peters joined in 1981. It seems that as more men, especially those who were chiefs, sought to extend their leadership over Coqualeetza, there was decreasing room for women to participate as directors of the organization. Women's leadership in the Coqualeetza centre shifts again in the last two decades of the twentieth century, however. Throughout the rest of the 1980s, the ratio of women to men was much more even, with women even outnumbering men on the board by two in 1989. In the last decade of the twentieth century, the gender balance shifted again, and women began to consistently outnumber men by 1995. In 1998, 1999, and 2000, the board was entirely made up of female directors. This increase in women's involvement on the board of the centre correlates with their growing political power, as women were not elected to positions as Stó:lō chiefs until this same period.[66] Of course, even at the close of the twentieth century, women's presence on the Coqualeetza board was much higher than their presence on chiefs' councils, suggesting the gendered split between cultural education and formal political power continued to be a formative social dynamic throughout the period.

Conclusion

Ultimately, this analysis of the Coqualeetza occupation shows that even as Stó:lō people—regardless of gender—united against settler colonialism, the gendered division of labour which cast political work as masculine and heritage work as feminine meant that women's presence and power at the site were underemphasized at the time, and have been largely absent from memories of the occupation ever since. Stó:lō women struggled for acceptance in typically male political environments, but as the example of women like Andrew shows, we know that this gendered division was permeable. While invader masculinity influenced Stó:lō gender dynamics to a significant degree, Stó:lō women involved with the Coqualeetza centre during the 1970s were able, like the women in the Kw'eqwá:líth'á sx̱wōx̱wiyá:m, to mobilize toward the improvement of their communities—regardless of their exclusion or marginalization from political leadership. In addition, unlike the men in the sx̱wōx̱wiyá:m, the male activists involved with the Coqualeetza occupation respected women's presence during the occupation, though they sometimes did not fully recognize women's power thereafter—a tendency which is replicated in shared Stó:lō memories about the action. For this reason, it is crucial to focus on Stó:lō women's contributions to the Coqualeetza occupation, a tactic which centres historical actors who have thus far been marginal in accounts of Stó:lō pasts. Moreover, for Stó:lō and other Indigenous communities, reclaiming women's historic power may be key in battling both settler colonialism and what Green calls the "colonizer patriarchy" that still exists within Indigenous communities.[67] As Elsie Redbird argues, "If the erosion of sovereignty comes from dis-empowering women, its renewed strength will come from re-empowering them."[68] Contextualizing this history of the occupation within the narrative of the Kw'eqwá:líth'á sx̱wōx̱wiyá:m reminds us of the historic roots of Stó:lō women's power, and the potential this power has for future Stó:lō feminist action.

Notes

1 To my teachers, partners, and friends in Stó:lō territory, especially Iyeselwet/Denise Douglas, Larry Commodore, and Marian Bisaillon, who taught me so much about Coqualeetza and the occupation, and to archivists Tia Halstad and Patricia Raymond-Adair: y'alh yuxw kw'a's hò:y! Thanks also to Mary-Ellen Kelm, Keith Carlson, and the editors of this collection for encouraging me to develop my ideas on the occupation. The research for this chapter was supported by funding from the Social Sciences and Humanities Research Council of Canada.

2 The Stó:lō are the Indigenous peoples whose territory encompasses much of what is now known as the Lower Mainland in southwestern British Columbia. The Halq'eméylem word stó:lō means "river," a translation that signifies the close connection between Stó:lō, "the river people," and the river now known as the Fraser. Historically, people in these communities developed shared language, economic and social systems, and intellectual heritage. Today there are more than two dozen Stó:lō First Nations, also known as bands, who continue to share this knowledge and culture and maintain their connection to their homelands.

3 In this chapter, I use Kw'eqwá:líth'á to refer to both the historic site prior to colonization and to the oral tradition about it; when speaking about the site in the twentieth century, I use Coqualeetza because although it is the anglicization of the Halq'eméylem place name, this spelling has become ubiquitously used by Stó:lō organizations and individuals and is still used today. See Galloway, *Dictionary of Upriver Halkomelem*, 194–95.

4 Marian Bisaillon and Larry Commodore, interview with author, 11 July 2014; McDowell, "This Is Stó:lō Indian Land"; Stanbrook and Doyle, "Seventeen Natives Charged in Coqualeetza Clash," 1, 20; Woods, "Coqualeetza: Legacies of Land Use," 74.

5 Ouellette, *The Fourth World*; see especially "Aboriginal Women and Feminism," 88–91.

6 Anderson, "Affirmations of an Indigenous Feminist"; Green, "Taking Account of Aboriginal Feminism"; Huhndorf and Suzack, "Indigenous Feminism: Theorizing the Issues."

7 Green, "Taking Account of Aboriginal Feminism," 25.

8 Two fairly recent major works on Stó:lō and Coast Salish pasts and presents undoubtedly contribute to the field in important ways, but neither focuses on gender: Bierwert, *Brushed by Cedar, Living by the River*; and Carlson, *The Power of Place, the Problem of Time*. Some exceptions to this include Bedard, "Becoming Xwiyálemot"; and Benson, "When There's Work to Be Done, Our Hands Go Out."

9 For example, Archibald, *Indigenous Storywork*; Buker, "Walking Backwards into the Future with Our Stories"; Gardner, "Tset Híkwstexw Te Sqwélteltset, We Hold Our Language High"; Maracle, *I Am Woman*; Pennier, *Call Me Hank*; Point, "Intergenerational Experiences in Aboriginal Education"; Bolton, *Xwelíqwiya: The Life of a Stó:lō Matriarch*; Victor, "'Searching for the Bone Needle'"; and Victor, "X̲ex̲á:ls and the Power of Transformation." Maracle's *I Am Woman* is the sole publication focusing on gender, women, and feminism from a Stó:lō perspective.

10 For instance, though these works are significant, especially in their reproduction of Stó:lō voices, because of their social and historical positions, the (mostly male) authors have tended to see gender as a fixed biological fact determined by sexual characteristics and ignore the significance of women due to colonial heteropatriarchy.

See works by anthropologists Franz Boas, Wilson Duff, Charles Hill-Tout, Diamond Jenness, Marian Smith, Wayne Suttles, as well as by Chilliwack-based amateur anthropologists Casey and Oliver Wells.

11 Wesley, "Twin-Spirited Woman." Keith Carlson is also beginning a project on Stó:lō women and place names.

12 Andersen and O'Brien, *Sources and Methods in Indigenous Studies*; Archibald, *Indigenous Storywork*; Brown and Strega, *Research as Resistance*; Denzin, Lincoln, and Smith, *Handbook of Critical and Indigenous Methodologies*; Kovach, *Indigenous Methodologies*; Smith, *Decolonizing Methodologies*, 1st ed.; Wilson, *Research Is Ceremony*.

13 I am especially grateful to Lumlamelut Wee Lay Laq/Laura Wealick, Naxaxalt'si/Albert (Sonny) McHalsie, Tsel'x̲at/Maxine Prevost, and Ts'i:wethot/Josette Jim, who have shared time with me and taught me the protocols I know. I am grateful to Drs. Keith Carlson and John Lutz for including me in the 2011 Stó:lō Ethnohistory Field School run by the Universities of Saskatchewan and Victoria, which also facilitated much of this learning. I have also taken to heart Jo-Ann Archibald's discussion of her own practice doing research as a Stó:lō person within Stó:lō communities, and how this might look different for a non-Indigenous person; see Archibald, *Indigenous Storywork*, 143–51.

14 Ironically enough, the only time I have experienced this type of critique of my work was with white settler interview partners. I followed the process described above and engaged in several subsequent conversations with three people involved. See Knickerbocker, "'What We've Said Can Be Proven in the Ground,'" especially n7 and n86.

15 Nickel, "'You'll Probably Tell Me That Your Grandmother Was an Indian Princess.'"

16 According to Q̲wí:qwélstom/Wenona Victor, sx̲wō̲x̲wiyá:m both represent Stó:lō "ways of knowing" and affirm Stó:lō sovereignty. Victor describes sx̲wō̲x̲wiyá:m as containing multitudes, arguing against their easy classification into any single form of knowledge: sx̲wō̲x̲wiyá:m are "equally scientific as they are ethical, historical, political, economical [*sic*], legal." Additionally, Victor rejects the easily assumed dichotomy between sx̲wō̲x̲wiyá:m and sqwélqwel, where the former are assumed to be legends and the latter, histories of real events; this binarization can lead to the assumption that sqwélqwel happened and sx̲wō̲x̲wiyá:m did not. Such an interpretation is inaccurate, for "they both recount real events." The distinction Victor does identify is that sqwélqwel can be oriented around a particular family or community, whereas sx̲wō̲x̲wiyá:m are shared by all Stó:lō individuals. However, even this differentiation is not clear-cut, for sx̲wō̲x̲wiyá:m can be connected to a family and still part of broader Stó:lō culture, and there are sqwélqwel that have value for all Stó:lō even though they are related to particular families. It seems the two ways of approaching history are more similar than scholars in the past have understood them to be. Keith Carlson has described the slippage between the two as being both "a series of sometimes unrelated happenings occurring simultaneously within the different rooms of a house," and also as "a single play unfolding simultaneously on two separate stages separated by a passageway." See Carlson, *The Power of Place, the Problem of Time*, 64; and Victor, "X̲e:x̲á:ls and the Power of Transformation," 89–91.

17 Because Stó:lō protocol affirms that it is important to tell sx̲wō̲x̲wiyá:m fully, without leaving out any details, I cannot offer summaries of the following examples, and unfortunately there is not enough space in this chapter to reproduce them in their

entirety. The notes for each example contain references to publications where the full sx̱wō̱x̱wiyá:m can be found.

18 McHalsie, Schaepe, and Carlson, "Making the World Right," 6–7.

19 Hill-Tout, "Ethnological Studies of the Mainland Halkomelem, a Division of the Salish of British Columbia, 1902," in *The Mainland Halkomelem*, 57–58; Óyewot/ Amy Cooper, as quoted in T'xwelátse et al., *Man Turned to Stone*, 33.

20 T'xwelátse et al., *Man Turned to Stone*, 22; Felix, *The Mosquito Story*.

21 Hill-Tout, *The Mainland Halkomelem*, 57–58. Though "Kw'eqwá:líth'á" is the Halq'eméylem place name and thus the preferred term, I use "Coqualeetza" in the rest of this chapter because the English spelling has become ubiquitously used by Stó:lō organizations and individuals; see Galloway, *Dictionary of Upriver Halkomelem*, 194–95.

22 Hill-Tout, *The Mainland Halkomelem*, 59. Ralph Maud, on p. 15 of his introduction to Hill-Tout, muses that perhaps Captain John and his family were not the best choice of interlocutors: due to their significant involvement in Methodism, he writes, Captain John "was perhaps not too eager to discuss the pagan doings of the old days." I see Maud's point here, and also want to affirm that just because Stó:lō individuals converted to Christianity, they did not necessarily stop participating in historic spiritual practices and/or become invalid sources of community knowledge. Recent scholarship has shown various ways that Indigenous Christians blended their new beliefs with their existing practices and traditions. The faith of Captain John and his male family members should not delegitimize what they shared with Hill-Tout.

23 Hill-Tout, *The Mainland Halkomelem*, 58.

24 Hill-Tout, 57.

25 Ralph Maud, in Hill-Tout, *The Mainland Halkomelem*, 58n12. Maud notes that Dan Milo told Oliver Wells the Kw'eqwá:líth'á sx̱wō̱x̱wiyá:m in 1970, and Bob Joe told Norman Lerman in 1976.

26 T'xwelátse et al., *Man Turned to Stone*, 22.

27 Woods, "Coqualeetza: Legacies of Land Use," 75. Woods reproduces Dan Milo and Bob Joe's retelling of the Kw'eqwá:líth'á sx̱wō̱x̱wiyá:m, writing that their particular version emphasizes the need for "respectful, harmonious relations between men and women based on the recognition that the power of women and the spirit world is stronger than physical strength and personal greed."

28 Carlson, *The Power of Place, The Problem of Time*, 134–42; Duff, *The Upper Stalo Indians of the Fraser Valley*, 80–81; Suttles, "Private Knowledge, Morality, and Social Classes among the Coast Salish," 3–13.

29 Carlson, *The Power of Place, The Problem of Time*, 30.

30 Carlson, *The Power of Place, The Problem of Time*.

31 Carlson, "The Numbers Game: Interpreting Historical Stó:lō Demographics," in *A Stó:lō-Coast Salish Historical Atlas*, 77; Carlson, *The Power of Place, The Problem of Time*, 92; Fraser, "Journal of a Voyage from the Rocky Mountains to the Pacific Ocean Performed in the Year 1808," entry for 24 June 1808, in *The Letters and Journals of Simon Fraser*, 115; Harris, "Voices of Smallpox around the Strait of Georgia"; Kelm, *Colonizing Bodies*.

32 Barnston, "Journal Kept by George Barnston, 1827–8," 28–32. Barnston reported several instances of Indigenous aggression towards the fort, as well as the fire

itself and a great meeting of Xwélmexw people at the fort several days afterwards. Barnston was not able to understand the passionate conversations these "leading men" had, but it seems after this meeting, there were no further instances of sabotage at the fort, and indeed Xwélmexw began to capitalize on their relationships with the fort, manoeuvring the fur traders into working in ways that benefited themselves.

33 Carlson, *The Power of Place, The Problem of Time*, 218; Carlson, *You Are Asked to Witness*, 71. Carlson reminds us that in comparison to settler holdings, this was not overly generous; settlers could pre-empt 160-acre farms and purchase an additional 450 acres.

34 Carlson, "Indian Reservations," in *A Stó:lō-Coast Salish Historical Atlas*, 94; Carlson, *You Are Asked to Witness*, 74. Stó:lō were also prohibited from pre-empting other land for the purposes of farming.

35 Keith Carlson, personal communication, 4 October 2019.

36 Bierwert, *Brushed by Cedar, Living by the River*, 61–62; Coqualeetza Cultural Education Centre, "About Us"; McDowell, "This Is Stó:lō Indian Land," 20–22; Woods, "Coqualeetza: Legacies of Land Use," 74–75.

37 Huhndorf and Suzack, "Indigenous Feminism," 5; Tsosie, "Native Women and Leadership."

38 Hokowhitu, "Taxonomies of Indigeneity," 84.

39 Barr, *Peace Came in the Form of a Woman*; Fiske, "Colonization and the Decline of Women's Status"; Pesantubbee, *Choctaw Women in a Chaotic World*.

40 Mark Point, interview with Melissa McDowell, 30 May 2002, Stó:lō Archives (hereafter SA), Sardis, British Columbia.

41 Wells, *Salish Weaving: Primitive and Modern*.

42 See Bobb et al., *Classified Word List for Upriver Halq'eméylem*, ii. The front matter for this Halq'eméylem word list gives forty-four Stó:lō individuals as co-authors; of these, thirty are women. See also Archibald, *Indigenous Storywork*, 59; and Galloway, introduction to *Dictionary of Upriver Halkomelem*, xviii.

43 Knickerbocker and Nickel, "Negotiating Sovereignty," 69–71.

44 "About Us," Coqualeetza Cultural Education Centre website.

45 SA, File 1148, Coqualeetza site reference material, Skulkayne Band Council Resolution, dated to 1970. "Skulkayne" is an anglicization of "Sq'ewqeyl," now represented in English as "Skowkale."

46 Archibald, *Indigenous Storywork*, 60. This terminology decision is purely for clarity's sake: though there was only one organization, it is alternately referred to by several names.

47 Patricia Raymond-Adair, personal communication with author.

48 Stanbrook, "Indians Frustrated by Negotiations for Coqualeetza Complex." From a survey of the advertisements in the *Stó:lō Nation News* promoting classes and activities at the Coqulaeetza centre, the activities relating to the carving shed seem to be the only ones consistently led by men. These were consulted at the Stó:lō Archives.

49 McDowell, "This is Stó:lō Indian Land," 21.

50 SA, RG-10: Clarence Pennier to Jean Chrétien, 24 July 1974; Judd Buchanan to Bill Mussell, 27 August 1974.

51 SA, RG-10, Judd Buchanan to Bill Mussell, 27 August 1974. Other First Nations

organizations also vocally supported the Coqualeetza centre: George Manuel, president of the National Indian Brotherhood, wrote to the government, urging them to negotiate with Stó:lō about the land claim in February 1976.

52 SA, RG-10, Alex Patterson to Judd Buchanan, 4 February 1976; ibid., J.R. Holmes to Judd Buchanan, 1 March 1976. Campagnolo and Holt were the other two MPs who likewise expressed their concerns to Buchanan.

53 Marion Bisaillon, interview with author, 11 July 2014; Spears, "Troops Were 'Away' When Invaders Came."

54 I have discussed this particular moment elsewhere; see Knickerbocker, "'We Want Our Land.'"

55 SA, RG-10, Harold Gideon to Clarence Pennier, 1 December 1976; Gideon, "Quarterly Funding, 1976-77, Coqualeetza Education Training Centre," 1 December 1976.

56 Coqualeetza Cultural Education Centre, "About Us." These numbers do not take into account the roughly forty people who were in the building at the moment the army breached the doors; I have been unable to find the names of all of those in attendance.

57 SA, Mark Point, interview with Melissa McDowell, 30 May 2002.

58 McDowell, "This Is Stó:lō Indian Land," 27.

59 McDowell, 24.

60 Marian Bisaillon, interview with author, 11 July 2014.

61 In Stó:lō communities, cohabitating with one's partner is the equivalent of being married to them so in the broad sense, some people might consider Bisaillon to have been part of Stó:lō communities at the time, even if her home community was elsewhere.

62 SA, Larry Commodore, interview with Melissa McDowell, 24 May 2002; these same sentiments were shared again with me during our interview on 11 July 2014.

63 See SA, RG-10, Harold Gideon to Clarence Pennier, 1 December 1976; Gideon, "Quarterly Funding, 1976–77, Coqualeetza Education Training Centre," 1 December 1976.

64 SA, RG-10, anonymous, "Briefing Notes—Coqualeetza Hospital Property," 1 December 1976, 1.

65 McDowell, "This Is Stó:lō Indian Land," 34. In 1995, the Stó:lō Xwexwilmexw Treaty Association officially laid claim to Stó:lō territories, including the Coqualeetza site, in the contemporary BC Treaty Process.

66 Much of Stó:lō women's alienation from formal political roles, however, also has to be contextualized within the frame of settler-colonial policy and history, which, as discussed above, undermined and delegitimized Indigenous women's positions within their own communities.

67 Green, "Taking Account of Aboriginal Feminism," 22.

68 Redbird, "Honoring Native Women," 135–36.

CHAPTER 2

Sámi Feminist Moments: Decolonization and Indigenous Feminism

ASTRI DANKERTSEN

In this chapter I explore how feminism is articulated and performed in the land of the Sámi, the only people in Europe with official Indigenous status. The Sámi people inhabit a large area across middle and northern Norway, Sweden, Finland, and the Kola Peninsula of Russia. This area is called Sápmi in the Northern Sámi language. While I will discuss issues that are relevant for Sápmi as a whole, most of my examples are from the Norwegian context, the area where I have done most of my own work. There are several Sámi languages, many endangered or deemed extinct, largely because of forced assimilation policies. Historically, the Sámi have pursued livelihoods such as reindeer herding, fishing, fur trapping, and farming, with reindeer herding the occupation that most distinguishes them from the majority population of the respective states that they inhabit. However, today most Sámi people do not follow these traditional livelihoods but earn their money from professions in the public and private sectors—much like most other people in the Nordic countries.

In contrast to other colonized peoples in the world, there is no specific start or end to the colonization of Sápmi. Sápmi has no Christopher Columbus. This means that concepts such as colonialism and postcolonialism do not really fit the complex reality of the Sámi people. The "post" in postcolonialism also complicates the use of this concept, since the Sámi people, like other Indigenous peoples, still live in societies where colonialism is an ongoing process. I nevertheless argue that the theoretical contribution from this perspective is useful for understanding the situation of Sámi people today. Sámi people live in states dominated and governed by a non-Sámi majority, and we need to consider how colonization, both past and the present, continues to shape Sámi society and the everyday life of Sámi individuals.

In the last few years, feminist, queer, and transgender issues have emerged as topics of discussion in Sámi society, with organizations, politicians, and others raising questions that challenge gender performance and relations in Sámi society. Sámi people today live in a world where the local and global, old ideas and new intermingle in everyday life and the public sphere, all of which in turn recreates what it is to be Sámi. I use the concept of "Sámi feminist moments" to explore how feminism is articulated and performed in present-day Sápmi. I define Sámi feminist moments as instances where different knowledge traditions meet or collide and where feminist ideas and norms are articulated from a Sámi standpoint. This concept is inspired by Helen Verran's concept of "postcolonial moments," wherein

> disparate knowledge traditions abut and abrade, enmeshed, indeed often stuck fast, in power relations characteristic of colonizing, where sciences usually line up on the side of the rich and powerful. Postcolonial moments interrupt those power relations, redistributing authority in hope of transformed contexts for the exercise of power. A postcolonial moment is not about retrieving a lost purity by overthrowing and uprooting an alien knowledge tradition. Rather, it might effect an opening up and loosening.[1]

A postcolonial moment is therefore a moment when different knowledge traditions meet. Through analyzing these meetings through the lenses of power relations and considering how they unfold, whether they are successful or not, and how they transform the relationship between the colonized and the colonizers, we arrive at a more dynamic understanding of change and continuity in societies facing the challenges of colonialism. I use this concept as an inspiration for analyzing how feminism is articulated and performed from a Sámi point of view, and how colonization affects the relevance of feminism for Sámi individuals in present-day Sápmi.

A problem that is often mentioned when discussing the role of colonization in the Nordic countries is the specific ways these countries have framed their present-day society and self-image. Traditionally, the Nordic countries have not been considered participants in European colonialism. They thus have a corresponding self-image of being more "humane" and promoters of peace, even though historic research has documented that individuals from the Nordic countries also profited from and participated in the slave economy, in addition to participating in the internal colonization of minority groups such as the Sámi.[2] The Nordic countries, as a part of the Western cultural and socio-economic world, have also been and still are part of (post)colonial processes linked to power and authority in a global context. We can thus talk about a Nordic colonial complicity, with discourses, ideologies, and practices of domination with corresponding political and economic advantages.

We need to adopt an understanding of culture that includes colonial perspectives and change, as it is impossible to return to a mythical past that maybe never existed. Sámi people live in states where feminism has been an integrated part of official policies for a long time, which in turn shapes how young Sámi women and men articulate themselves as gendered human beings in an intercultural space.[3] Sámi youth do not simply reproduce a frozen or stereotypical image of Sámi culture, but insist that Sámi society has to change in ways that are beneficial not only for Sámi women but for Sámi society as a whole, in order to push back against colonial patriarchy. In this way, Sámi women can challenge the colonial narrative of a static, romanticized Indigenous people.

Gender in Sápmi: Myths and Realities

Rather than seeing feminism and Indigenous feminism as monolithic and categorically rigid processes, I want to explore how feminism is articulated and performed in different ways and in different Sámi contexts. Instead of trying to explain the position of Sámi women in relation to near-mythical descriptions of "pure" and "authentic" traditional culture, we need to understand how Sámi people live and see their future today. We need to examine how feminism is articulated and performed in people's everyday life and in the public sphere. Feminism is more than just statements about being feminist; actions are what matters. Feminism also involves statements and actions that can be classified as performed feminism, whereby individuals intend to change the power structures between men and women in Sámi society. Looking at these dimensions highlights different positionalities within Sámi society.

Inspired by Márgara Millán's concept of transnational feminism, I understand feminism as a travelling, multi-local concept in Sámi context.[4] Joyce Green reminds us, Indigenous feminism is not without its critics, many who insist it is "un-traditional, inauthentic, non-libratory for Aboriginal women and illegitimate as an ideological position, political analysis and organizational process."[5] Yet, for Green, Indigenous feminism raises important issues related to colonialism, racism, and sexism, with sometimes unpleasant but useful synergies.

Green's assertions are relevant to Sámi research as well. Despite growing awareness of Indigenous feminism in communities and academia, there is much work that still needs to be done, particularly as feminism is sometimes understood as oppositional to Indigenous perspectives.[6] I argue that by analyzing "moments," we can open up the discussion to a more dynamic analysis of different feminist positions within Sámi society today. As Torjer Olsen points out:

> Whiteness and non-whiteness, indigeneity and non-indigeneity, and even women and men, are not binaries. There are spaces in between. Within indigenous communities there is diversity and difference. Even though indigenous peoples are seen as belonging to marginalized and vulnerable communities, there are also differences within them in terms of power as well as internal relations of privilege and oppression. Gender studies, with its explicitly critical perspective on power and normativity, clearly has something to offer to indigenous studies.[7]

Following Olsen, I suggest that we need perspectives on gender and feminism in Sámi societies that take into account the complexity of Sámi societies today, including differences between groups and individuals in Sámi societies, and the varied power relations that are entangled in these different positions. Sápmi has gone through linguistic, cultural, material, economic, technological, and social changes during the last century that have had some specific effects on gender relations in Sápmi. We can see some of these through population-based studies such as the SÁMINOR study, initiated by the Centre for Sámi Health Research at the University of Tromsø, a centre that has several Sámi researchers. SÁMINOR examines the health and living conditions in regions in Norway with both Sámi and Norwegian populations. The results indicate that the level of formal education is much lower among Sámi over the age of sixty-five than in the non-Sámi population in the same area. Among Sámi men aged thirty-six to sixty-four, the level of education is much higher, but still lower than in the non-Sámi population. Sámi women in the same age group with higher education, however, outnumber non-Sámi women.[8]

While Sámi women dominate in higher education, Sámi men are more likely to retain their ties to traditional primary industries such as fishing and reindeer herding. Inger Marie Kristine Nystad explains that boys' high school drop-out rates can be linked to the expectation that they take over the reindeer herd and the family traditions linked to this livelihood. The regulation of the reindeer herding industry along with economic and technological changes have also led to the exclusion of many men from this industry. According to Nystad, the gender roles for young men have become quite narrow, stuck between "myth and modernity," where the mythical "traditional gender role" becomes an obstacle for young men, since they can fulfill neither the expectations of Sámi society nor the expectations of the larger society with regard to education and career.[9] Sámi women, on the other hand, have been pushed out of herding altogether.

Sámi researcher Rauna Kuokkanen argues that prior to Scandinavian government interventions, men and women were given equal privileges and had equal rights to property ownership and inheritance in the Sámi reindeer-herding communities.[10] The capitalization of reindeer herding has, especially since the 1960s, led to a push to make the occupation more economically profitable through rationalization and mechanization. This, in turn, according to Kuokkanen, has reduced the involvement of women and led to a masculinization of reindeer herding. Sámi women thus left the "traditional Sámi lifestyle" for education and employment elsewhere. However, as Astri Buchanan, Maureen G. Reed, Gun Lidestav point out,

> The increased level of formal education among women ... suggests that women may be well positioned to become more influential in institutions that affect reindeer husbandry, including RHPs [Reindeer Herding Plans], local government and Sámi Parliament. This would serve to shift power dynamics in reindeer herding communities, make women's roles more visible and improve access by reindeer herding communities to a greater pool of intellectual potential to address their relative weakness within the power relations that shape the regulatory environment in which they operate.[11]

Women can thus be an important resource for the reindeer herding industry, since dealing with climate change, large-scale resource extraction, industrialization, colonization, and social and political changes, in addition to the increasing focus on economic profit, will be a challenge for years to come. Buchanan, Reed, and Lidestav's article is a good example of how gendered perspectives can provide new insight into issues that are relevant to Sámi societies today, and why there is a need to address the complexity of gender perspectives in Sámi research.

This was illustrated with the so-called Tysfjord case, where eleven women and men from the small Sámi-Norwegian municipality of Divtasvuodna/Tysfjord, with approximately 2,000 inhabitants, came forward in Norway's national media with their histories of sexual abuse. When the Tysfjord case exploded in the media, Sámi researcher Astrid Eriksen, originally from Tysfjord herself, published an article on emotional, physical, and sexual violence among Sámi and non-Sámi populations in Norway. Erikson and her co-authors document that almost half of the Sámi female respondents (49.1 percent of Sámi women against 34.7 percent of non-Sámi women) reported that they had experienced violence, and that Sámi women were more likely to report emotional, physical, and sexual violence than non-Sámi women were.[12] In the small multi-ethnic municipality of Tysfjord there are now twenty-seven registered victims and thirty-eight registered perpetrators.[13] While both the victims and the perpetrators were both Sámi and non-Sámi, the case was especially dramatic for the Sámi community, since most of them belonged to the Lule Sámi, a group that constitutes a small minority within Sámi society and whose language and culture still is in a precarious situation as a result of colonization and forced assimilation.[14]

Complicating matters, many involved were directly or indirectly connected to the local Læstadian congregation, a conservative pietistic Lutheran revival movement. In Tysfjord, the Læstadian congregation has also been of great importance for the survival of the Sámi language and community, a place where people could take care of each other, grieve and feel a sense of belonging, something very important for many in the community at a time when the discrimination they experienced was tough to bear alone. Researchers such as Guttorm Gjessing,[15] Jens-Ivar Nergård,[16] and Marit Myrvoll[17] have pointed out how the Sámi maintained and transformed certain Sámi religious practices through Læstadianism. There are, for example, certain similarities between the Læstadian "stirrings," "lijgudis" in the Lule Sámi language, a kind of religious ecstasy that is practised in Læstadianism, and the traditional Sámi shamanic trance. The importance of the Laestadian congregation in building a sense of community extended across Tysfjord's Sámi community to include those not active in the congregation.

While Christianity was not a part of Sámi culture historically, the Læstadian religious movement is of great significance in many small Sámi communities today, demonstrating the complexity of colonization. Yet, it is also problematic in its control over women's sexuality and bodies. When sexuality is a private matter, it can be challenging to address sexual violence and sexual harassment publicly.[18] Mixed with a fear of further marginalization due to ethnic discrimination, violence toward Sámi women becomes a taboo that one cannot address.[19]

The gendered norms and ideals of Læstadianism still shape how gender is articulated and performed in these Sámi communities. This includes staying away from pre-marital sex, makeup, dancing, and alcohol, and the expectation that women not speak in public. Women's sexuality is controlled through modest clothes and behaviour, and sexuality is something that is regarded as a private matter within marriage.[20] In pietistic Lutheran movements like Læstadianism, a woman may be thought partly to blame when she experiences sexual violence, as the violence is believed to be connected to her lack of modesty and submissiveness required of a good Christian.[21]

Though violence is a problem for men and women in all societies, Rauna Kuokkanen claims that Indigenous women are particularly vulnerable to violence. She argues that this must be understood in the context of colonialism, racism, and sexism. Because of the challenges that Indigenous people experience politically and in their everyday life as a result of discrimination and marginalization, members of Indigenous communities are often reluctant to raise violence against women as a problem, fearing that this will cause further discrimination.[22] This silencing of sexism and violence against Indigenous women is relevant for Indigenous communities as a whole. As Kuokkanen states, "How do you build Indigenous self-determination if women don't feel safe and free from violence in their own communities?"[23] In a small and vulnerable Sámi community that still suffers from the effects of forced assimilation policies and marginalization, sexual violence affects more than just those who are abused directly: it has a negative impact on the whole community through the trauma, broken relationships, and distrust that disrupt the healing process of the local Sámi culture. Discrimination against Indigenous women is not only a threat to women themselves but to Indigenous societies as a whole, since it threatens the very existence and dignity of Indigenous communities.

Yet, predominant myths about Sámi culture as traditionally peaceful complicate the understanding of violence against Indigenous women. Such violence is seen as something inherently "un-Sámi" and, therefore, not something that can be dealt with critically within Sámi culture.[24] Indeed, Kuokkanen suggests that tradition is often treated as something that is immune to criticism, which further marginalizes Indigenous women.[25] Myth of peacefulness can be linked to that of the "noble savage," invented by Rousseau in the mid-eighteenth century to glorify the "natural" life, which led to the notion of "inferior" races and legitimized colonization, slavery, and genocide.[26] This mythical perception of Sámi culture is not a constructive position for Sámi individuals today, since it leaves no critical position for Sámi women and men to take action and make positive change.

There is also a problematic myth about strong Sámi women that is ironically mobilized to uphold unequal gender relationships. Developed in the 1970s amid the Sámi ethnopolitical movement, the myth of the strong Sámi women was a way to distinguish Sámi women from the majority population. Sámi women were presented as equal to men, linked to notions of an almost matriarchal Sámi society in the past and to Sámi spirituality, with its goddesses and emphasis on the female primal force in nature. "Authentic" gender roles thus became linked to an idealized past rather than to the reality of Sámi women in the present. While the ideal of strong Sámi women has been beneficial for Sámi women, this myth has also been used by men who, as Jorunn Eikjok puts it, have either internalized the myth or benefit from the patriarchal system of today's society through silencing women who speak up against gender inequality in Sápmi.[27] For Eikjok, this myth thus becomes an excuse for many Sámi men and women not to take action and try to change the society for the better.[28] This does not mean that strong Sámi women have never existed in Sápmi (historically and today), however.[29] As she notes, Sámi society (in common with many other Indigenous societies and Nordic societies) has a relatively egalitarian societal structure compared to other societies in the world.[30]

The complex intercultural space that Sámi live in today is also relevant when analyzing how people negotiate and perform gender in Sápmi. Notions of "traditional Sámi gender roles" give the impression of a pure, authentic past, where gender and Sámi culture were not yet contaminated by Westernization. But as Sámi feminist scholars Eikjok and Kuokkanen remind us, ideas of femininity and masculinity are constantly changing as cultures change and evolve.[31] Using concepts like "traditional gender roles" and "Sámi traditions" risks freezing an Indigenous culture in time and space with no possibility of change, or positing a culture and tradition that has been polluted or even lost because of colonialism.

However, it may also be argued that the idea of the traditionally strong Sámi woman is "a strategic use of positivist essentialism in a scrupulously visible political interest" to strengthen group identity in a simplified, collectivized way in order to achieve feminist goals within Sámi and mainstream society.[32] In this way, the idea of the strong Sámi woman becomes a tool for Sámi feminism, where feminism is rooted in Sámi culture, norms, and values.[33]

Feminist Moments in the Public Sphere

Sámi feminist moments, where feminist ideas and norms are expressed from a Sámi perspective, may happen in both private and public spheres. An example of a public moment was the speech by Liisa-Ravna Finbog, representative of the Sámi Women's Network, at the 2019 Oslo Women's March. In her speech to 14,000 participants, Finbog announced that Sámi women were now breaking the silence on the need for gender equality in Sámi societies.[34] This was a historic event, since it was the first time that the Women's March in Oslo had both a Sámi speaker and a Sámi banner. It demonstrated that feminism is becoming an important part of Sámi society, where Finbog and other Sámi women now are setting the agenda not only in Sámi society but also within the majority society. Finbog's speech can be seen as a way of intervening politically in Sámi society and at the same time Indigenizing the Women's March in Oslo, a march that for many years had focused on international women's issues and other minorities but where Sámi issues and Sámi women were quite invisible. This speech thus serves as a good example of what I call a Sámi feminist moment: it is a public statement, it comes from a Sámi position, and it actively criticizes the harassment of women inside the Sámi community, with the purpose of improving gender equality within Sámi society.

According to feminist scholar Beatrice Halsaa, Sámi feminists chose to set aside feminism as a specific Sámi political agenda in the 1970s in the interest of fighting for Sámi rights and protection of Sámi territories and resources.[35] The struggle against Norwegianization and neocolonialism was too important to ignore, as evidenced by the Alta controversy, a series of massive protests in Norway in the late 1970s and early 1980s concerning the construction of a hydroelectric power plant on the Alta river in Finnmark county, Northern Norway. This is why Sámi feminism has developed with a distinctly political, decolonizing purpose, since the overall fight for Sámi rights at the time was so important that feminist issues had to wait. However, this can also be analyzed as a failure by mainstream feminism in Nordic societies to meet the needs of Sámi women, a failure to acknowledge the contribution of Sámi women in mainstream Nordic feminist movements, and a failure of the Sámi rights movement to account for gender inequality.

While Sámi women's issues for a long time were not that publicly visible, it is important to remember that the Alta controversy also contributed to the organization of women in Sápmi. The activism provided a space where Sámi women could meet, network, and develop organizational and leadership skills that in turn became important for Sámi society as a whole. In the aftermath of the Alta controversy, Sámi women established organizations such as the women's organization Sáráhkká, named after a Sámi goddess, and Sámi NissonForum. These organizations in turn became important for future leaders such as President Aili Keskitalo, who in addition to holding political office has been a Sáráhkká board member. This was significant given the lack of a self-identified feminist amongst Sámi politicians.

Indeed, in 2014, a Sámi television and radio program broadcast in Norway, Sweden, and Finland featured a panel of interviews with prominent Sámi politicians that revealed that none of the leaders of the political parties represented in the Swedish and Finnish Sámi Parliaments identified themselves as feminists.[36] Min Geaidnu's Ol-Johán Sikku explained, "I have trouble defining the word feminism. Therefore, I prefer saying that I prioritize working for equality."[37] However, the president of the Norwegian Sámi Parliament, Aili Keskitalo, proudly answered yes when asked if she was a feminist. The chair of the Swedish Sámi Parliament, Stefan Mikaelsson, also affirmed being feminist; Mikaelsson is openly queer/trans and has proudly worn nylon stockings and nail polish in public, insisting it is important that young people see different expressions of identity and that people in Sámi society change their attitudes toward traditional gender norms.[38] This example shows us the complexity of present-day Sámi politics, where the Sámi politicians from different countries position themselves differently in relation to feminism, though all of them could to some extent be understood as representatives of "Sámi tradition." Their responses show us that there is not one opinion, but many.

Another event that can be analyzed as a Sámi feminist moment is the public statement made by Ellinor Marita Jåma, leader of the Sámi Reindeer Herders' Association of Norway (NRL). In a 2015 interview with the weekly Sámi TV program Árdna, Jåma said:

> I have felt pressure from people emphasizing that I am a female leader and what it entails . . . Not directly harassment, but a lot of rumour-mongering. I have experienced threats and other things that are linked to people who maybe don't have a good view of women. . . . I will not judge all men alike, but I understand very well why there aren't more women who are active members of NRL if women generally are met with the kind of attitude that I have experienced in the last year.[39]

Jåma is the second female leader of the NRL and the youngest person ever to hold this position in Norway. In the interview, she pointed out that she raised this issue because she wants to change the organization for the better and include more women and young people in the NRL. When asked about the harassment, Jåma stated that on the one hand, she has been accused of sleeping her way to her position, and on the other, she has been accused of being a lesbian because "no one gets in her pants."[40] Jåma noted that she is South Sámi, which is a minority language group in Norway's Sámi society. People will sometimes speak to her in North Sámi, even though they know that she does not speak that language. In fact, Jåma pointed out, the South Sámi are often accused of not speaking Sámi, which is true for many because of the marginalization of Sámi people and the Norwegianization policy. Jåma often answers in South Sámi when she encounters that kind of attitude. She also noted that she has been quite open about the fact that she does not know everything about reindeer husbandry, especially in the North Sámi area—Jåma is from a reindeer-herding family in the South Sámi region.

The interview went viral in Sámi mainstream and social media, and several Sámi politicians expressed support for Ellinor Marita Jåma. Others, such as the former candidate for the leadership position in NRL, Ellinor Guttorm Utsi, maintained that these kinds of conflicts should be dealt with internally in the organization rather than in the media. Discussing such topics in the media might give the impression that these kinds of things only happen in Sámi organizations, when they are quite common in other organizations as well.[41] However, the deputy leader of the NRL, Per John Anti, supported Jåma, stating, "We must change how we behave toward our female members."[42] Vibeke Larsen, at that time the parliamentary leader of the Labour Party in the Norwegian Sámi Parliament, asserted: "Threats and harassment of women is a symptom of the existence of attitudes that one would not expect in a professional trade organization like NRL. Society has a way to go before we can say that we have full gender equality."[43]

Marit Kirsten Anti Gaup, who was the Sámi Parliament representative for the Labour Party, confirmed there was an expectation that "a woman should preferably remain silent and agree. Only then will she be accepted. I have experienced that people almost have told me that I am stupid when I have spoken."[44] Beaska Niilas, who was the leader of the Norwegian Sámi Association (NSR), chose to refer to Sámi traditions in declaring that this kind of behaviour toward women is unacceptable. "And it is strange," he said in an interview, "since historically it has not been common to trample on women—they should be praised and lifted up."[45]

We can thus see how Sámi politicians use a variety of strategies to condemn suppression of women in the Sámi society. Per John Anti focuses mostly on the NRL and the need for men in the organization to change, with no reference to Sámi culture as a whole. Vibeke Larsen takes a clear feminist standpoint, relating the situation Jåma described to a lack of gender equality in Sámi society, arguing that this needs to be dealt with. Jåma has written a master's thesis in psychology about attitudes toward Sámi people and clearly has a theoretical understanding of the issue as well. Her position can be characterized as a postcolonial or intersectional feminist standpoint, as a young woman and a South Sámi (a minoritized language within Sámi society). Her focus is on attitudes toward women in Sámi society and on what needs to change in order to be more inclusive of Sámi women.[46]

Ellinor Guttorm Utsi's statement focuses mostly on the position of the Sámi as a minoritized people. The attitude that sensitive and problematic issues should not be addressed in public because this can cause further discrimination against the Sámi and give people an unfair impression of Sámi culture as generally oppressing women is common both among the Sámi and in other Indigenous and minoritized groups. Utsi's point is that the situation in the NRL is not specific to Sámi organizations or reindeer herders but is found in organizations everywhere. While Indigenous communities differ regarding women's position in society, it is also important to remember the role of colonization and how that has shaped Indigenous societies. As Kim Anderson points out, "It was not long before [Europeans] realized that, in order to dominate the land and the people that were occupying it, they needed to disempower the women."[47]

Marit Kirsten Anti Gaup relates the issue to her own experiences in Sámi society, noting that it is a culture that believes women should not hold public office but should remain silent and agree with male leaders. When women do speak up, they are often ridiculed. While criticizing culture for oppressing women is a classic feminist position, Gaup also links her critique to Christianization and Sámi society. As previously mentioned, the attitudes she describes are quite common in many Sámi communities with ties to Læstadianism and other forms of Christianity. The norms in these religious communities clearly say that women should not speak in public. Gaup thus aligns herself with a critical feminist Indigenous perspective.

Beaska Niilas's statement resembles Marit Kirsten Anti Gaup's response, but he takes a more traditional Indigenous position, claiming that it is in fact "un-Sámi" to harass women, and that women historically have had a strong position in Sámi societies. Here we can clearly see what Eikjok and Kuokkanen call "the myth of the strong Sámi woman."[48] However, Beaska Niilas does not appear to dismiss or undermine Jåma's goal of changing the NRL and Sámi culture as a whole to become more inclusive and welcoming to women. Instead, he uses this myth actively to criticize men who harass women, construing them as "un-Sámi" and thus not included in the Sápmi Beaska Niilas wants to see. He seeks to root feminism in a traditional Indigenous perspective, making space for Sámi feminism from a Sámi perspective. It becomes a Sámi feminism that deploys a strategic essentialism to open up discussions of feminism as something that is inherently Sámi.

Sámi Feminist Moments in Everyday Life

Rather than essentializing both feminism and Sámi culture and gender roles, we need to look at what Sámi women actually do. In everyday life, feminism can be performed or articulated in various ways. In 2013 I interviewed Hilde, a Sámi woman who recounted an incident that can be defined as sexual harassment. Hilde is an educated woman with strong opinions and a tough, outgoing, and cheerful disposition. In the area she is from, the Sámi language was for a long time at risk of disappearing. In the 1980s and 1990s, some local parents engaged in ethnic politics were able to partly reverse this tendency, establishing a Sámi day care and Sámi language instruction in school. However, the language situation in the area remains quite critical.

The incident happened at Hilde's workplace and involved a meeting with two middle-aged men from the Finnmark interior, an area where a majority of the population still speaks Sámi fluently. When they arrived, Hilde greeted them and showed them the way to where their meeting was being held. As Hilde accompanied them, the two men joked among themselves in Sámi, clearly assuming that Hilde did not understand what they were saying. In the interview, Hilde described them telling sexually explicit jokes and making comments about her body. At first, Hilde pretended not to understand or take notice of the conversation, simply showing them to their destination. She was both a little angry and a little amused, and when she later met them again she spoke to them in Sámi, asking politely about their meeting but with a clear implicit reference to their earlier conversation. The men were shocked that she spoke Sámi, and quite embarrassed.

The men had debased Hilde from both a gendered and a cultural perspective. Their behaviour can be linked to both their gender and their position as Sámi from the Finnmark interior, where the assimilation policy was not as firmly enforced and where Sámi language and traditional knowledge remain strong. We can see how these men placed Hilde in a position where she was disempowered because of both her gender and her background from a Sámi area that has been marginalized within Norwegian and Sámi society. And this was not an isolated incident.

Hilde mentioned a similar incident when she and some fellow students were at a bar together. The other young women were Norwegians who did not know Sámi culture very well. While they were drinking and having a good time, two middle-aged Sámi men entered the bar and started talking to the Norwegian girls with what Hilde described as a clear sexual agenda. She was amused, since it was obvious that her Norwegian friends did not know how to handle the situation, continuing to talk to the men in a polite and friendly way even though they were uncomfortable with the situation. Possibly, the young Norwegian women were trying to avoid being labelled racists. After a while, Hilde decided to help those "poor girls" who obviously did not know how to handle "those old Sámi pigs," as Hilde characterized the men. She addressed the men in Sámi in a facetious manner, signalling indirectly that their behaviour was unacceptable. The men then left their table.

During the interview, Hilde was quite entertained by these incidents, but her views about the way these men behaved were also clear. Though she was joking, there was also an explicit moral to the story: Hilde does not approve of the way some Sámi men behave toward women. At the same time, her way of performing feminism in a Sámi context could easily be missed by someone unfamiliar with the culture and its communicative ideals. In these episodes, Hilde used a traditional way of handling conflict in combination with her feminist ideals, and through this was able to communicate that the men's behaviour was unacceptable to her as a woman. In Sámi culture, indirect communication and silence are common ways of expressing one's opinions.[49] An example that is frequently mentioned in the scholarship is an old childrearing technique called "narrideapmi," a technique in which one jokes with and teases children in an indirect way to correct them rather than confronting them directly.[50] In an article on cultural norms in mental health treatment, the "Sámi way of communicating" is described "as being less verbal, more indirect, using hints and body language and not complaining."[51] Authors Dagsvold, Møllersen, and Stordahl quote a participant who explains:

> The way to tell others you're having a hard time is very indirect, cautious, roundabout, maybe as a joke. . . . Everyone understands

> ... everyone understood ... if you just said ... a little ... and then ... you almost didn't need to say anything, and people understood.... in your family ... they can tell by looking at you ... how you are. I think body language is widely used in the Sámi culture.[52]

Hilde's response to the incidents can also be understood as conveying discontent in an oblique and humorous way. While her manner of communication followed traditional Sámi practice, the content can be seen as an indirect way of performing a feminist critique of sexual harassment. Hilde's retelling of the stories can also be understood as a way of communicating her opinions on how some Sámi men behave, and the ways in which she and other young Sámi disapprove of this behaviour. While not a confrontational form of feminism, the content and agenda of her statements are a way of articulating or performing a Sámi feminist cultural critique. Narrideapmi can thus be an example of how to identify Sámi feminism from a Sámi point of view: as Sámi feminist moments in everyday situations, expressed through jokes. Jokes can thus in themselves be Sámi feminist moments, performed as part of everyday life. Hilde's stories also demonstrate the advantages of this perspective, since the analysis of these episodes draws on both gender and colonial perspectives.

Sámi Feminist Moments As Becoming

As I have shown in this chapter, feminism is a kind of political enactment that highlights how the situation of Sámi women can be identified and improved in Sámi society today. I argue that we need to analyze how Sámi individuals engage in feminist discourses both on national and international levels, and how this in turn reflects the Sámi society of today. There is a need for Sámi feminist research that critically examines feminism and gender relations in Sámi society from a Sámi point of view, rather than a discussion of feminism that does not take into consideration the specific situation of the Sámi people. If Sámi society is analyzed using non-Sámi ideals and norms for feminist expression and performance, actual feminist moments in Sámi society can be overlooked. Rather than reproducing myths about gender roles and strong Sámi women, or unjustly characterizing Sámi culture as oppressive for women per se, I argue that feminist moments allow us to see feminist change in Sápmi.

While there is a need for Indigenous perspectives that critically engage in debates about hegemonic Western intellectual structures and how these are a significant part of colonialism that "depended on modes, structures, epistemologies, and approaches of the West," adopting an essentializing perspective on Indigenous culture can be just as damaging.[53] As Kuokkanen reminds us, this way of understanding culture "can suggest racist notions of a frozen culture," with corresponding views of authenticity and "traditional practices," leaving no room for change in Indigenous cultures.[54] Rather than reproducing the dichotomies between Indigenous and non-Indigenous cultures, and the implicit hegemonic relationship between the "West" and the "inauthentic," colonized "rest," we need to analyze Indigenous societies from their own point of view. We need to understand how Indigenous people engage in both local and global debates and dialogues, in relation to Indigenous communities that are continuously trying to preserve and take back their cultures while constantly changing, and individuals seeking ways to express themselves that incorporate both old and new elements and transform them into new ways of being Indigenous. Feminist interventions from Sámi women can thus create space for articulating women's needs. Rather than being a threat against Sámi traditions, Sámi feminist moments represent critical instances where Sámi women intervene in both their own society and the majority society, challenging the power relations between the colonized and the colonizers, women and men, and opening the way for new reflections about the future of Sápmi.

Notes

1 Verran, "A Postcolonial Moment in Science Studies," 730.
2 Palmberg, "The Nordic Colonial Mind."
3 Bhabha, *The Location of Culture*.
4 Millán, "The Traveling of 'Gender' and Its Accompanying Baggage," 6.
5 Green, *Making Space for Indigenous Feminism*, 1st ed., 20.
6 Green, *Making Space for Indigenous Feminism*, 1st ed.
7 Olsen, "This Word Is (Not?) Very Exciting," 194.
8 Lund et al., "Population Based Study of Health and Living Conditions in Areas with Both Sámi and Norwegian Populations—the SÁMINOR Study."
9 Lund et al.
10 Kuokkanen, "Indigenous Women in Traditional Economies."
11 Buchanan, Reed, and Lidestav, "What's Counted As a Reindeer Herder?," 360.
12 Eriksen et al., "Emotional, Physical and Sexual Violence among Sámi and Non-Sámi Populations in Norway."
13 Quist, "Etterforsker 31 overgrepssaker i Tysfjord."
14 Dankertsen, "Samisk artikulasjon."
15 Gjessing, "Sjamanistisk og Læstadiansk ekstase hos samene."

16 Nergård, "Læstadianismen—kristendom i et samisk kulturlandskap"; Nergård, *Den levende erfaring.*
17 Myrvoll, "'Bare gudsordet duger.'"
18 Olsen, "Kall, skaperordning og mak."
19 Kuokkanen, "Violence against Women, Indigenous Self-Determination and Autonomy in Sámi Society"; Kuokkanen, "Gendered Violence and Politics in Indigenous Communities."
20 Eggen, "Troens Bekjennere"; Olsen, "Læstadianisme og seksualitet"; Olsen, "Kall, skaperordning og makt."
21 Norbakken, "Når ord mangler."
22 Kuokkanen, "Gendered Violence and Politics in Indigenous Communities."
23 Knobblock and Kuokkanen, "Decolonizing Feminism in the North," 276.
24 Kuokkanen, "Violence against Women, Indigenous Self-Determination and Autonomy in Sámi Society."
25 Kuokkanen, "Violence against Women, Indigenous Self-Determination and Autonomy in Sámi Society," 439. For further discussion of Indigenous tradition and women, see, LaRocque, "Re-examining Culturally Appropriate Models in Criminal Justice Applications"; Eikjok, "Indigenous Women in the North"; Enloe, *The Curious Feminist*; Martin-Hill, "She No Speaks and Other Colonial Constructs of 'the Traditional Woman'"; Green, "Cultural and Ethnic Fundamentalism"; Smith, "Native American Feminism, Sovereignty, and Social Change"; Denetdale, "Chairmen, Presidents, and Princesses"; Kuokkanen, "Violence against Women, Indigenous Self-Determination and Autonomy in Sámi Society."
26 Ellingson, *The Myth of the Noble Savage.*
27 Eikjok, "Indigenous Women in the North."
28 Eikjok, "Gender, Essentialism and Feminism in Sámiland."
29 Kuokkanen, "Myths and Realities of Sámi Women."
30 Kuokkanen. See also Solem, *Lappiske rettstudier*; and Bäckman, "Female—Divine and Human."
31 Eikjok, "Gender, Essentialism and Feminism in Sámiland"; Kuokkanen, "Myths and Realities of Sámi Women"; Kuokkanen, "Violence against Women, Indigenous Self-Determination and Autonomy in Sámi Society"; Kuokkanen, "Gendered Violence and Politics in Indigenous Communities."
32 Spivak, "Subaltern Studies: Deconstructing Historiography," 205.
33 Kuokkanen, "Myths and Realities of Sámi Women."
34 Aarnes and Husøy, "8.marstoget: Vill jubel for 14-åringenes oppgjør med sexisme i skolegården."
35 Halsaa, "Mobilisering av svart og Sámiske feminism."
36 Kejonen and Eira, "Partiledarna: Vi är inte feminister."
37 Ol-Johán Sikko, in Kejonen and Eira, "Partiledarna: Vi är inte feminister." This statement and all subsequent quotes from Norwegian media were translated by the author.
38 Stefan Mikaelsson, in Letmark, "För mig känns det bra att vara queer."
39 Ellinor Marita Jåma, in Pulk and Smuk, "Har opplevd trusler og ryktespredning som leder i NRL."

40 Larsen and Måsø, "Trakassering av kvinner: Dette tar vi internt i organisasjonen."
41 Larsen and Måsø.
42 Larsen and Måsø.
43 Larsson et al., "Etter trakasseringsavsløringene—flere kvinner bekjenner at de er sjikanert."
44 Larsson et al.
45 Larsson et al.
46 Jåma, "Vi vet bare at de har en annerledes kultur, men vi lærer ikke å forstå den."
47 Anderson, *A Recognition of Being*, 59.
48 Eikjok, "Gender, Essentialism and Feminism in Sámiland"; Kuokkanen, "Towards an 'Indigenous Paradigm' from a Sámi Perspective"; Kuokkanen, "Gendered Violence and Politics in Indigenous Communities."
49 Bongo, "Samer snakker ikke om helse og sykdom."
50 Balto, *Sámisk barneoppdragelse i endring*; Balto, "Traditional Sámi Child-Rearing in Transition."
51 Dagsvold, Møllersen, and Stordahl, "What Can We Talk About, in Which Language, in What Way and with Whom?," 6.
52 Dagsvold, Møllersen, and Stordahl, 6.
53 Kuokkanen, "Towards an 'Indigenous Paradigm' from a Sámi Perspective," 415.
54 Kuokkanen, 418.

CHAPTER 3

"It Just Piles On, and Piles On, and Piles On": Young Indigenous Women and the Colonial Imagination

TASHA HUBBARD, WITH JOI T. ARCAND, ZOEY ROY, DARIAN LONECHILD, AND MARIE SANDERSON

In her article "Ontologies of Indigeneity: The Politics of Embodying a Concept," Sarah Hunt explains that the "processes of colonialism in North America involved representational strategies that transformed Indigenous peoples and their lands conceptually and materially, in order to facilitate their displacement and to render them less than human."[1] As an educator and filmmaker, I have wanted a film that I could screen in the classroom that illustrates the way Indigenous women are conceptualized as "Indian maidens" and "sexual squaws" in the colonial imagination. I wish to do so in order to begin conversations about the resulting material harm these conceptualizations create for Indigenous women and girls. The "Indian maiden" and "sexual squaw" tropes often go unchallenged and are replicated throughout different media. This chapter examines these stereotypes and their impact through the lens of a hybrid documentary *7 Minutes* and the experiences of Indigenous women who took part in the project. First, I discuss the theoretical foundations of the film, which connects harmful misrepresentations to one young woman's lived experience of a harrowing escape from sexual violence in Saskatoon, Saskatchewan. I follow this with a description of the creative process involved in producing the film.

Next, I take a cue from Elizabeth Archuleta, who says "we have a responsibility to acknowledge and integrate the many insights offered by Indigenous women," and that those insights that come from their own lived experiences should be seen as theory.[2] I have invited several of the young Indigenous women who contributed to the film to share their experiences and ideas on misrepresentations of Indigenous women. Their words make up the section called oskinikiskwēwak, or young women.

Foundations

In reflecting on my motives in making *7 Minutes*, I find the work of Maile Arvin, Eve Tuck, and Angie Morill in close alignment. They speak of the way Indigenous feminism gives us the tools "to contest the rampant misrepresentations of Indigenous peoples and their lives in school curricula, the media, and the sociological imagination.[3] Further, Luana Ross expresses how Indigenous feminism "privileges storytelling as a way to decolonize and empower our communities," and in my film work I strive to contribute to these efforts.[4] Existing Indigenous feminist scholarship maintains that Indigenous women and their bodies have been conflated with land and are colonial contact zones for conquest and erasure. Emma LaRocque argues that "white North American cultural myths" have led to racist and sexist stereotypes of Indigenous women.[5] These stereotypes are enduring and are perpetuated by their repeated appearance in media representations. According to LaRocque, the entire spectrum of stereotypes of Indigenous women contributes to a "dehumanizing portrayal of Aboriginal women as 'squaws,' which renders all Aboriginal female persons vulnerable to physical, verbal and sexual violence."[6] Echoing LaRocque, Janice Acoose maintains that the representations found in popular culture "create very powerful images that perpetuate stereotypes, and perhaps more importantly, foster dangerous cultural attitudes that affect human relations."[7] These human relations play out in several ways, including the belief that Indigenous women are always available to men and are ultimately disposable. The way Indigenous women are viewed in the colonial imagination ultimately increases the potential for violence.

In my preparation for teaching and in the research process for the film, I looked at several sites where harmful representations occur. Mark Anderson and Carmen Robertson, in *Seeing Red: A History of Natives in Canadian Newspapers*, explain how newspapers "have long imagined Aboriginal women within the stereotypical binary of the Indian princess/Indian 'squaw,'" and that "these essentialized images" are normalized and perpetuated in popular culture.[8] Newspapers, while not a visual medium, were the main source of information at the time of the Canadian prairies' settlement and have contributed to the colonial mindset that views Indigenous women as objects of conquest and violence. Anderson and Robertson expand: "The passivity of the princess renders a malleable construct not just unthreatening but sexually attractive as a paternalistic and patriarchal construction."[9] The princess construct is also perpetuated within advertising images, as discussed by Cecily Devereux. She shows how a "white colonial economy" depends on the erasure of Indigenous people "through the appropriation and consumption of its representation and the exchange of women across racial and cultural categories as commodities with a specifically sexual value."[10] The "Indian Maiden" trope, used to sell merchandise, frames Indigenous women as objects to be bought, used, stolen, and even destroyed.

Damaging messages are also found in Hollywood film depictions of Indigenous women. From the silent era until today, Indigenous women are most often represented in certain categories: the helping maiden assisting a white man in his goal, or the sexualized squaw. Elise Marubbio goes into detail about these categories in *Killing the Indian Maiden: Images of Native American Women in Film.* She also unpacks the way sexualization of Indigenous women in film contributes to historic and contemporary incidents of violence against Indigenous women, which continue to rise: "These numbers and the reality that Native women find themselves measured against these stereotypes suggest that a cultural ambiguity toward Native American women still exists, and that it is often played out violently on their bodies."[11] The high numbers of missing and murdered Indigenous women and increased incidents of relentless harassment are rooted in the belief that Indigenous women do not have agency and are therefore always available as sites of violence without consequences.

Sarah Deer, in *The Beginning and End of Rape*, explains that the lack of legal protection for Indigenous women is woven into the American legal system, resulting in a current situation where "predators may target Native women and girls precisely because they are perceived as marginalized and outside the protection of the American legal system."[12] The lack of protection for Indigenous girls and women within the entire legal system is a concern north of the border as well. Thomas McMahon cites the following statistic from Amnesty International: "If you are an Indigenous woman or girl in Canada—whether you live on reserve or in an urban area, regardless of your age or socio-economic status—the simple fact that you are an Indigenous woman or girl means that you are *at least 3 times more likely to experience violence*, and *at least 6 times more likely to be murdered* than any other woman or girl in Canada."[13] McMahon suggests that the Canadian legal system as a whole not only fails to protect Indigenous women and children from violence, it actively contributes to the violence.[14] Indigenous women report that police routinely ignore complaints of harassment and sexual assault, and are even perpetrators themselves. The

Figure 3.1. From *7 Minutes*. Actor Darian Lonechild portraying Marie Sanderson during her seven-minute walk home in Saskatoon. Photo credit: George Hupka.

court system often fails to convict perpetrators, and the courts themselves have been known to dehumanize the victims through the use of stereotypes.

The Making of *7 Minutes*

Around the time that I was searching for film resources with which to broach these topics in the classroom, Marilyn Poitras and I decided apply to the National Screen Institute IndigiDoc program as a producer/director team. Our proposed short film about the imagery of Indigenous women was accepted, but we were still lacking a strong story to anchor the film. I eventually found our story by scrolling through social media, where I read a young Cree nursing student's status. One evening during the fall of 2014, Marie Sanderson left a library in Saskatoon, using the seven-minute walk home to plan her next day. She didn't know that a man was stalking her the entire evening with the intent to get her in his van. When he revealed himself, his first question was to ask if she was "Native American." The film, called *7 Minutes* because of the short length of time it should have taken for her to walk home, is a re-enactment of what happened, told by Marie in her own words.

In her article discussing feminism within Indigenous women's documentaries, Patricia Demers highlights "the honesty of a personal, direct voice" in activating justice and redress.[15] Although Marie does not appear in the film, I felt it was absolutely necessary that it be her voice telling her story. To create the basic storyline of the film, I interviewed Marie in a sound booth at the

University of Saskatchewan. We sat in a room lit only by a lamp, and I began by asking her about her ambitions, which were based in her experiences as a child. We gradually started to talk about her move to the city and the night that she left the library at 9:00 p.m., after a full day of classes and studying. She walked the short walk, not knowing that a man, a fellow student, had targeted her in the library and followed her out, getting his van in the process. She walked her route with her usual awareness, but he stayed far enough back until she turned off the busy street onto her own side street. When she was half a block away from her house, he started calling out to her, asking her if she was "Native American" and telling her to get into his van. She didn't answer and instead kept focused on reaching safety without revealing her house to him. After pulling his van up closer to her, the man got out and started walking in circles around her. She recalled that it was getting dark and that she was tired and now scared of what he was going to do to her. In order to distract him, Marie told the man she wasn't feeling well and would give him her number to call her another night. He agreed and as he turned his back to get something from his van, she turned and ran from him and was able to run a few blocks farther to her friend's house. The two watched out the window as the man drove around the neighbourhood looking for Marie.

In the interview, Marie tells her story calmly but her voice catches at times, revealing how much the incident impacted her. She has her own theory about her experience:

> I think in our culture and in our society, how Indigenous women are shown in media, in movies, and in television, we're shown to be very quiet and docile and allowing anything to happen. When I was walking home and he approached me, he asked me if I was an Indian. . . . People just think that they can [treat Indigenous women like this] because there's no consequence whatsoever, and I know this because with the incidents I've been through, nothing ever happened to the men. . . . It's something that happens so often that it just piles on and piles on and piles on, so how can you feel safe even doing anything?

Using the audio recording of the narrative, I created the script for the film, but I also wanted to visually contextualize what had happened to Marie within the larger framework of colonial violence. I commissioned Cree artist and graphic designer Joi Arcand because of her work around the concept of the "Indian Maiden."

Figure 3.2. Cree artist and graphic designer Joi Arcand's work "Indian Maiden" challenges stereotypes about Indigenous women.

Joi's contribution to the film was both inspiration and participation. I had been interested in her "Indian Maiden" series in the way it challenges colonial representations of Indigenous women and simultaneously reconceptualizes them, taking them out of the colonial frame and into spaces that better represents their agency in the world. In an interview with Leena Minifie, Joi says, "I created the SuperMaidens to lift up the imagery of Indigenous women out of the past. I created it for my niece who is turning 12 this year and for her mom who is one of the SuperMaidens, [and] for Indigenous women doing work in their communities who aren't often portrayed in the media."[16] She explains it is a continuation of earlier work, and that she saw this piece as referring back to "a 1800's [*sic*] Wild West Burlesque poster featuring 14 burlesque dancers dressed in feather headdresses and posed in awkward positions." Then Joi continued, "I knew I wanted to get 14 Indigenous women together for the shot. I began to think about what the women were up to in the image and why they would be gathered together like that and that's where the idea for turning them into superheroes came from."[17] Indigenous women, like Marie, set goals for themselves that break the harmful moulds enforced by colonial representations. However, they must still confront the imagery that exists, as

Figure 3.3 and 3.4. Actor Darian Lonechild portraying Marie Sanderson as she encounters stereotypes in her daily life. Photo credit: George Hupka.

well as the repercussions of those representations and how they are situated within non-Indigenous people's imaginations.

Joi and I began the process by discussing the range of harmful imagery and decided to create two pieces. The first was an "Indian maiden" T-shirt for a background performer to wear around "Marie" in her day-to-day life. We also decided on a fictional event poster featuring a "sexy Pocahontas" type wearing a headdress, inspired by real images available for similar events in bars. The fictional Marie encounters these scenarios as she walks around the

Figure 3.5. Actor Darian Lonechild portraying Marie Sanderson being followed by a man on a bike. Photo credit: George Hupka.

city. We filmed these two scenes at sixty frames per second, allowing time for the viewer's eye to register the images.

During the research process, producer Marilyn Poitras and I witnessed an incident that underscored exactly what we are trying to call out with the film, and reminded us that we weren't just dealing with issues from the past. Marie was walking with us along the street where she walked home when a man on a bike homed in on her. He kept going in front of her, demanding that she acknowledge him. Marie ignored him altogether and walked past him, and although we told him to go away, he wouldn't leave her alone. This inspired the film's third scene, where a man on a bike circles the fictional Marie. For this scene, we asked a young Indigenous tattoo artist, Tanis Worme, to design a "sexy headdress pinup tattoo," which she then drew on the actor on the bike. This nod to the ongoing and relentless struggles of Indigenous women was important for further contextualizing Marie's experiences.

Another one of the layers of the film is the way in which the police responded to the original incident. Marie and other young women I spoke with said their concerns were usually dismissed and not taken seriously, despite the way in which these incidents restrict the women's freedom of movement and sense of well-being. In her interview for the film, Marie explained: "It affects me because I keep thinking that one of these times it's going to be more worse than the other times. I've been lucky where I've been able to get out and get help, but at the same time the help doesn't really do what it's supposed to do.

It's more like 'we'll take a description of what happened, we'll take a statement,' but that's about it." When Indigenous women see the film, they respond overwhelmingly with their own similar stories, relating to the treatment by the stalker and the protector/police as a common experience.

This reflects some of the testimonials given during a recent Human Rights Watch investigation. In the final report, titled *Submission to the Government of Canada on Police Abuse of Indigenous Women in Saskatchewan and Failures to Protect Indigenous Women from Violence*, instances of excessive violence, opposite-sex strip searches, and other offences are documented. The report also notes that "calls to the police by Indigenous women and girls seeking help with violence are frequently met with skepticism and victim-blaming."[18] When complaints are treated in this manner, Indigenous women feel isolated and intimidated and are less likely to report further incidents, while the men involved face no consequences for their actions. In a climate like this, the imperative to listen to and believe Indigenous women's stories is pressing and necessary.

oskinikiskwēwak[19]

Several young Indigenous women were collaborators in making *7 Minutes*, including the actual Marie; Darian Lonechild, the actor who portrayed Marie; and Zoey Roy, the assistant director. I met with Darian and Zoey to discuss their initial thoughts about participating in this chapter and what questions should be asked of the three of them. Marie, Darian, and Zoey then sent in their written answers, which have been edited for clarity.

Tasha: Why did you decide to be a part of the making of the film? What were your goals? Can you reflect on your experience? What did you learn?

Marie: At first, I was hesitant about participating in the film. This was because I did not want to be recognized by the man or by my school. It was very much the same feeling I had with whether or not I should report the incident. I just wanted to forget it happened because it happens so often—why should I focus on the one incident? It took some encouragement from others to say that this should garner as much attention possible. It has to be talked about. Once others in the community realize how often it happens, then the conversation can shift to prevention and protection.

Darian: When I heard about the auditions for this film, I knew I wanted to try out for it. The story is something that is a familiar experience for

Indigenous women living in urban settings. Being an Indigenous woman who has spent time learning and researching the systemic violence that Indigenous women face, I knew that playing the role of Marie would not only help me grow my understanding of what our women go through but also help educate the public that Indigenous women are human beings and deserve the right to feel safe in their daily lives. When I landed the role of Marie, my goal was to honour her experiences as an Indigenous woman who found herself at risk for doing everyday activities that others take for granted. I imagined myself in these situations without the cameras being there. The situations that Marie found herself in are lived realities for Indigenous women.

Zoey: Filmmaking, or the capturing of the narratives of Indigenous people where they are the ones in control, is really important to me. Any opportunity that I can have to be a part of that process I would take on if I believe I could contribute to it. And this topic is really important because I myself, as an Indigenous woman, have had my own experiences of feeling like prey in the simple tasks of walking to school and to the store. I don't have those moments anymore. I still need to reclaim that space within myself and be there for that little girl who was scared. It is so unpredictable. You don't feel in control. So being a part of the making of this film gives me back some of that control. I knew that the people who would see it, Indigenous girls who would see it, would understand that it is not their fault. I want them to know that they are not alone. It can be an isolating feeling.

I've had four friends who I grew up with who have gone missing or who have been murdered in 2016. Just because I'm in university and I feel like I'm successful doesn't mean that I am immune. And I want people to remember that these girls have names. They have families.

Tasha: What are your thoughts about the popular representations of Indigenous women, such as "Indian maidens," "sexy Pocahontas," and other over-sexualized or submissive portraits of Indigenous women? Can you discuss your personal experience with these images?

Marie: It is degrading that these caricatures are still out there in the media—for example, Adam Sandler's movie *The Ridiculous 6*. The film is supposed to be funny with the use of old stereotypes and derogatory language. And then you hear people saying, "It's just a movie, suck it up." It piles on you. Then there's Halloween and music festivals, annual celebrations that butcher the meaning behind Indigenous headdresses and dress women in skimpy, hypersexualized "Reservation Royalty" costumes. It makes every insult seem like it's acceptable teasing without realizing the damage it does. In my personal experience, I've heard nice people, very nice people with good intentions, say things that are so absurdly racist and stereotypical that I was shocked those words even came out of their mouths. But that's the society we live in, where the media makes these kinds of things seem okay.

Darian: The false representations and sexualizing images of Indigenous women in the media, and especially Disney, has been something I have grown up watching. The moment I started observing the beautiful women in my life such as my mother, aunties, and grandmothers, I witnessed strength and resilience. Through the teachings given to me by my mother and grandmothers, I found my way as an Indigenous woman.

About three years ago I was approached by a company in Saskatoon that hosts birthday parties and events for young girls with Disney Princess themes. Because my hair is long and black and I have dark skin, I was asked to play Pocahontas for an upcoming event. I felt conflicted over this situation because of the false representation and the true, disturbing story of her. Also, the costume that Pocahontas wears is much different than the dresses that the rest of the Disney Princesses wear. It is revealing on the shoulders and legs, which is not historically accurate to what Indigenous women wore before contact with Europeans. I asked women in my community about what I should do, and one person told me that I should look past these issues and show young Indigenous girls that they can be princesses too. After much careful thought I declined the role, because I knew that I hold a responsibility as a young Indigenous woman to correct false images and represent the strength and resilience my grandmothers have.

Zoey: Pocahontas and other depictions of Indigenous women in the media gives permission to perceive and believe that Indigenous women and girls are less valuable. The police and the way they react to the cases of Indigenous women and girls who go missing validate that permission.

Tasha: Have you experienced similar situations to the one depicted in the film?

Marie: Of course. I've been followed by vehicles in the past. I've been physically grabbed; I've been groped; I've been talked to in inappropriate ways. The most helpless I've ever felt was this one summer day, in broad daylight, I was grabbed by this man I did not know. People saw but nobody did anything. There were parents sitting outside with their kids playing. I had managed to get away and the police were called. I was crying because he had handled me so rough and was yelling into my ear what he was going to do to me. All they did was drive him home and told me he just found me pretty, and they told him to stay away from me. It made me feel like I was a waste of their time.

Darian: During the three-day period we spent filming, I found myself recognizing these situations in my own life growing up. A memory I have was being yelled at by what appeared to be white males in a passing vehicle when I was simply walking to the park from the convenience store near my home. I remember that uncomfortable feeling all too well. I wondered, did I do something wrong? Or was it for being a brown girl in a white neighbourhood? I am fortunate enough to have not been stalked by anyone as Marie was. But it does not mean I don't live with that fear when I am leaving my night class at the university or walking to my vehicle in a parking lot.

Tasha: Zoey, in the fall of 2016, you entered a Spirit of Halloween store in Saskatoon and found a girl's "Native American" costume. You attempted to have it removed from the store. Can you tell me about that?

Zoey: I went into that store with my fourteen-year-old-niece. She isn't taught to be proud of her Indigeneity through school. Depictions of Indigenous people, and more specifically Indigenous women, are not widely shared in a way that she can connect to. Even old archival pictures that are shared most of the time are of men or chiefs. Where are the women? And then we walk in and we see this costume of an Indian princess for little girls.

I needed to show her that you can be vulnerable and brave when it comes to standing up for your people. And use these moments of ignorance by other people as teachable moments, where we don't condemn

Figure 3.6. Stereotypical "Indian Princess" costume found in local Halloween stores. Photo credit: Zoey Roy.

those who don't understand, but where we can open up a space to have meaningful dialogue so that we can all learn and all grow. And through my work with trying to educate the public and Spirit of Halloween, I think meaningful dialogue was the success. My niece now knows how to stand up for herself when she feels she is on the receiving end of injustice. She knows. And so do my other young relatives, and that makes me proud.

There was a strong chance that the company wasn't going to pull the costumes or acknowledge their wrongdoing. We are combining ethics with capitalism. So I knew I needed to prepare myself to be disappointed.

Statement from Spirit of Halloween: *"Understanding certain sensitivities, we always strive to present our costumes in a responsible and respectful manner. While we respect the opinion of those who are opposed to the sale of any cultural or historical costumes, we are proud of our costume selection for men, women and children."*

Zoey: And when that [statement] came out, I needed to take a step back, and after talking to some of my teachers, I learned that it was my ego that wanted to achieve some sort of tangible success from this venture. But I was told that it was a success because it generated meaningful conversations among groups that are comfortable with the conversation but also with groups who are not. This is part of the work—to lighten the load for the next seven generations. Ultimately that's what we are doing. Sometimes we want to be the hero, but that isn't why we do the work. We aren't going to be the beneficiaries of the work we do now and we have to be okay with that.

Continuing to Walk on the Land We Belong To

As a filmmaker, I have occasionally been asked why I make films that critique my homelands, as though I don't love where I live. This is not the case. My process seeks to call out the structural and gendered violence that makes it difficult for Indigenous people to feel welcome in their own territories. This process comes from the love I have for our people, knowing that violence is not what our ancestors envisioned for us. Art, according to Gabrielle Hill and Sophie McCall, has the ability to "create productive sites of discomfort, disconnection, and disruption."[20] I wonder if I get asked that question because some audiences are discomforted by seeing the way they are implicated in Indigenous peoples' oppression. The film *7 Minutes*, using an Indigenous feminist framework, attempts to illuminate the way colonial concepts of Indigenous women cause harm in very real ways. As Archuleta explains, "When Indigenous women speak out against oppression and become visible we politicize our continued existence and signal to the United States, Canada, Australia, and other colonized nations that assimilation or continued threats of violence have

Figure 3.7. Actor Darian Lonechild portraying Marie Sanderson. Photo credit: Ted Whitecalf.

not worked despite more than five hundred years of trying to erase, ignore, or keep us silent."[21] The young women who worked with me on the film refuse to be silent in the face of misrepresentations and sexual violence. They continue to walk on the land they are from. To bring this point home, the film ends with "Marie" walking to school, undeterred in her determination to meet her goals, despite the colonial imagination that tries hard to rob her of humanity.

Notes

1 Hunt, "Ontologies of Indigeneity," 30.
2 Archuleta, "'I Give You Back,'" 89.
3 Arvin, Tuck, and Morrill, "Decolonizing Feminism," 10.
4 Ross, "From the 'F' Word to Indigenous/Feminisms," 5.
5 LaRocque, "Aboriginal Women," 73.
6 LaRocque, 74.
7 Acoose, *Iskwewak Kah' Ki Yaw Ni Wahkomakanak*, 39–40.
8 Anderson and Robertson, *Seeing Red*, 193.
9 Anderson and Robertson, 193.
10 Devereux, "Finding Indian Maidens on eBay," 30.
11 Marubbio, *Killing the Indian Maiden*, 231.
12 Deer, *The Beginning and End of Rape*, 9.
13 McMahon, "Canada's Legal System Hates Indigenous Women," 4.
14 McMahon, 4.
15 Demers, "Location, dislocation, relocation," 312.
16 Arcand and Minifie, *When Raven Becomes Spider*.
17 Arcand and Minifie.
18 Human Rights Watch, *Submission to the Government of Canada on Police Abuse of Indigenous Women*.
19 oskinikiskwēwak, meaning young women in nêhiyawewin (Cree), is also the title of Joi Arcand's exhibition at Gallery 101 in Ottawa, curated by Laura Margita. Used with permission.
20 Hill and McCall, *The Land We Are*, 13.
21 Archuleta, "'I Give You Back,'" 92.

CHAPTER 4

"Making an Honest Effort": Indian Homemakers' Clubs and Complex Settler Engagements

SARAH NICKEL[1]

On a late spring day in 1965, Frances Decker, chair of the Mount Currie Indian Homemakers' Club's Health and Welfare Committee, sat down to write an important letter. Faced with the imminent eviction from the local school where the Homemakers' Club operated near Pemberton, British Columbia, Decker appealed to Jack Letcher, the British Columbia Superintendent of the Department of Indian Affairs, to intervene. Building her case for a permanent Homemakers' Club office, Decker outlined the important work the club and, more specifically, its Health and Welfare Committee had accomplished since the committee's inception in 1962. Under the direction of the Department of Indian Affairs, the committee's purpose was to "[improve] the living conditions on the Reservation by endeavouring to show the women how they could help themselves, and to fill in as best we could, the gap between their revenue, what the Department can do for them, and emergent conditions."[2] The committee's social welfare activities included repairing homes, mending clothing and bedding, holding a "Beautify Mount Currie" home improvement contest, planting trees, and providing transportation for patients needing medical attention. This essential work was made possible, Decker argued, by Indigenous women's dedication, the club's fundraising efforts, and access to space in the school basement, where the club could store its equipment and materials and where members could work.

In May 1965, however, John Lawrance, District Superintendent of Indian Schools, insisted the school could no longer accommodate the club. In the flurry of debate that ensued between Decker, Shirley Arnold (the

Indian Affairs social worker assigned to supervise the club), Lawrance, and Letcher, Lawrance defended his actions as protecting the school children's best interests, as the club materials obstructed the children's play area.[3] Insisting he had nothing against the Homemakers' Clubs or their work, he categorized the dispute as a "struggle for control between groups, one white dominated and the other more Indian."[4] Arnold acted as a moderator between Decker and Lawrance, reassuring the club women that Lawrance meant no harm. Meanwhile Letcher was content to let Arnold and Lawrance sort it out among themselves, resulting in the eventual relocation of the Homemakers' Club from the school basement to the community hall. This debate happened at Mount Currie, but it could have happened anywhere across Canada. The interactions between each of the players here is indicative of the many layers of settler intervention and oversight the broader Indian Homemakers' Club network, of which Mount Currie was a part, endured, demonstrating the racial and gendered nature of Indigenous women's voluntary work.

The Mount Currie Indian Homemakers' Club was just one of hundreds of clubs operating in Canada's West during the 1960s. These clubs were part of a wider national and transracial movement designed to improve Indigenous women's domestic skills, leadership potential, and community standards of living. Saskatchewan had the earliest clubs in Canada, introduced in 1937. Modelled after the non-Indigenous women's institute, the Association of Homemakers' Clubs of Saskatchewan (HCS) formed in 1911, the Indian Homemakers' Clubs were initially administered through the Agricultural Extension division at the University of Saskatchewan.[5] It was Thomas Robertson, the Inspector of Indian Agencies, who introduced the notion of extending the Homemakers' Clubs to surrounding First Nations communities, and in 1937, members of the HCS at the University of Saskatchewan established the first Indian Homemakers' Club on the Red Pheasant Reserve, northwest of Saskatoon.[6] Here Indigenous women adopted the HCS mandates and took courses on sewing, child care, gardening, and non-Indigenous food preservation techniques.[7]

By 1940, Homemakers' Clubs were active in fourteen reserve communities across Saskatchewan, and clubs quickly spread to other provinces (including British Columbia by 1942, and Alberta by 1952). It was around this time that the Department of Indian Affairs took over responsibility, forming the national Indian Homemakers of Canada (IHC) network.[8]

By the mid-1950s, the IHC network was a staple feature in Indigenous communities, with over 200 clubs operating in the provinces and territories by

1956 (see Figure 4.1).[9] Not surprisingly, club numbers were highest in Quebec and Ontario, with eighteen and forty-five clubs, respectively. In comparison, the Maritime provinces had eleven clubs, and the western provinces 110. Forty-four of those were in Manitoba, thirty-three in Saskatchewan, fourteen in Alberta, and nineteen in British Columbia.[10] Membership numbers fluctuated throughout the 1950s and 1960s, but by 1969 Alberta's numbers had flattened considerably, with only nine active clubs, while British Columbia boasted an incredible forty-five Homemakers' Clubs (see Figure 4.1 and Table 4.1). And yet despite their popularity and clear impact on Indigenous communities and Indigenous women, relatively little is known about the Homemakers' Clubs, their regional characteristics, and their impact on the Indigenous women's political movement and Indigenous-settler relationships.[11]

Using examples from the Indian Homemakers' Clubs in British Columbia, Alberta, and Saskatchewan, I explore Indigenous women's complex engagements with the expectations of settler domesticity, religion, and nationalism, as well as the personal and professional relationships with settlers involved in the clubs. In many ways, these clubs were rife with contradiction. They were sites of unequivocal settler domesticity (marked by an emphasis on "modern" or Euro-Canadian sewing and homemaking practices), but they also cultivated and preserved women's leadership and rights, and cultural strength and pride. Although the landscape of the Indigenous women's movement has broad similarities across the provinces, including the genesis of clubs under the Women's Institute structure, oversight by the Department of Indian Affairs, and a strong focus on domestic work as a tool of community betterment, there are also significant divergences—particularly in the late 1960s, where shifting provincial needs created different political trajectories. Examining these themes reveals the broad variations of Indigenous women's political work, as well as strong intersections between Indigenous women, white social workers, and religious and Indian Affairs officials.

Figure 4.1. Indian Homemakers' Clubs, 1953–69.

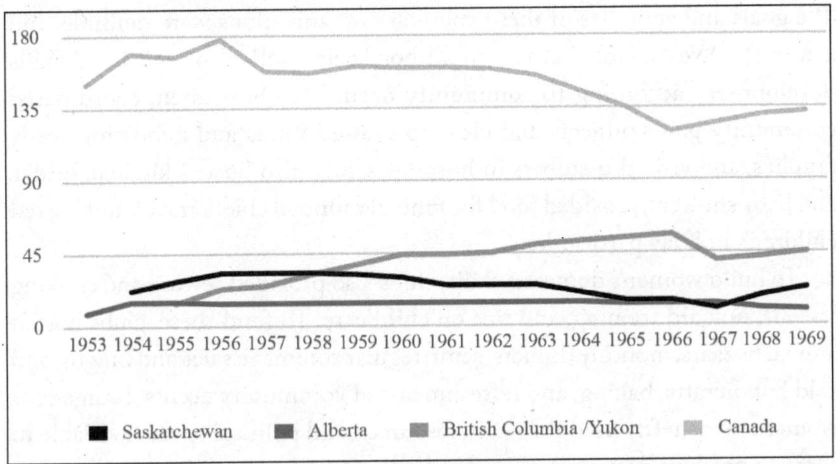

Source: Canada, Department of Citizenship and Immigration Report of Indian Affairs Branch for the Fiscal Year Ending 31 March 1953–1963.

Table 4.1. Homemakers' Clubs and Other First Nations' Women's Organizations as of 1 September 1969.

Location	Homemakers' Clubs	Other Indian Women's Organizations	Total
Maritimes	5	7	12
Quebec	10	2	12
Ontario	35	22	57
Manitoba	5	8	13
Saskatchewan	23	16	39
Alberta	9	26	35
British Columbia	45	0*	45

Source: Canada, Department of Citizenship and Immigration Report of Indian Affairs Branch for the Fiscal Year Ending 31 March 1970, 114.

**Previous research suggests the BC Native Women's Society and Native Sisterhood of British Columbia were created before 1969, but these are not included here.*

Community Improvement and Skills Development

The goals and activities of these voluntary organizations were multiple, and across the West clubs focused on ad hoc social welfare projects and skills development according to community need. Members, then, coordinated community paint projects and cleanups, raised funds and goods for needy families, and visited members in hospital. Clubs also hosted kitchen, bridal, and baby showers, provided food for funerals, funded chiefs' travel, and hosted children's holiday parties.[12]

To build women's domestic skills, clubs also provided sewing and cooking lessons, first aid training, and tips on child care. To fund these, clubs hosted annual bazaars, monthly dinners, semi-regular rummage sales and bingos, and sold handicrafts, baking, and refreshments at community events. Indigenous women, then, deftly used the skills, resources, and political spaces available to them to produce decisively activist responses to their conditions.

As I have argued elsewhere, this produced a distinctly socio-political and oftentimes feminist mandate within the clubs.[13] Just as Dankertsen and Knickerbocker document in their chapters in this volume, unique feminist expressions among Sámi and Stó:lō, so too did the Homemakers' Clubs practise a particular brand of activism—often Indigenous feminist in practice if not in ideal—driven by Indigenous women's relentless desire to address pressing socio-political needs within their communities and advance their skills and well-being. This mentality that women needed to take on an active role in their communities was apparent in activities and even club names such as the Cowichan Homemakers' Club, aptly nicknamed the Active Annies.[14]

Home-Based Work

Of course, activism is not always as explicit as that described in Knickerbocker's chapter, and the Homemakers' Clubs, in many ways, represent subtle and evolving political expressions. Domestic work, for example, played a central role in club activities where members taught others to repair and remodel donated clothing, as well as to make new clothing and linens for sale or personal use. Between the 1940s and late 1960s, sewing served a broad range of social welfare, economic, and cultural goals—some of which were premised on Indian Affairs' mandate to redirect Indigenous women's domesticity to align with settler ideals, and others that emerged from women's own socio-political needs and their desire to actively better their communities. Similar to what Katya MacDonald has observed regarding twentieth-century handmade work in two

Indigenous communities, the types of items made and women's motivations for making such objects varied considerably.[15]

At the end of the Second World War, clubs across Canada obtained discarded military clothing to repurpose into shirts, dressing gowns, and pajamas for community members in need.[16] In 1948, Indian Affairs reported: "There were also many shipments of pajamas and dressing gowns, made by the various Clubs, which were checked and sorted for reshipment to Indian Hospitals and other points where these articles as well as shipments of salvaged clothing, were required."[17] This continued throughout the 1950s and into the 1960s with clubs frequently writing to social workers and Indian agents for access to surplus RCMP clothing to "make ... over in to children's clothing" and blankets for families in need.[18] This resourcefulness enabled clubs to make meaningful contributions to community well-being, and also filled a significant service gap for Indian Affairs.

In fact, through their work in communities, the Homemakers' Clubs were indispensable, providing services that usually fell within the domain of Indian Affairs. Department correspondence is rife with references to this service work, and officials even rationalized existing service gaps by emphasizing the absence of Homemakers' Clubs in the area. In Alberta's Hobbema district Indian Agent E.A. Robertson, in submitting a requisition to the Inspector of Indian Agencies for clothing and materials for the old, destitute, and sick individuals in his agency, explained: "There are no active Homemakers' Clubs in the Agency and previous supplies given out to individual members of the Band have not been put to proper use."[19] With no Homemakers' Clubs yet established in Alberta, Robertson, clearly aware of the growing Homemakers' networks in neighbouring provinces, viewed the clubs as a necessary resource to address socio-economic need on reserve. Likewise, in British Columbia's Kootenay agency, Agent J.S. Dunn, with no "active Homemakers' Club" to turn to, was forced to provide clothing for fifty-seven individuals in his agency.[20] Where clubs were active, these tasks fell to Indigenous women, but in their absence, Indian Agents were forced to develop a response.

The Homemakers' Clubs, then, freed up Indian Agents by taking on vital social welfare duties and presumably influenced Indian Affairs' bottom line. Since the Department rarely provided financial support to the clubs, did not pay women for their labour, and relied on donated RCMP and military uniforms for supplies, officials could address community needs for little to no cost. The existence of active Homemakers' Clubs in each agency was a considerable financial advantage to Indian Affairs. This not only offers new insights into social welfare on reserves, but also challenges dominant deficiency-based narratives (visible in Department correspondence and attitudes) about the clubs helping Indigenous women, when in reality Indigenous women were helping others.

The clubs also served Indigenous communities, and many bands demonstrated their support for club activities by providing materials, space, and moral support to the women. In June 1956 the St. Mary's Club in Cranbrook received $35 from the band trust account to purchase buckskin for sewing lessons, and later that same year the Spallumcheen band council approved a $25 allocation in matching funds to its Homemakers' Club for Christmas gifts and candy for ninety-six children on reserve.[21] This initiative, according to D.M. Hett, Superintendent of the Okanagan Agency, reflected the women's "great effort to keep their community active, and to create social interest for the members," and thus Hett spoke in favour of the council resolution. Similar resolutions appeared in Alberta's Hobbema Agency, with the Samson and Ermineskin bands' Homemakers' Clubs requesting funds for flannelette, thread, and other sewing materials.[22] Hett, and others, were likewise supportive of Homemakers' Club efforts to improve infrastructure on reserve. At Spallumcheen, the Homemakers' Club requested $50 from band trust money to purchase a stove for cooking lessons and general band use, and elsewhere other clubs made similar purchases of stoves, furniture, paint, dishes, and other materials that promoted the Homemakers' objectives as well as improved the general community infrastructure.[23] It was difficult, then, to ignore the impact the clubs had on community life.

Domestic work also served social purposes and provided space for sharing knowledge and facilitating socio-economic and even cultural resistance. Indeed, like many Indigenous communities across the West, the women of the Paul band in Alberta created their Homemakers' Club specifically to share knowledge of sewing. Social worker W.R. Broderick explained: "The suggestion was made by one of the women that since the younger women, graduates of the day school, do not know the fundamentals of sewing, one of their own older women would teach them the basic ideas of some article."[24] Women brought together a number of resources to make this happen, including bringing their own fabrics and sewing machines, using the initial start-up resources from Indian Affairs, and even soliciting extra sewing materials from band council funds.[25]

It is curious that members of the Paul band, despite attending day schools, where according to the literature, sewing and other domestic skills

Figure 4.2. British Columbia Indian Homemakers Association display at 1971 PNE International Bazaar. Photograph by Bob Tipple. City of Vancouver Archives, CVA 180-6851.

were prioritized, came to the Homemakers' Club to learn sewing from older women.[26] Historian Katya MacDonald's work on handmade items helps us see greater nuance in how these skills manifested outside the schools in complicated ways. In the Paul Club, for instance, in addition to making clothing and linens for everyday use, the club purchased buckskin, beads, needles, and thread to produce traditional clothing and regalia.[27] At the Shulus Club, in British Columbia's Nicola Valley, club members "decided to learn how to make buckskin gloves[,] so [they] got a lady on our Reserve to teach [them]."[28] The objective of the Senyeemin Homemakers' Club in Penticton, British Columbia, was to produce "Indian arts and crafts," and thus its name, Senyeemin—the nsyilxcən/Okanagan word for weaving—both reflected and propelled this aspiration.[29] These activities blur the lines between skills gained in colonial institutions and those in community, as well as the division between so-called traditional and modern materials.

It was not simply the case that the type of sewing work practised in Homemakers' Clubs was either an extension of Euro-Canadian domestic skills learned in the schools or clubs, or a holistic expression of tradition in response to this training. Instead, Indigenous women sewed multiple types of objects and garments that fit their interests and needs. And while at times this generational knowledge sharing could strengthen communities—filling gaps in cultural knowledge—to resist generations of settler-colonial erasure, in other instances it was simply a way for women to make popular items to sell in craft fairs or for personal use.

Some handmade items produced a revenue stream for the Homemakers' Clubs when they were auctioned off in local fundraisers and at events like the Pacific National Exhibition (PNE) in Vancouver and the Armstrong Fair in the Okanagan Valley.[30] Figure 4.2 shows the range of items sold by members of the British Columbia Homemakers' Clubs, including woven shawls, beadwork, moccasins, baskets, carvings, and visual art. Other items were incorporated directly into club events, such as a fashion show organized for the 1967 meeting of the Interior Indian Homemakers' Clubs in Kamloops, British Columbia. Here members showcased contemporary and traditional garments made by members of surrounding Homemakers' Clubs and raised money through raffles and ticket sales. Some models, such as thirteen-year-old Lucy Michel from Kamloops, displayed their own creations—in this case, a "pink homespun A-line skirt topped with a pink print homespun top with long raglan sleeves and a scarf to match."[31] For many women, sewing the latest fashions was in keeping with the times, which saw the use of personal sewing machines and store-bought patterns to produce clothing many could otherwise not afford. Homemakers' Club members were no exception to this trend.[32] Many fashion show participants also produced traditional regalia, including "smoked deer hide in Shalish design," as well as beaded moccasins and bags, thus demonstrating the continued value of these items and the ongoing skills development needed to create them. And while women and girls represented the majority of participants, club activities and membership were not gender specific. In fact, the lone male participant of the 1967 Kamloops fashion show, Henry Jules—described as "the only man who took sewing lessons at Deadman's Creek"—modelled his two western-style shirts in the show, demonstrating the wide reach of club activities.[33]

In many communities, the clubs were a hub for social and service-based activities, which were accomplished with limited outside financial support. To attract new and self-sustaining clubs, Indian Affairs advertised a sewing machine and $50 worth of sewing materials for each group.[34] W.S. Arneil, the Indian Commissioner for British Columbia, maintained that this "capital investment" would "increase the treasury making other projects possible."[35] What Department reports fail to mention, however, is that Indian Affairs was not actually paying for these machines and supplies, but rather approving their purchase and arranging for discounts from suppliers. The actual funds came from band trust accounts. When the Enoch Indigenous women in Alberta's Hobbema district organized their Homemakers' Club in 1952, their regional supervisor of Indian agencies, R.G. Gooderham, requested funds for the sewing machine to be charged to "Band Account #120."[36] Shortly after, the club learned that Indian Affairs' Reserves and Trusts Division was "quite in accord with the purchase of the sewing machine from Enoch Band funds," and with approval via band council resolution from the Enoch Band chief and council, the purchase of two sewing machines "to be used to training purposes in the Indian Day Schools and Homemakers' Clubs," was made.[37]

The band's capacity to provide for the Homemakers' Club and the club's ability to make good use of these funds continued to be questioned, however. And the club's success was pinned on the ability of social worker Broderick to "manage" the women. Regional Supervisor G.H. Gooderham insisted Broderick was "making an honest effort to try and improve the social conditions of this Band, which has lately come into such wealth [*sic*], by establishing clubs and creating interests on the reserve that will keep them out of temptation elsewhere."[38] This tension between wealth and temptation is indicative of the assumption that wealth for Indigenous peoples, who are pathologized as perpetually impoverished, leads to immoral behaviour. The presumed disjuncture between Indigenous peoples and wealth, well researched by Alexandra Harmon and John Lutz, means that any move toward economic success must be managed externally.[39]

Emphasizing Department of Indian Affairs support in initializing the clubs preserves a problematic and false image of Indigenous peoples as eternally reliant on the state. Of course, band communities generally had the funds to purchase sewing machines and materials, but through another layer of settler-colonial control were required to request (through band council resolutions) that these purchases take place. This meant that Indigenous women wanting to initiate a Homemakers' Club needed to first speak to their often-male chief and council to seek approval, and then have chief and council submit a band council resolution to Indian Affairs. And through all this, women received the message that Indian Affairs was providing for them because they could not provide for themselves.[40] In fact, in 1955 Regional Supervisor R.F. Battle expressed surprise that women of the newly formed Wabaman Homemakers' Club in Alberta were getting along well and "making good use of the grant."[41]

Complex Settler Engagements

Indian Affairs social workers, who were assigned to regional offices to oversee, initiate, and manage Homemakers' Clubs, conveyed a similar message about women's dependency and need for improved domestic skills and economic self-sufficiency. Social workers were "new to the department in the postwar years," historian Mary Jane McCallum explains, and they "were especially responsible not only for encouraging work placement but for ensuring that Native people spent their leisure time in responsible ways, away from 'danger spots.'" With fewer than ten social workers active across Canada, McCallum notes that "their surveillance was fairly targeted and dependent upon their connection with local religious and civic organizations."[42] In 1950s western Canada, M. Meade oversaw activities in Saskatchewan, W.R. Broderick in Alberta, and Shirley Arnold in British Columbia. McCallum has demonstrated how these workers helped place a number of young Indigenous women as domestic labourers and nurses in the cities (largely through partnerships with residential schools and the Department of Indian Affairs), but they also worked closely with the Homemakers' Clubs.[43] Social workers would comment on the progress Indigenous women were making toward "bettering themselves" and their communities, and Homemakers' Club members were required to provide updates on club activities and request materials such as painting and sewing supplies. Social workers then remarked on the women's capacity to keep their clubs active, raise money through bake sales and other fundraisers, and maintain community morale and pride through paint-ups and cleanups.[44]

In the Edmonton agency in 1954, Broderick encouraged the women of Paul's band to continue a group they had initiated to plan a special occasion. After some thought, the group "decided to carry on, using the organization set-up for the Indian Homemakers' Club."[45] Welcoming the newly formed West Coast Namu Homemakers' Club to the IHC in 1962, Shirley Arnold announced that joining the network of forty-nine active clubs with a membership of over 600 women brought privileges, such as the sewing machine and materials, as well as responsibilities "towards the common goal of service to their families and communities."[46] IHC members were regularly reminded of their obligations as women and mothers to keep sanitary homes, to provide adequate nutrition and health care, and to contribute to the overall health, wellness, and happiness of their communities.

Often this type of oversight could take on tones of moral regulation, as it did in 1955 when Sister Pauline, who oversaw the Fort St. James Club in northern British Columbia, reported her attempts to eliminate alcohol manufacturing and consumption in the community. She explained: "I spoke to them on the responsibility they had towards their families and their need of family prayer and good example in their homes."[47] From her position of religious authority, Sister Pauline spoke in a condescending and paternalistic manner about community shortcomings, presuming, of course, that she rather than Indigenous peoples knew what was best. This need to guide the morality of Indigenous women and families not only fit within a broader pattern of moral regulation within the Homemakers' Clubs but was also characteristic of historical engagements between settlers and Indigenous peoples, as Jean Barman, Robin Jarvis Brownlie, Joan Sangster, and Adele Perry have confirmed.[48]

When we consider these broad patterns of oversight grounded in settler-colonial attitudes, it is not surprising that even settlers who were not directly involved in the Homemakers' Club network offered unsolicited interventions. In November 1955, Lois E. Hamilton of the Imperial Order Daughters of the Empire (IODE) appealed to Director of Indian Affairs Colonel H.M. Jones to determine how her organization might "adopt" a Homemakers' Club. Hamilton explained that she had just recently learned about the clubs and believed "a very practical way to assist in helping the Indians to appreciate full citizenship rites was for organizations such as ours to take an interest in the Indian women by adopting one of these clubs."[49] With an air of superiority and presumption, Hamilton requested a list of clubs, contact names, and directions for how to move forward with such an adoption. Jones responded with a somewhat contradictory mix of incredulity that Hamilton would presume to want to adopt a club without knowing anything about it or what such an adoption might look like, and praise for her organization's interest in such a noble cause. He was not clear on the implications of such a plan to adopt a Homemakers' Club, but enclosed a copy of the IHC constitution nevertheless. He did, however, also explain the logistical challenges of Hamilton's plan, noting there were currently 167 active clubs—many located in remote areas—and that "each group operates independently as the movement has not been developed to the point of having a national or provincial executive."[50] Rather than direct Hamilton to speak to the clubs themselves about their needs or interest in the IODE's involvement, Jones suggested Hamilton contact one of the eight Indian Affairs' social workers assigned to the Homemakers' Clubs. Through this correspondence, both Hamilton and Jones perpetuated the continuing socio-political dispossession of Indigenous women, discussing the most advantageous ways to "help" Indigenous peoples realize the value of citizenship and modern society without ever consulting the women or assuming them competent enough to manage their own affairs.

And yet, Indigenous women in the Homemakers' Clubs developed complex and genuine relationships with settlers. While this does not negate the inequities between these parties, it does complicate our understanding of the relationships between them. Social workers occupied unique and intricate spaces as facilitators of the assimilative tendencies of the IHC and of the limited gender roles upheld within them; as allies supporting women in their clubs and facilitating their work; and as gendered allies and friends who forged and upheld important personal relationships amid these structures. Homemakers' Club presidents, in particular, maintained frequent correspondence with the social workers. Often these letters offered some club updates but were also personalized with details about the women's lives and community happenings. In 1962 Namu Homemakers' Club President Kitty Carpenter wrote to Shirley Arnold, updating her on the club's unique plans to represent the labour rights of women working at the local fish plant. Beyond the usual niceties expected in such correspondence, this letter maintained a degree of warmth and familiarity as Carpenter discussed community events, including a recent fire and her current travels with her husband on his commercial fishing ventures. Instead of a professional letter closing, Carpenter signs off with "loads of love to you dear."[51] Certainly, official club business and Arnold's expectation for updates motivated this letter, but it is clear that at the very least Carpenter viewed this friendship as genuine. And while Arnold's responses maintained an air of professionalism, her 16 February 1962 reply to Carpenter expresses sincere concern over the fire and caring thoughts toward the women in the club. In this letter, Arnold also departs from her typical closing of "yours truly" adding "yours very truly," which denotes a similar degree of affection toward Carpenter.[52] These friendships were not isolated but part of a noticeable trend in the surviving documentation.

These types of personal and professional relationships also extended beyond the IHC network, speaking to the complexity of intersectionality at work here. Throughout the 1950s and 1960s Homemakers' Clubs supported Euro-Canadian and religious organizations such as the Lions, the Catholic Women's League, and hospital associations. Homemakers' Clubs frequently held fundraisers for these organizations and participated in their events, demonstrating Indigenous women's broad definitions of "community." In the Bella Coola district, Carpenter noticed white settler women had formed a women's institute, and she was hopeful that both groups would work together.[53]

Elsewhere, in preparation for Canada's centennial celebrations, Stó:lō Chehalis Club members organized "a supper to honour our centennial pioneers," and several other clubs across the West joined centennial committees to help organize Canada Day festivities.[54]

On the surface, it appears that Indigenous women were complicit in continued colonization efforts and the nostalgic memorializing of Canada's settler-colonial project. In part, that may be true. But it is also true that Indigenous women navigated their complex relationships with the settler state and their Indigenous political communities carefully. In many ways, Homemakers' Club members' support for nationalistic activities that accepted and even glorified continued settler colonialism is surprising, but women acted within overlapping contexts of a growing Indigenous rights movement and their everyday lives as part of a broader Canadian community. Women, then, could concurrently advocate for better reserve conditions and services for Indigenous peoples and be good neighbours who celebrated the creation of Canada.

Many clubs also structured their activities according to their religious beliefs. We have seen how many clubs were overseen or run by religious officials, and Homemakers' Clubs often used their resources to support religious efforts and individuals within their communities, viewing these as part and parcel of community well-being. In British Columbia, the Vernon Homemakers' Club provided breakfast for the first communicants in their community, the Stellaquo Club at Fraser Lake raised money to build a new church, and Penticton Senyeemin Club members used their funds to bring Father Blackquire home for Christmas.[55] The Chehalis Club also got its start through mobilizing to refresh the local church, and many club members blended their religious affiliations and activities with those of the Homemakers' Clubs.[56] And yet, the earlier example of Sister Pauline using the Fort St. James Club to intervene into supposed immoral activities surrounding alcohol production and consumption in the community offers nuance to these relationships. As a site of colonial encounter, religion is necessarily complex, but as the club members' engagements with the various churches demonstrate, Indigenous peoples participated in religion in ways that were meaningful to them.[57]

In many ways, these religious and nationalistic gestures epitomized the IHC's ideological underpinnings and church influence. Indeed, the organization's emphasis on producing useful and patriotic citizens was explicitly outlined in its constitution and in its motto, "For Home and Country." Further, women's connections to church and country, through various historic and contemporary sites, were celebrated in club names such as the Maple Leaf Homemakers' Club in Chilliwack and the Our Lady of Fatima Club in Chehalis, as well as through the women's activities.

There could be strong contradictions between women's affinity with the Canadian nation, their religious beliefs, and close relationships with state actors, and the complex colonial legacy and continued beliefs in Indigenous rights. An Indigenous feminist analysis enables us to see that while these women certainly acted as individuals—choosing to develop friendships and alliances as they pleased—they did so within the broader structures of colonialism, gender oppression, and the growing Indigenous and feminist rights movements.

Regional Networks and the Shifting Indiginous Women's Movement

The IHC played a key, if uneven, role in the Indigenous women's rights movement, particularly as women united within and across the provinces to further their socio-political causes. Cross-provincially, the clubs communicated semi-regularly and often attended the same regional conferences. The 1954 Homemakers' Convention for the prairie provinces, for example, took place at Duck Lake, Saskatchewan, and welcomed delegates from British Columbia, Alberta, Saskatchewan, and Manitoba.[58] It was not until the late 1950s that provincial club numbers increased to the extent that demanded independent provincial conventions, and though these became the norm in the 1960s, it was not uncommon for women to attend provincial conferences other than their own. It was this type of political travel and dialogue that connected provincial networks to the national IHC. The conventions provided space for Indigenous women to get to know one another, to share the activities of their clubs, and to comment on shared challenges and issues. Typically, one or two delegates—generally executive members—from each club would attend the conventions; thus the total number of attendees could number in the hundreds. Since a single Homemakers' Club, whose membership could range between fifteen and forty, organized conventions, hosting a regional convention was no small feat. The organizing committee would have to draw up budgets and funding requests, arrange accommodations (including local billets), secure a conference location, and arrange for speakers. It is through this turn toward provincial organizing that we begin to see a strong national movement as well as regional variations.

Despite similarities in how the clubs were initiated and a national constitution that guided club structures and activities, each province developed its unique organizational style. In British Columbia, clubs expanded dramatically in the 1960s and began to take on more overt forms of political activity, whereas those in Alberta and Saskatchewan faced significant declines in membership. On the surface it might appear that Indigenous women in British Columbia were simply more interested in socio-political organization than their prairie counterparts were, but this was not the case. Across the country (and indeed the world), Indigenous women were becoming increasingly vocal against their political, social, and economic dispossession via settler-colonial policy, and they began organizing in greater numbers. In British Columbia, this shift took place within the existing Homemakers' Club framework, whereas in Alberta and Saskatchewan it took place outside. For British Columbia clubs, a turning point came in 1968, when, frustrated by the limitations of the Indian Homemakers' Clubs constitution and the Department of Indian Affairs' resistance to Indigenous women's changing mandates (which included lobbying for better reserve conditions, education, and health care through policy change rather than through women's domestic work alone), the clubs united to form an independent political organization, the British Columbia Indian Homemakers' Association (BCIHA). Through this amendment, Indigenous women in British Columbia repurposed an existing structure and network. Similar politicization happened in Alberta and Saskatchewan, but unlike British Columbia members, who decided to alter their clubs to reflect their new political dynamic, women in the prairie provinces largely abandoned their Homemakers' Clubs and began new Indigenous women's political organizations. In 1969 Alberta's political landscape included only nine Homemakers' Clubs but twenty-six Indigenous women's organizations, while Saskatchewan maintained twenty-three Homemakers' Clubs and sixteen other organizations.[59]

In Alberta, the decline of the Homemakers' Clubs was cause for concern among membership and Indian Affairs officials, and both made concerted efforts to shore up dwindling numbers. In response to women's concerns, in 1966 Alberta Community Development Officer William Wacko suggested sending delegates from the fledgling Alberta Homemakers' Clubs to the British Columbia Homemakers' Club convention in Duncan. Wacko and the Alberta delegates hoped they might build on British Columbia's political successes and implement these at home. Appealing to his superiors to fund the travel and expenses for ten delegates, Wacko explained: "You may not know that Homemakers Clubs in Alberta have become very inactive, whereas in British Columbia these clubs are very active and it appears that their scope of concern is much broader than the stove and the sewing machine. In order to give some Indian ladies in Alberta an opportunity to meet with Native Homemakers women in British Columbia, the Regional Community Development Section in Indian Affairs has agreed to pay the travelling expenses of ten Indian ladies—one from each Agency—to attend this conference."[60] Curiously, while Indian Affairs officials in British Columbia resisted the politicization of Homemakers' Clubs (refusing to fund and support the new "lobby group"), Wacko appeared to view women's broadening socio-political agenda as aspirational and worth pursuing. This divergence likely resulted from Indian Affairs officials' varied experiences with women's activities and the presumed threat these might pose. In British Columbia, the Homemakers' Clubs integrated overt critique of Indian Affairs into their proposals for better services and conditions—something the Department of Indian Affairs did not look kindly upon.[61] In Alberta, women had not yet begun the same lobbying efforts within the clubs, and therefore their activities appeared supportive of rather than threatening to the Department's status quo.

At the Duncan conference, Alberta delegates Josette Many Guns (Gleichen) and Emma Minde (Hobbema) were impressed with the youthfulness of the executive membership and the cooperation between younger and older women in the organization, noting the Alberta clubs were primarily populated by older women.[62] Margaret Makosis of Saddle Lake appreciated the multiple programs the British Columbia clubs offered to young people in terms of children in care, entertainment, and education, and saw an opportunity for her club to mirror these efforts. For Cecile Gambler, the Duncan convention reminded her of what was lacking in Alberta. She explicitly contrasted the divergent interest in and development of the clubs between the provinces, explaining: "I was so disappointed about our district when the chairman announced that there were about fifty Homemaker's Clubs all over British Columbia."[63] Gambler noted, however, that the Alberta women learned strategies to attract new membership and to handle diminishing membership during their time in Duncan. Overall, the women left the convention with a strong conviction that their clubs could and should be reinvigorated.

But by 1969 it seemed few Indigenous women shared the Alberta delegates' enthusiasm, as provincial club numbers had dropped to a paltry nine (down from the 1957 peak of thirty-four clubs).[64] Yet far from indicating the demise of women's socio-political work, however, this decline in Homemakers' Clubs was matched by a dramatic increase in other women's political organizations. Of these, perhaps the most well-known was the Voice of Alberta Native Women's

Society (VANWS), a coordinating organization of Treaty and Métis women created in 1968 to "communicate and exchange information among the various Native Women's groups and organizations across the province."[65] The very idea that a coordinating organization was needed in 1968 is indicative of the number and diversity of existing organizations. Indeed, the idea for VANWS emerged after Alice Steinhauer, Mary Ruth McDougall, and Christine Daniels attended a Native Women's Conference at Fort Qu'Appelle in 1967. Interested in holding their own conference for Alberta women, as an "opportunity for native women to express their concerns and mutual interests and to endeavour to define their goals for a better future in their communities," the concept of a new organization was formed.[66] Throughout the late 1960s and early 1970s, Indigenous women in Alberta would become heavily involved in VANWS, local organizations (in communities such as Edmonton, Calgary, Lethbridge, Fort Saskatchewan, Standoff, and Saddle Lake), as well as in newly formed national Indigenous women's organizations such as the Native Women's Association of Canada and Indian Rights for Indian Women (IRIW).[67]

The Saskatchewan movement followed a similar trajectory, with the development of several local women's organizations (from communities such as Regina, La Ronge, Prince Albert, and Yorkton). In spring 1971, Indigenous women across the province formed a steering committee to determine how they might create a provincial women's rights organization. In September that year, the Saskatchewan Indian Women's Association (SIWA) was formed with Irene Tootoosis as president. By 1973, SIWA had taken over the Homemakers program and remained active in the women's rights movement, liaising with the national IRIW as well as the more male-dominated Federation of Saskatchewan Indian Nations (within which SIWA gained formal recognition).[68] Also predominant at this time was the Saskatchewan Native Women's Movement (later the Saskatchewan Native Women's Association), formed in 1971 by Treaty, non-Status, and Métis women who wanted to combat racism, sexism, poverty, and educational disadvantages, as well as seek recognition of Indigenous women's rights.[69] With the exception of SIWA, these organizations and others would not immediately supersede the Homemakers' Clubs, but they did draw a number of women from their ranks, creating a significant void within the Homemakers' Club network.

In British Columbia, the provincial Homemakers network remained strong through the independent BCIHA, but women also joined emerging organizations such as the BC Native Women's Society (also founded in 1968), the Native Sisterhood of British Columbia, the Makwalla Club of Vancouver, and local women's clubs in Kamloops, Chase, Campbell River, Comox, Penticton, Prince George, Fort St. James, Terrace, and Burns Lake.[70] The BCIHA, along with the BC Native Women's Society, would dominate the political scene for Indigenous women and worked to place women's concerns on the agenda of the male provincial organization, the Union of BC Indian Chiefs. Overall, despite these provincial differences in terms of the longevity and continued relevance of Homemakers' Clubs, in each province these clubs provided a foundation and forum for women's socio-political work.

Conclusion

In many ways, the Homemakers' Clubs represent a number of strange contradictions. They were grounded in sentiments of nationalism and Euro-Canadian gender norms—built out of the Canadian women's institutes and taken up by the Department of Indian Affairs—and yet from an Indigenous feminist perspective, they were also sites of resistance and political capacity building. Looking at the complexity of Indigenous women's early work and activism, as well as the intricate and shifting relationships with non-Indigenous stakeholders, we see how the clubs could be both complicit in settler-colonial mores and resistant to them. The clubs both delineated and separated Indigenous space for women to do things that were meaningful to them, but at times also solidified state assimilation efforts. Certainly women used the clubs in ways that fit the Department of Indian Affairs mandate toward improved domesticity, but they also solved everyday issues of needing paid work, providing social and economic support for community members, improving community conditions, and facilitating political consciousness. As the Indigenous women's political movement gained ground in the late 1960s, the contribution of the Homemakers' Clubs was clear and the club's motto, "For Home and Country," took on new meaning in an era where homes were undeniably and unapologetically political.

Notes

1 Thank you to Amanda Fehr for her insightful comments on the earliest iteration of this piece, as well as to the anonymous reviewers for their thoughtful contributions. Some of the research findings here also appear in *From Suffragette to Homesteader: Exploring One Woman's Memoir on Life in England and Canada, 1870–1930* published by Fernwood Press. Thank you to Fernwood for permission to reproduce. Financial support for this research was provided by the Social Sciences and Humanities Research Council of Canada.

2 Library and Archives Canada (LAC), RG10-C-IV-7, File 987/24-5, Volume 13461, File Part 1, Homemakers' Clubs, 1965/04–1967/11, Letter from Frances E. Decker, Mount Currie Homemakers' Club, to Mr. Letcher, Superintendent, Department of Indian Affairs, Vancouver, BC, 28 May 1965.

3 LAC, RG10-C-IV-7, File 987/24-5, Volume 13461, File Part 1, Homemakers' Clubs, 1965/04–1967/11, Letter from Frances E. Decker, Mount Currie Homemakers' Club, to Mr. Letcher, Superintendent, Department of Indian Affairs, Vancouver, BC, 28 May 1965; Letter from Miss S.J. Arnold, Welfare Consultant, to Mrs. J.O. Decker, 23 July 1965; Letter from J.C. Lawrance, District Superintendent of Schools, to Miss Shirley Arnold, 21 July 1965; Letter from Miss S.J. Arnold, Welfare Consultant, to Mrs. J. Decker, 17 August 1965.

4 LAC, RG10-C-IV-7, File 987/24-5, Volume 13461, File Part 1, Homemakers' Clubs, 1965/04–1967/11, Letter from J.C. Lawrance, District Superintendent of Schools, to Miss Shirley Arnold, 21 July 1965.

5 Milne, "Cultivating Domesticity," iii.

6 LAC, RG10, Box 1, File 987/24-5, Constitution and Regulations for Indian Homemakers' Clubs, Indian Affairs Branch, Department of Citizenship and Immigration, Ottawa, 1951, 6; Milne, "Cultivating Domesticity," 63n59.

7 Milne, "Cultivating Domesticity," 63.

8 Leger-Anderson, Women's Organizations in Saskatchewan, 163; Magee, "'For Home and Country,'" 32; Moran, *Sai'k'uz Ts'eke Stoney Creek Woman.*

9 LAC, RG 10, Volume 8482, File 1/24-5, Reel C-13816, General—Homemakers' Club Correspondence, 1955–1958, Memorandum to W from C. Roberts, Indian Affairs Branch, Department of Citizenship and Immigration, 10 April 1957.

10 LAC, RG 10, Volume 8482, File 1/24-5, Reel C-13816, General—Homemakers' Club Correspondence, 1955–1958, Homemakers' Clubs, Statement as of 1 August 1956.

11 Barkaskas, "The Indian Voice"; Magee, "'For Home and Country'"; Harris and McCallum, "'Assaulting the Ears of Government.'"

12 LAC, RG10-C-IV-7, File 901/24-5-1, Volume 13462, File Part 2 (Folder B), Homemakers Club—Conferences, 1965/04–1968-08, Homemakers' Club Convention, 21 and 22 April 1965, Chilliwack, BC; ibid., File Part 2, (Folder 1), File 901/24-5-1, Homemakers' Club—Conferences, 1965/04–1968/08, Minutes of the Interior Homemakers' Clubs (1967), I.O.O.F. Hall, Kamloops, 30 March–1 April 1967.

13 Nickel, "'I Am Not a Women's Libber, Although Sometimes I Sound Like One.'"

14 LAC, RG10-C-IV-7, Volume 13462 (File Part 2, Folder 1), File 901/24-5-1, Homemakers' Club—Conferences, 1965/04–1968/08, Minutes of the Interior Indian Homemakers' Clubs (1967), I.O.O.F. Hall, Kamloops 30 March–1 April 1967.

15 MacDonald, "Making Histories and Narrating Things."

16 Canada, Department of Citizenship and Immigration, *Report of Indian Affairs Branch for the Fiscal Year Ending 31 March 1945.*

17 Canada, Department of Mines and Resources, *Report of Indian Affairs Branch for the Fiscal Year Ended 31 Mach 1948,* 220.

18 LAC, RG10, File 982/24-5, Box 389, File Part 2, Kootenay Okanagan District Office—Homemakers' clubs—Kootenay-Okanagan District, 1947–1966, Letter from D.M. Hett to W.S. Arneil, 8 December 1955, re: Spallumcheen Band—Homemakers' Club; LAC, RG10, Box 1, Volume 11466, File 972/24-25 (Part 1), Various Annual Statements—Homemakers' Clubs, 1955–1969, Letter from Mrs. Doreen Robinson, Klemtu, to Miss Arnold, 18 November 1959; Letter from Miss Shirley Arnold, Social Worker, to Mrs. Doreen Robinson, Klemtu Homemakers' Club, 2 December 1959.

19 LAC, RG10, Volume 8483 File part 2, File 774/24-5, Reel C-13817, Edmonton, Hobbema District—General Correspondence and Accounts Regarding the Homemakers' Club, 1942–1964, Letter from E.A. Robertson, Indian Agent, to G.M. Gooderham, Inspector of Indian Agencies, Calgary, 4 March 1947.

20 LAC, RG10, File 982/24-5, Box 389, File Part 1, 1999-01431-6, Kootenay Okanagan District Office—Homemakers' clubs—Kootenay-Okanagan District, 1947–1966, Letter from J.S. Dunn, Indian Agency Kootenay Agency, to Major D.M. MacKay, Indian Commissioner for BC, 12 February 1947.

21 LAC, RG10, Box 389, File 982/24-5 (Part 1), Kootenay Okanagan District Office—Homemakers' Clubs—Kootenay-Okanagan District, 1947–1966, Voucher form for Kootenay Agency Trust Account, Cranbrook, 22 June 1956; Letter from D.M. Hett, Superintendent, Okanagan Agency, to W.S. Arneil, Indian Commissioner for BC, 7 December 1956.

22 LAC, RG10, Volume 8483 (File Part 2), File 774/24-5, Reel C-13817, Edmonton, Hobbema District—General Correspondence and Accounts Regarding the Homemakers' Club, 1952–1965, Band Council Resolution—Samson Indian Reserve, n.d.; Band Council Resolution—Ermineskin Indian Reserve, 26 March 1952; Band Council Resolution—Samson Band of Indians, n.d.

23 LAC, RG10-C-IV-7, Volume 13462 (File Part 2, Folder 1), File 901/24-5-1, Homemakers' Club—Conferences, 1965/04–1968/08, Minutes of the Interior Homemakers' Clubs (1967), I.O.O.F. Hall, Kamloops, 30 March–1 April 1967.

24 LAC, RG10, Volume 8483 (File Part 2), File 774/24-5, Reel C-13817, Edmonton, Hobbema District—General Correspondence and Accounts Regarding the Homemakers' Club, Letter from W.R. Broderick (Miss), Social Welfare Worker, to Superintendent of Welfare, 14 December 1954.

25 LAC, RG10, Volume 8483 (File Part 2), File 774/24-5, Reel C-13817, Edmonton, Hobbema District—General Correspondence and Accounts Regarding the Homemakers' Club, 1952–1965, Band Council Resolution—Samson Indian Reserve, n.d.; Band Council Resolution—Ermineskin Indian Reserve, 26 March 1952; Band Council Resolution—Samson Band of Indians, n.d.

26 MacDonald, "Making Histories and Narrating Things"; Miller, *Shingwauk's Vision.*

27 LAC, RG10, Box 389, File 982/24-5 (Part 1), Kootenay Okanagan District Office—Homemakers Clubs—Kootenay-Okanagan District, 1947–1966, Letter from D.M. Hett to W.S. Arneil, 8 December 1955, re: Spallumcheen Band—Homemakers'

Club; Letter from W.S. Arneil, Indian Commissioner for BC to Indian Affairs, Ottawa, 6 December 1955; MacDonald, "Making Histories and Narrating Things."

28 LAC, RG10-C-IV-7, Volume 13462 (File Part 2, Folder 1), File 901/24-5-1, Homemakers' Club—Conferences, 1965/04–1968/08, Minutes of the Interior Homemakers' Clubs (1967), I.O.O.F. Hall, Kamloops, 30 March–1 April 1967.

29 LAC, RG10, File 982/24-5, Box 389, File Part 2, Kootenay Okanagan District Office—Homemakers' Clubs—Kootenay-Okanagan District, 1947–1966, Letter from W.S. Arneil to H.M. Jones re: Senyeemin Homemakers' club—Penticton Reserve, Okanagan Agency, 18 September 1951.

30 LAC, RG10, File 673/24-5, Box 281, File Part 2, Yorkton District Office—Homemakers' Clubs, Yorkton District, 1967, Cowessess Homemakers' Club exhibiting at the Indian Pavilion, 1967; City of Vancouver Archives, CVA 180-6851—British Columbia Indian Homemakers Association display at the 1971 P.N.E. International Bazaar; LAC, RG10-C-IV-7, Volume 13462 (File Part 2, Folder 1), File 901/24-5-1, Homemakers' Club—Conferences, 1965/04–1968/08, Minutes of the Interior Homemakers' Clubs (1967), I.O.O.F. Hall, Kamloops, 30 March–1 April 1967.

31 LAC, RG10-C-IV-7, Volume 13462 (File Part 2, Folder 1), File 901/24-5-1, Homemakers' Club—Conferences, 1965/04–1968/08, Minutes of the Interior Homemakers' Clubs (1967), I.O.O.F. Hall, Kamloops, 30 March–1 April 1967.

32 Bower, "From Wanting In to Opting Out."

33 LAC, RG10-C-IV-7, Volume 13462 (File Part 2, Folder 1), File 901/24-5-1, Homemakers' Club—Conferences, 1965/04–1968/08, Minutes of the Interior Homemakers' Clubs (1967), I.O.O.F. Hall, Kamloops, 30 March–1 April 1967.

34 Canada, Department of Citizenship and Immigration, *Report of Indian Affairs Branch for the Fiscal Year Ending 31 March 1953*; LAC, RG10, Volume 8483, File Part 2, File 774/24-5, Reel C-13817, Edmonton, Hobbema District—General Correspondence and Accounts Regarding the Homemakers' Club, 1942–1964, Letter from G.H. Gooderham, Regional Supervisor of Indian Agencies, to Superintendent, Welfare Service, Indian Affairs Branch, 14 August 1952; Letter from Acting Superintendent, Reserves and Trusts Division to G.H. Gooderham, Regional Supervisor of Indian Agencies for Alberta, 19 August 1952.

35 LAC, RG10, File 982/24-5, Box 389, File Part 2, Kootenay Okanagan District Office—Homemakers' Clubs—Kootenay-Okanagan District, 1947–1966, Letter from H.M. Jones, Superintendent–Welfare Service, to W.S. Arneil, Indian Commissioner for BC, 10 June 1953.

36 LAC, RG10, Volume 8483, File Part 2, File 774/24-5, Reel C-13817, Edmonton, Hobbema District—General Correspondence and Accounts Regarding the Homemakers' Club, 1942–1964, Letter from G.H. Gooderham, Regional Supervisor of Indian Agencies, to Superintendent, Welfare Service, Indian Affairs Branch, 14 August 1952.

37 LAC, RG10, volume 8483, File Part 2, File 774/24-5, Reel C-13817, Edmonton, Hobbema District—General Correspondence and Accounts Regarding the Homemakers' Club, 1942–1964, Letter from Acting Superintendent, Reserves and Trusts Division to G.H. Gooderham, Regional Supervisor of Indian Agencies for Alberta, 19 August 1952; Letter from G.H. Gooderham, Regional Supervisor of Indian Agencies to Superintendent, Welfare Service, Indian Affairs Branch, 14 August 1952.

38 LAC, RG10, Volume 8483, File Part 2, File 774/24-5, Reel C-13817, Edmonton, Hobbema District—General Correspondence and Accounts Regarding the Homemakers' Club, Letter from G.H. Gooderham, Regional Supervisor of Indian Agencies, to Superintendent, Welfare Service, Indian Affairs Branch, 14 August 1952.

39 Harmon, *Rich Indians*; Lutz, *Makúk*.

40 Later, as the clubs expanded, the Department of Indian Affairs did generate a budget line for the Homemakers' Clubs to provide limited financial support, but even this was reluctant, as Indian Affairs officials continued to encourage Indigenous women to seek alternatives to department monies. Magee, "'For Home and Country,'" 28.

41 LAC, RG10, Volume 8483, File Part 2, File 774/24-5, Reel C-13817, Edmonton, Hobbema District—General Correspondence and Accounts Regarding the Homemakers' Club, 1952–1965, Letter from R.F. Battle, Regional Supervisor of Indian Agencies, to Superintendent of Welfare, 24 March 1955.

42 McCallum, *Indigenous Women, Work, and History*, 65.

43 McCallum, 62.

44 LAC, RG10, Box 1, Volume 11466, File 972/24-25 (Part 1), accession V84-85/368, Various Annual Statements—Homemakers' Clubs, Letter from Miss Shirley Arnold, Social Worker, to Mrs. David Carpenter, Bella Bella, BC, 27 November 1957; Letter from Miss Shirley Arnold, Social Worker, to Mrs. Margaret Hunt, Campbell Island, BC, 20 June 1958; Letter from Miss Shirley Arnold, Social Worker, to Mrs. Doreen Robinson, Klemtu, BC, 24 June 1957.

45 LAC, RG10, Volume 8483 (File Part 2), File 774/24-5, Reel C-13817, Edmonton, Hobbema District—General Correspondence and Accounts Regarding the Homemakers' Club, Letter from W.R. Broderick (Miss), Social Welfare Worker, to Superintendent of Welfare, 14 December 1954.

46 LAC, RG10, Box 1, Volume 11466, File 972/24-25 (Part 1), Various Annual Statements—Homemakers' Clubs, 1955–1969, Letter from Miss. S.J. Arnold, Regional Welfare Supervisor, to Mrs. Ruby Dickson, Pres., Namu Homemakers' Club, Namu, BC, 16 February 1962. Namu is located on British Columbia's northwest coast, just south of Bella Bella.

47 LAC, RG 10, Volume 11481, Box 1, File 971/24-5, accession V84-85/288, Homemakers' Clubs—Homemakers' Club Bulletin, 1 October 1955.

48 Sangster, "Criminalizing the Colonized"; Barman, "Taming Aboriginal Sexuality"; Perry, "The Autocracy of Love and the Legitimacy of Empire"; Brownlie, "Intimate Surveillance."

49 LAC, RG 10, Volume 8482, File 1/24-5, Reel C-13816, General—Homemakers' Club Correspondence, 1955–1958, Letter from Lois E. Hamilton, The Imperial Order Daughters of the Empire, to Colonel H.M. Jones, Director of Indian Affairs, Department of Citizenship and Immigration, 25 November 1955.

50 LAC, RG 10, Volume 8482, File 1/24-5, Reel C-13816, General—Homemakers' Club Correspondence, 1955–1958, Letter from H.M. Jones, Director to Mrs. G.L. Hamilton, National Convener of Immigration and Canadianization, The Imperial Order Daughters of the Empire and children of the Empire (Junior Branch), 9 December 1955.

51 LAC, RG10, Box 1, Volume 11466, File 972/24-25 (Part 1), Various Annual Statements—Homemakers' Clubs, 1955–1969, Letter to Miss Arnold from Kitty Carpenter, 7 February 1962.

52 LAC, RG10, Box 1, Volume 11466, File 972/24-25 (Part 1), Various Annual Statements—Homemakers' Clubs, 1955–1969, Letter to Kitty Carpenter from Miss Shirley Arnold, 16 February 1962.

53 LAC, RG10, Box 1, Volume 11466, File 972/24-25 (Part 1), Various Annual Statements—Homemakers' Clubs, 1955–1969, Letter to Miss Arnold from Kitty Carpenter, 7 February 1962.

54 LAC, RG10-C-IV-7, Volume 13462 (File Part 2, Folder 1), File 901/24-5-1, Homemakers' Club—Conferences, 1965/04–1968/08, Minutes of the Interior Indian Homemakers' Clubs (1967), I.O.O.F. Hall, Kamloops, 30 March—1 April 1967, Report of the Chehalis Club by Mrs. Pat Charlie.

55 LAC, RG10-C-IV-7, Volume 13462 (File Part 2, Folder 1), File 901/24-5-1, Homemakers' Club—Conferences, 1965/04–1968/08, Minutes of the Interior Indian Homemakers' Clubs (1967), I.O.O.F. Hall, Kamloops, 30 March–1 April 1967.

56 Sto:lō Research and Resource Management Centre (SRRMC), Oral History Collection, Rose Charlie, interview with Koni Benson, Chehalis First Nation, Agassiz, BC, 3 June 1998.

57 For more on the complex relationships between Indigenous peoples and Christianity, see Bradford and Horton, *Mixed Blessings*.

58 LAC, RG10, Volume 8483, File 501/24-5-1, Reel C-13817, Manitoba Regional Office—General Correspondence and Accounts Regarding the Homemakers' Convention, 1954–1956, Letter from J.P.B. Ostrander, Superintendent – Welfare Service, to R.S. Davis, Regional Supervisor of Indian Agencies, Winnipeg, 3 May 1954.

59 Magee, "For Home and Country," 46.

60 LAC, RG10-C-IV-7, File 901/24-5-1, Volume 13462, File Part 2 (Folder B), Homemakers' Club—Conferences, 1965/04–1968-08, Letter to [blank], from Wm. J. Wacko, Senior Community Development Officer, n.d., re: Homemakers Convention, Duncan British Columbia, 12 April to 14 April 1966.

61 LAC, RG10, Volume 13462, Homemakers' Club—Conventions, 1969–70, File 901-24-5-1, Rose Charlie to Regional Director J.V. Boys, 3 July 1969.

62 LAC, RG10-C-IV-7, Volume 13462, File Part 2 (Folder 2), File 901/24-5-1, Report of the Cowichan Homemakers' Club Conference, Josie Many Guns, 1966; Report of Duncan Homemakers' Conference, Mrs. Margaret Makosis, Saddle Lake Reserve, 1966; Letter from W.J. Wacko, Senior Community Development Officer – Indian Affairs Branch – Alberta to Mrs. Shirley Gillkin, Duncan, BC, 5 April 1966.

63 LAC, RG10-C-IV-7, File 901/24-5-1, Volume 13462, File Part 2 (Folder 2), Cowichan Homemakers' Club Conference, Duncan, BC, Mrs. Emma Minde, Hobbema, Alberta, 1966.

64 Magee, "For Home and Country," 46; LAC, RG10, Volume 11481, Box 1, File 971/24-5, Homemakers' Club, October 1955 Homemakers' Club Bulletin; LAC, RG10, Volume 11466, Box 1, File 972/24-25 (Part 1), Various Annual Statements—Homemakers' Clubs, Letter from W.S. Arneil, Indian Commissioner for BC, to Indian Affairs Branch, Ottawa, 5 May 1955.

65 Provincial Archives of Alberta (PAA), GR1979.0152, File 0023, Voice of Alberta Native Women's Society—General, 1970–1972, 1972 VANWS Conference: An Evaluation, September 1972, 4.

66 PAA, PR1999.0465/0080, Alberta Native Women's Association, Voice of Alberta Native Women Society History.

67 PAA, GR1979.0152, Box 10, File 0115, Indian Rights for Indian Women's Conference; Conferences and Training Courses, 1972–73; PR1999.0465/0079, Alberta Native Women's Association, 1969–1972; GR1979.0152, File 0023, Voice of Alberta Native Women's Society; General, 1970–1972.

68 "Indian Women Want a Far Greater Role," 14; "The Saskatchewan Indian Women's Association," 9.

69 LAC, RG6-F, Box 38, File 9316-D, Citizenship Sector—Saskatchewan Native Women's Association – Developing Leadership of Native Women, 14 February 1979–18 May 1979.

70 UBC, Rare Books and Special Collections, Leonard and Kitty Maracle Fonds, Box 4, File 4-21, Makwalla Native Women's Association, 2nd Annual Meeting of the Makwalla Native Women's Association, 21 April 1974; Box 4, File 4-12, B.C. Native Women's Society—Reports, Memos, 1975.

Part II
Queer and Two-Spirit Identities, and Sexuality

CHAPTER 5

Reclaiming Traditional Gender Roles: A Two-Spirit Critique

KAI PYLE

With this chapter, I hope to expand our understanding of the ways in which heteropatriarchy can sometimes prevail even as we attempt to dismantle it. During the 2015/2016 school year, I worked as co-facilitator of an Indigenous youth group whose goal is to promote healthy relationships and end domestic abuse and sexual assault. As part of our work, we decided to spend a day talking about "traditional gender roles," using a curriculum that was created by a prominent national Indigenous organization in the United States. However, as the other facilitator and I looked it over, we became concerned. The material was full of references to hunter-gatherers, with women as childbearers and men as warriors. No specific peoples—including the Haudenosaunee, with which most of the youth identified—were mentioned. I asked my co-facilitator, who is a part of the same nation, "Aren't the Haudenosaunee historically an agricultural people with a very strong tradition of female leadership? Shouldn't we be teaching these kids about their own people, rather than this generalized 'Native' stuff?" She agreed, and we redesigned the material.

Experiences like these have led me to develop a critique, based in my own Two-Spirit identity, of oft-proposed "traditional gender roles" in Indigenous communities. My lived experiences as a Métis/Anishinaabe Two-Spirit person, combined with my readings of scholars in Native feminism and queer Indigenous studies, cause me to question the ways that heteropatriarchy is often present even when we attempt to decolonize our attitudes toward gender and sexuality.[1] Calls for a return to traditional gender roles are deeply intertwined with concern about Indigenous authenticity: What are the truest or purest forms of Indigenous gender roles? What kinds of gender roles were present before colonization? Likewise, such calls raise questions about the nature of tradition: What does it mean for something to be traditional? How are certain practices and ideas determined to be traditional? Is being traditional reason enough for us to follow certain paths? If not, how do we determine what is the best pathway into the future? Though the demand for authenticity is a powerful spectre for Indigenous peoples, decolonization means recognizing that change has always been a part of our traditions, and that we are in control of our own cultures. Two-Spirit people, as I will show, are doing some of the most fruitful work in this direction, and expanding on Hanson's assertion of the centrality of Two-Spirit people, I argue that no attempts to decolonize Indigenous gender are complete without taking Two-Spirit experiences into account.

The first part of this chapter deconstructs the ways that ideas about traditional gender roles often have strains of heteropatriarchy running through them. These strains of heteropatriarchy include restricting women's and Two-Spirit people's actions, conflating the diverse traditions of Indigenous people into generic "Indigenous" roles and flattening all pre-colonization history into a single imagined "traditional" period of time. In the second part of this chapter, I examine some of the critiques that Two-Spirit people have specifically expressed regarding gender in Indigenous communities, such as the lack of flexibility in roles for people who do not conform to the male/female binary, and the ways modern Two-Spirit people have been deemed less authentic than their ancestors, resulting in being excluded from community activities like ceremony. I conclude with a few examples of how Two-Spirit people are shaking up expectations surrounding traditional gender roles and in doing so, are helping to create futures for Indigenous people that are not mired in colonial heteropatriarchy.

Heteropatriarchy and "Traditional Gender Roles"

Indigenous feminists and other women of colour writers have amply dissected how modern gender is shaped by and used as a tool of colonization.[2] One of the goals of colonizing Indigenous peoples has always been to eliminate Indigenous understandings of gender, and in particular to subjugate Indigenous women and Two-Spirit people, whether through outright destruction or through assimilation. Nineteenth- and twentieth-century Indian boarding schools in the United States and residential schools in Canada were primary locations for indoctrinating Indigenous peoples into colonial roles.

From the moment they arrived, Native children were separated into groups of boys and girls and marched off to be forcibly outfitted with clothing and hair made to fit white standards.[3] Today the assimilative project continues through institutions like schools, foster care, welfare, and health care, as well as in the form of the ever-present white-dominated media that saturates our daily lives. The results of this project are visible in the legacy of misogyny, homophobia, transphobia, domestic violence, sexual assault, and other forms of abuse in Indigenous communities today.

In response to this assault on Indigenous peoples and ways of life, one approach to redressing gendered violence in Indigenous communities has been a call to return to "traditional gender roles." M. Annette Jaimes and Theresa Halsey cite Native women such as Laura Waterman Wittstock, Beverly Hungry Wolf, and Clara Sue Kidwell, who argue that "recovery of traditional forms [of gender roles] is more than ever called for."[4] Over the past several decades, as Indigenous peoples delved deeper into the history of gendered domination, many scholars and community laypeople alike began to revisit ideas of gender that predated colonization. Some of these ideas of gender were still known to Elders and still practised, while others were rediscovered through archival documents. Over time, certain tropes based in these rediscoveries have become near standard understandings in Pan-Indian circles.[5] Politically savvy Native politicians drop references to how they honour and respect "our" women, or to how their men are warriors in the fight for sovereignty. Even scholars such as Paula Gunn Allen have argued that all Indigenous peoples were originally matriarchal, which Elders from various communities I have spent time in dispute.[6] I have heard Anishinaabe people claim that our ancestors were matrilineal, for example, when Elders have repeatedly told me that we have always passed down our clans through the male line. These claims point to a climate in which Indigenous people consider it desirable to reclaim some kind of "traditional" gender roles, where "traditional" generally signifies "before European contact."

While it is admirable that people are concerned with addressing gendered colonization, we must take care to question where these tropes come from and what purposes they serve. Though many may claim that their people have always held women in high regard, Indigenous women themselves have pointed out repeatedly that misogyny and sexism are deep-rooted problems within Native communities. The logic of claiming "high regard" for women while ignoring the present reality of these problems can lead to silencing Native women. Diné scholar Jennifer Nez Denetdale writes about how Diné women have been kept out of leadership positions in tribal government on the basis that "traditional" women's roles, though "highly regarded," do not include such positions.[7] Images of male warriorhood in the American Indian Movement contributed to men keeping women off the frontlines and discounting the role they played behind the scenes in furthering the movement's achievements. The American Indian Movement and other parts of Indigenous activist movements in 1970s Canada and the United States were significant in helping to strengthen Pan-Indian identities; Scott Richard Lyons recalls that the actions of people in the Red Power movement helped even Indigenous people who were not directly involved develop a stronger sense of pride in being Indian.[8] Furthermore, some of the people active in the movements of the 1970s, like Chantal Fiola's relative Eddie Benton-Banai, went on to become respected spiritual and political leaders within their communities. As a result, the effects of the attitudes of American Indian Movement members have become widely dispersed throughout Indigenous North America, often closely interwoven with Pan-Indianism in general.

The real problem with many of the gender roles presented as traditional today, particularly in Pan-Indian circles, is that they reproduce colonial heteropatriarchy under a thin Indigenous veneer. Heteropatriarchy purports to establish a biological root of gender, claiming empirical differences between men and women that determine their aptitudes, inclinations, and abilities. At the same time, it places these qualities in a hierarchy in which men are superior to women and deserve control over women. The demands of heteropatriarchy regulate behaviour according to these gendered prescriptions. Among these prescriptions, sexuality is a very prominent concern, and heteropatriarchy mandates a particular heterosexuality (always within patriarchal frameworks, so that the man is in the leading, controlling position) that nobody is capable of living up to in practice. And while heteropatriarchy exists as an ideal enforced by individuals and infrastructures, its ideology simultaneously insists that it is a natural thing arising simply from "the way things are," and that those who do not fulfill its requirements are deviants.[9]

Heteropatriarchy is intimately tied up in the colonial project. The settler-colonial nation-state requires compliance with heteropatriarchy in order to continue its colonizing project. Settler men become leaders of the family and the nation who subdue the "wilderness" (and the Indigenous) through force, while settler women participate by colonizing through domestication of the newly conquered spaces. Settler children, the products of "proper" heterosexual relations, are icons of the nation-state's future, and often serve as symbols whose protection demands further colonization through calls to "protect our children's futures." Additionally, a key part of the colonization of Indigenous people through assimilation has involved forcing them to conform to heteropatriarchal ideology. For example, American officials, viewing agriculture as a male enterprise, attempted to force Native women to stop farming and to make Native men take on those roles instead. Similarly, boarding schools taught girls skills such as sewing, cooking, and housekeeping in an attempt to coerce them into white heteropatriarchal roles.[10]

Because of our history of colonization and assimilation, Indigenous people have also internalized heteropatriarchal ideas, and these ideas are sometimes even invoked for a purpose similar to the settler state's invocation: to protect and strengthen the (in this case, Indigenous) nation. Same-sex marriage bans in the Cherokee and Navajo nations were passed through appeals to tribal sovereignty, arguing that "homosexual activists" aimed to destabilize their nationhood.[11] In support of the ban, many invoked a "tradition" of heterosexuality. It may seem easy to point to this as a case of colonized mentalities, particularly due to the clear influence of Christianity in these settings. Joanne Barker writes that both the Cherokee and Navajo passed their bans "in the name of Christian patriotism," yet at the same time she cautions against asserting any sort of binary between assimilated Christians and unassimilated traditionals.[12]

In fact, heteropatriarchy can be found in even the most non-Christian Indigenous communities. At one Anishinaabe ceremonial event I attended, for example, the teachings given by both male and female Elders to young girls instructed them that their primary duty was to be demure, pure, and supportive of their male relatives. At the same time, boys were being instructed that they should be strong leaders. I have heard similar stories from other women and Two-Spirit ceremony participants; Emma LaRocque recalls one Elder who declared that "man is the law, and woman is to serve the man and to nurture the family."[13] Whether these are indeed identical to pre-contact teachings is not important. What matters is that these teachings today reinforce a status quo where women are subordinate to men. Although the etymology of "decolonization" may suggest an undoing of colonization, the goal of decolonization is not to recreate as perfectly as possible the ways of our ancestors. If certain forms of gender prescriptions are harmful toward women, no matter how ancient they may be, it is essential to deeply consider whether or not our Indigenous communities want to continue perpetuating those prescriptions.

Perhaps the clearest example of the way heteropatriarchy plays out in spiritual communities that consider themselves to be "traditional" (i.e., non-Christian) is the trope of Indigenous womanhood as motherhood. I have encountered the rhetoric of Native womanhood as motherhood in many groups that aim to decolonize spirituality and activism throughout the midwestern United States and western Canada. In the gender roles curriculum I described at the beginning of this chapter, for instance, the section on women's roles described women as being "multitaskers" due to their need to watch children while working, and as being "highly respected" for their ability to give birth. Meanwhile, the section on men's roles made no mention of children at all, thus equating womanhood and the domestic sphere. Emma LaRocque notes that even the extraordinarily nuanced book *A Recognition of Being* by Cree/Métis scholar Kim Anderson, which considers Indigenous women's gender roles extensively, tends to reinscribe childrearing as the ultimate designator of womanhood.[14]

In this trope, Indigenous womanhood is linked inextricably to the duty of motherhood, or of caring for the family and home more generally. Women's power is said to come almost exclusively from the power to give birth. Although this may seem less problematic because women's status is considered to be complementary but "equal" to men's, there are unavoidable difficulties with equating womanhood entirely with motherhood. Legal scholars Emily Snyder, Val Napoleon, and John Borrows write: "This motherhood rhetoric ultimately obscures, mischaracterizes, and too narrowly frames Indigenous women's options, choices, and contributions within their societies. This is particularly problematic when women's responsibilities and contributions as citizens are only framed in relation to nurturing and caring for the nation. While 'mothering the nation' is espoused as something to take pride in as a highly respected role, this discourse too often forecloses a multitude of other functions and roles that Indigenous women assume in their societies."[15]

Like colonial heteropatriarchy, the equation of womanhood with motherhood posits a biological link between women's bodies and their social roles, which ignores women who cannot give birth or do not wish to, as well as people who can give birth but do not identify with womanhood. As Snyder, Napoleon, and Borrows note, it can easily erase other roles that women currently have and historically had in Indigenous societies, such as their participation as traders, diplomats, leaders, healers, warriors, artists, and more. Likewise, teaching warriorhood and leadership as male traits contributes to the exclusion of Indigenous women from those positions, while also limiting the roles of men and boys to identities linked to violence and power.

By critiquing these tropes, I do not intend to demean women who find strength in motherhood or men who find meaning in warriorhood. In *Dancing on Our Turtle's Back*, for example, Leanne Simpson describes how her experience giving birth and becoming a mother helped her "to understand the deeper meanings of these theories" found in the Nishnaabe creation story.[16] At the same time, she also states that she is "not comfortable being confined to an essentialized version of Native womanhood defined by child birth [*sic*]."[17] My intention is to point out that when preached as universal values to the exclusion of other visions of womanhood and manhood, these roles reinforce heteropatriarchal ideology. I also do not mean to imply that these roles are not in fact "traditional" in the sense of being based in historical practices. Regardless of the fact that these may have been part of Indigenous gender roles in the past, however, today they are contiguous with heteropatriarchy to the extent that they may be complicit in its perpetuation.

It is also important that we interrogate the notion of "tradition" itself and question the idea that these gender prescriptions have been in place since time immemorial. First, the strange similarity of these tropes regarding gender across Indigenous communities in North America should be noted. There are over 500 Indigenous nations in the United States alone, and each has its own body of traditional teachings. Although Pan-Indianism has a crucial place in creating solidarity among Indigenous peoples, in this case it may be in danger of overwhelming individual traditions with heteropatriarchy-tinged, overgeneralized gender ideologies. Not in any sinister or intentional way, but simply because it is often easier, particularly for urban people who today make up half of the Indigenous population in the United States and Canada, to access these ideas than the teachings of their own people. Making a concerted effort to explore and excavate individual teachings of our own peoples may be one way to counteract the tendency to erase the diversity of Indigenous gender. When we perpetuate stereotyped, generalized roles as "traditional," we lose the opportunity to examine the individual teachings each Indigenous nation has about gender. If we do not intentionally seek out and explore these individual teachings from our Elders, eventually we will lose that knowledge, a knowledge rooted in tribally specific values and practices.

In addition, I often hear people in Indigenous communities speak of the "traditional" in unspecified terms that imply there is a singular, unified understanding of what "traditional" means. Perhaps influenced by the "ethnographic present tense" of the anthropological accounts that many people I know draw upon to assist in reclaiming traditional practices, "tradition" becomes eternal and atemporal. By refusing to acknowledge the impact of change over time, vague Pan-Indian gender prescriptions present a static idea of tradition that disavows Indigenous ability to transform ourselves and our cultures. To give only one example: among Anishinaabe people, ricing is now known as a "traditionally" male activity. In her book *My Grandfather's Knocking Sticks*, however, Brenda Child offers evidence that this is a relatively recent development, before which women were the primary participants and directors of ricing.[18] Even before European contact, Indigenous people engaged in creative innovation in areas ranging from technology to social structures. We can recognize the continuities that connect us to our ancestors' ways of doing things, but we cannot pretend that things have always been exactly the same. This does not make us any less "authentic" or less Indigenous. It simply reminds us that we are dynamic peoples who are actively enacting our own cultures.

Emma LaRocque poignantly sums up Indigenous people's responsibilities when it comes to assessing and enacting tradition in our communities:

> We are being asked to confront some of our own traditions at a time when there seems to be a great need for a recall of traditions to help us retain our identities as Aboriginal people. But there is no choice—as women we must be circumspect in our recall of tradition. We must ask ourselves whether and to what extent tradition is liberating to us as women. We must ask ourselves wherein lies (lie) our source(s) of empowerment. We know enough about human history that we cannot assume that all Aboriginal traditions universally respected and honoured women. (And is "respect" and "honour" all that we can ask for?).[19]

Looking to the history of gender and sexuality among Indigenous peoples, it is crucial to recognize the diversity in both ideal roles and in actual practice over a great span of time and space. I end this section with an appeal to other Indigenous people who are seeking justice for colonization and gendered violence. Just as we must not disavow change that has happened in the past, we must also take care not to reject change in the present simply because it is new. Our ancestors were not only passive objects of the changes caused by colonization, they were also active participants in creating and recreating their culture in ways that demonstrate both continuity and change. Contemporary Indigenous people can make strategic decisions about how we want to continue our traditions, and it is crucial that we decide to move forward with practices that do not replicate heteropatriarchal norms.

Two-Spirit Critiques

Because Two-Spirit people are particularly targeted by heteropatriarchy as deviants—of which Ramona Beltrán, Antonia Alvarez, and Miriam Puga provide poignant and devastating examples in Chapter 8—we are well placed to notice the ways that "traditional gender roles" have been made non-inclusive. Two-Spirit people are often especially harmed by appeals to tradition, as many Indigenous people have internalized the belief that only cis-gender heterosexuality is "traditional" and view LGBTQ Indigenous people as being overly colonized and even corrupted. Many Two-Spirit people are thus denied access to their communities and cultures. Even when they are able to access these things, too frequently the roles that Two-Spirit people could take in their communities have been forgotten. In the article "My Pronouns Are Kiy/Kin," Lindsay Nixon raises difficult questions that confront Two-Spirit people who wish to take part in ceremony:

> How then do I move through these spaces and honour creation in ways that connect to the Two Spirit life that surrounds me? How can I navigate moving between these defined spaces present at water ceremony—between keeping the fire and praying for the water? Would I be respected in both spaces if I tried to move in a fluid nature through and within them, like the fluidity I feel about the space my own embodied gender takes up within community? Could I occupy the women's space, for example, if I didn't wear a skirt? Could I keep the fire with the men if I did? Would I still be welcomed and accepted into ceremonial spaces that have previously filled my spirit in ways that I cannot describe, if I were honest about the ways that felt right for me to flow through those spaces like the very water we prayed over?[20]

These questions reveal the struggle that Two-Spirit people face in balancing their desire to participate in their communities and cultures and their desire to be true to themselves.

Since the 1970s, Two-Spirit people have begun to reclaim the stories of ancestors who were "like us." Researchers such as Will Roscoe, Walter L. Williams, Beatrice Medicine, and Sabine Lang have dug up archival records and oral histories that show that in some places and at some times, Two-Spirit people were accepted, highly regarded, and essential parts of their communities. Here too, however, tradition is sometimes weaponized against Two-Spirit people. Again and again I have heard Two-Spirit people, including myself, agonize over whether or not they are "traditional" enough to call themselves "Two-Spirit" or to call themselves by the word in their language used for a Two-Spirit person. "Two-Spirit" is often defined in terms of "traditional-ness," even by Two-Spirit people themselves. An article by Tony Enos published on 28 March 2017 in *Indian Country Today* stated that as opposed to being gay, which simply means being attracted to the same gender, "claiming the role of Two Spirit is to take up the spiritual responsibility that the role traditionally had. Walking the red road, being for the people and our children/youth, and being a guiding force in a good way with a good mind are just some of those responsibilities."[21] While these are all admirable things, requiring them of Two-Spirit people simply in order to claim the term itself forces Two-Spirit people to conform to unreasonable standards of tradition.

Another reason for this anxiety is the predominance of non-Indigenous (and certainly non-Two-Spirit) voices in defining Two-Spirit people historically. While pressure from living LGBTQ Indigenous people has convinced many writers to drop the outdated term "berdache" from their vocabulary, our ancestors continue to be described and analyzed primarily by non-Indigenous scholars. In most scholarly accounts, these authors make a strict division between historical "berdaches" (whether or not they use that word) and modern LGBTQ Indigenous people, through statements like "the last 'true' winkte who fully functioned in a traditional Two-Spirit gender role are said to have lived in the 1930s."[22] Even other Indigenous people reproduce the idea of there being a division between "true" Two-Spirits and modern Two-Spirits, with the implication being that modern Two-Spirits are not as authentic or traditional as our ancestors. This places the blame on Two-Spirit people for not continuing the traditional ways, rather than seeing the larger problem of the increasing colonization of Indigenous societies that no longer support Two-Spirit people.

Unfortunately, even attempts to empower Two-Spirit people can reinforce the idea that Two-Spirit people should be held to higher standards of "traditionalness" to be considered authentic. Historical studies have emphasized the "special roles" of Two-Spirit people, such as their roles as spiritual leaders, namegivers, medicine people, fortune tellers, and exceptional artisans. Native people, including Two-Spirit people themselves, repeat these roles as a way to boost the esteem of modern Two-Spirit people. Although these roles are important to know and recognize, they can sometimes obscure the fact that our Two-Spirit ancestors were also simply regular people who laughed, loved, worked, cried, and lived their lives, just as their non-Two-Spirit siblings did. Indigenous women and men today do not carry out all the same roles that they did 200 years ago, and though they may strive to reclaim some, we do not require them to do so before considering them men and women. Neither should Two-Spirit people be held to that impossible standard.

Despite these challenges, Two-Spirit people have often been successful in reclaiming and rebuilding traditions that are not steeped in heteropatriarchy. At the Great Lakes Gathering in the summer of 2016, a gathering for those concerned for the waters of the Great Lakes, the ceremonial breakout groups included a group for Two-Spirit-identified people. The tent was lined with flags printed with the message "Gender is fluid like nibi [water]." Lindsay Nixon expands on this: "Recently nîtisân Erin Marie Konsmo gifted me the first teaching I had ever received about the potentiality of genderless water. The fluidity of water taught wiya about the fluidity of wiya gender, of niya gender. While I would never devalue teachings and ceremony shared with me that associate feminine spirit to water, I also want to be honest about the ways that I experience my spiritual connection to water and other kin—human and otherwise."[23] Nixon's words reveal the possibility of Two-Spirit teachings that recognize the experiences of Two-Spirit people and connect them to their kin, as Nixon says, "human and otherwise." These teachings do not have to replace the teachings about men and women but can complement them and offer alternative ways of looking at gendered teachings.

In academia, Two-Spirit scholars are also doing fruitful work in creating new ways of looking at the place of queer Indigenous people in their communities. In a 2014 issue of the journal *Transgender Studies Quarterly*, transgender Stó:lõ/Tsimshian scholar Saylish Wesley describes a community-centred approach to creating space for Two-Spirit people within Indigenous nations. Wesley was unable to find evidence of precolonial roles of Two-Spirit people among her people, which meant she had to try a different method of developing her identity and community roles. She uses a methodology drawn from another Stó:lõ scholar, Jo-Ann Archibald's story-work, to recount how she was able to reconnect with her grandmother after struggling with their relationship due to Wesley's transition. After becoming her grandmother's apprentice in the art of basket weaving, they managed to reach an understanding that resulted in her grandmother coining a phrase in their language to refer to Wesley's identity and role. Since then, Wesley has even offered this phrase to other Two-Spirit Stó:lõ people as a possible name for their identity if they want it.

Relying as it does not on rigid conformity to imagined tradition but on existing relationships between Two-Spirit people and their kin, Wesley's account of the journey that she, her grandmother, and their community took together to reincorporate Two-Spirit people as valued members of their nation serves as a powerful model for other Indigenous people wishing to do the same.[24]

I want to end with a story from my own experience. I was at an Indigenous language camp when a group of women invited me to join their drum group to perform at the camp's ending ceremony, which I eagerly agreed to. In our last practice session together before the event, the eldest woman who was our leader informed us that we should all wear long skirts for the performance. Immediately I became anxious and unsure what to do as a Two-Spirit person. Finally, I got up the courage to go talk to the leading woman. I explained to her that I was Two-Spirit and that I did not feel comfortable wearing a skirt. She did not know what to do, having never encountered this issue, so together we called her Elder, a Cree woman in her nineties. After we explained the issue, she was quiet for a minute. When she spoke, she told us she did not know anything about Two-Spirit people. However, it had always been taught to her that wearing a skirt was about respecting oneself before the Creator. If a person felt that wearing a skirt would not be respecting them, would actually be disrespecting who they felt they are, then it was clear that they should do what would be respectful of their identity. With the Elder's blessing, I wore pants as we drummed and sang before the entire camp.

The attempt to (re)build healthy Indigenous gender roles is not merely an activity of academic interest. The youth I worked with as a group leader continuously brought up problems with gendered relationships in their community: men and women alike speaking of women badly and treating them poorly, queer and trans youth being excluded from cultural events, children raised with strict gender prescriptions that did not allow them to flourish. Influences of colonization, colonial trauma, and colonial heteropatriarchy have left indelible marks on the ways we relate to one another. The harmful effects of these forces are visible in the lives of our people from the earliest of ages. We must work against the hegemony of heteropatriarchal roles in our lives collectively and create ways of relating based in Indigenous ethics.

As we do so, it is utterly essential that Two-Spirit people be central actors in the efforts to reimagine and recreate gender roles in Indigenous communities. Indeed, in Chapter 8, Beltrán, Alvarez, and Puga outline their work creating culturally relevant curriculum for HIV prevention among Two-Spirit youth, noting the continued colonial erasure of and violence against these folks. Using

Indigenous feminist and queer theory, they demonstrate how we can improve health outcomes in Indigenous communities by providing decolonized and Indigenous-centred articulations of gender, sex, and sexuality that push past the gender binary and heteronormativity prevalent in health curricula and settler-colonial society. Here, I suggest that by putting Two-Spirit perspectives at the forefront, we may be better able to avoid the pitfalls of heteropatriarchy that harm not just Two-Spirit people but all Indigenous people. With gender and gendered relations so intimately tied up in the ability of Indigenous nations to survive and thrive, allowing Two-Spirit people to take the lead may open up new ways to think about sovereignty, self-determination, and nation as well.

Notes

1 Some of the readings that have been particularly influential in my thinking include Arvin, Tuck, and Morrill, "Decolonizing Feminism"; Driskill, "Doubleweaving Two-Spirit Critiques"; and the many contributors to Green, *Making Space for Native Feminism*, 1st ed.

2 For an overview of the Indigenous feminist project, see Arvin, Tuck, and Morrill, "Decolonizing Feminism," 9.

3 Hunt, "Embodying Self-Determination," 106.

4 Jaimes and Halsey, "American Indian Women," 334.

5 I use the term "Pan-Indian" throughout this chapter to refer to the communities, both physical and ideological, that diverse Indigenous peoples have created together based in a group identity as "Indian." While urban Indigenous communities often have developed Pan-Indian identities and practices due to the diversity of people in a small area, Pan-Indian ideas are also present within most tribal communities to some extent as a result of communication and interaction between them since the late 1800s and even before. While many Pan-Indian ideas and practices have their roots in the histories of specific Indigenous groups, things like powwows, the medicine wheel, and the concept of Turtle Island (to give a few examples) have become dispersed throughout Indigenous communities in North America to the extent that their roots have sometimes been forgotten.

6 Allen, *The Sacred Hoop*, 2.

7 Denetdale, "Chairmen, Presidents, and Princesses."

8 Lyons, *X-Marks*, xi.

9 Arvin, Tuck, and Morrill, "Decolonizing Feminism," 13.

10 Paxton, "Learning Gender," 174.

11 Barker, *Native Acts*, 189.

12 Barker, 190.

13 LaRocque, "Métis and Feminist," 55.

14 LaRocque, 63.

15 Snyder, Napoleon, and Borrows, "Gender and Violence," 611.

16 Simpson, *Dancing on Our Turtle's Back*, 41.
17 Simpson, 56.
18 Child, *My Grandfather's Knocking Sticks*.
19 LaRocque, "The Colonization of a Native Woman Scholar," 14.
20 Nixon, "My Pronouns Are Kiy/Kin."
21 Enos, "8 Things You Should Know About Two Spirit People."
22 Lang, "Various Kinds of People," 108.
23 Nixon, "My Pronouns Are Kiy/Kin."
24 Wesley, "Twin-Spirited Woman."

CHAPTER 6

Reading Chrystos for Feminisms That Honour Two-Spirit Erotics

AUBREY JEAN HANSON

In previous chapters, authors have identified Stó:lō cultural heritage sites (Madeline Knickerbocker), Homemakers' Clubs (Sarah Nickel), Sápmi (Astri Dankertsen), and the streets of Saskatoon (Tasha Hubbard et al.) as sites of Indigenous women's resistance and sovereignty. Here I introduce the erotic as a site of sovereignty. Lived erotics become contested sites, sites at which defiance, validation, and pleasure manifest through embodied practices. As such, the erotic is also an essential site of analysis and enactment for Indigenous feminisms. Two-Spirit perspectives, consequently, are crucial to feminisms that serve Indigenous peoples. Two-Spirit perspectives, further, demonstrate the need for nuanced, intersectional, decolonial feminisms. In seeking to advance Indigenous feminisms, it is necessary to dismantle the multiple and connected oppressive systems that threaten Indigenous self-determination in its diverse forms, and Two-Spirit erotics are a powerful catalyst for this work.

To examine these claims, I read the poem "Ya Don Wanna Eat Pussy" by the poet Chrystos, from her landmark 1988 collection *Not Vanishing*. Chrystos describes herself as a "First Nations Two-Spirited Lesbian" who was "born off-reservation, in San Francisco" to a "Menominee father and a euro-immigrant mother."[1] This particular poem from Chrystos's many works warrants close examination. The poem's speaker navigates a complex tangle of offences and solidarities in response to verbal violence—that is, to a series of oppressive comments. Reading this poem enables an interpretation of how sexism, homophobia, racism, and colonialism intertwine in the speaker's experience. To borrow the words of Janice Acoose (Saulteaux-Métis), this text is rife with "spaces for decolonization"[2]—sites at which colonial violence must be confronted and unsettled. As the acts of verbal violence in this text target gendered, queer, and racialized bodies, understanding them calls for robust decolonial feminist analyses. This short text—layered with silences both "sharp / & hot"[3]—therefore remains significant for understanding Indigenous feminisms: its continuing salience points to the persistent disconnects between some feminist discourses and the lived realities of Two-Spirit Indigenous people. In response to Chrystos's "Ya Don Wanna Eat Pussy," then, I ask how understanding Two-Spirit erotics as contested sites of sovereignty is necessary for Indigenous feminisms.

Intricate Positionalities and Two-Spirit People

In examining the erotic as a site of sovereignty, I am building upon important prior scholarship. Qwo-Li Driskill, Daniel Heath Justice, Deborah Miranda, and Lisa Tatonetti, for instance, describe "the notion of 'sovereign erotics'" as "an assertion of the decolonial potential of Native two-spirit/queer people healing from heteropatriarchal gender regimes."[4] The erotic, they suggest, is a powerful realm through which Indigenous people can disrupt and contest the mechanisms of oppressive, colonial systems that continue to govern gender and sexuality.[5] Likewise, Mark Rifkin examines erotics and sovereignty in order to contend that sexual self-determination undermines restrictive notions of Indigenous authenticity and opens up possibilities for Indigenous collective selfhood.[6] Such scholars also highlight the role of Indigenous literatures in disrupting colonial logics—acknowledging the potential inherent "in the act of telling our stories."[7] This insistence is one that I wish to emulate. In this chapter, then, I build upon prior scholarship that calls for attention to Two-Spirit perspectives in literary writing.

The reading that follows is meant to open up space for the sovereign, safe well-being of Two-Spirit people, and particularly—given continuing patterns of heteropatriarchal violence against certain bodies—women and people with non-binary gender identifications. The phrase "Two-Spirit people" used in my title requires some clarification: I need to take a moment to smooth the turbulence that occurs when intent descends into language. I use the term Two-Spirit because it invokes the possibility of understanding gender and sexuality through Indigenous frameworks—for instance by reclaiming and reviving traditional understandings—rather than through Eurocentric, colonially imposed frameworks. This term is meant "to be inclusive of Indigenous people who identify as GLBTQ or through nationally specific terms from Indigenous languages."[8] However, I echo the caution that "there is no single umbrella term that can be effectively used for non-heteronormative genders and sexualities within Native communities."[9] Likewise, my analysis works in service of queer Indigenous women and trans folks, particularly because of the perspectives in the poem I examine, but again, these are categories that are not coherent or comprehensive.

I recognize that the systems of heterosexism, patriarchy, and colonialism lead to violence—whether through academic-ontological restriction or brutal, back-alley attacks—against all bodies that do not align with the ideals of white, heteronormative masculinity. While I focus on Chrystos's writing in this chapter, I have been reading poetry by Qwo-Li Driskill, for instance, who articulates such beautiful and visceral reminders that "sexism is the root of homophobia,"[10] and that homophobia far too often manifests as devastating violence against those who dance in the spaces between posited gender binaries—particularly when such homophobia is compounded by racism. My arguments here, in short, are meant to be made in solidarity with all people who identify against gender-based, sexuality-based, racialized violence.

I turn to the poem "Ya Don Wanna Eat Pussy" by Chrystos because it offers a clear and troubling portrayal of the complex violence that occurs when "systems of oppression"[11] compound each other. In citing Sherene Razack's work here, I signal my wish to build upon her understanding of such systems as "interlocking" or as "mutually constitute[ing] each other."[12] This particular poem is productive for an analysis of such systems because it explicitly addresses oppression along the synchronous axes of gender, sexuality, and race/Indigeneity. The poem speaks to the potential complexity of Two-Spirit people's positionings while also opening up considerations of what it means to challenge violence aimed at multiple categories of difference.

Reading Chrystos in Context

"Ya Don Wanna Eat Pussy" is part of Chrystos's first published collection, which has already celebrated its thirtieth anniversary. *Not Vanishing*, as its title conveys, is itself an insistence. Before the poems, Chrystos sets out some of the urgent priorities that shape her work, providing context to challenge the "many myths & misconceptions about Native people" that might mislead readers.[13] She sets out this context by insisting, "I am not the 'Voice' of Native women . . . I am not a 'Spiritual Leader' . . . My purpose is to make it as clear

& inescapable as possible, what the actual material conditions of our lives are. . . . Don't admire what you perceive as our stoicism or spirituality—work for our lives to continue in our own Ways . . . we are not Vanishing Americans."[14]

This set of warnings anchors the writing that follows in Chrystos's particular experiences while gesturing firmly to the social and political realities that affect Indigenous people. This framing is important because it positions the collection of poems as a challenge to colonial violence. Chrystos here repudiates the colonial myth that Indigenous peoples are disappearing, as well as the dehumanizing practice of fetishizing or appropriating Indigenous voices, cultures, and beliefs. Her poems are acts of resistance and self-expression. Respecting Chrystos's writing as articulations of self-determination, I read her poem with insistence, for a few main reasons.

First, I insist that it is essential to continue listening to the voices of Indigenous women like Chrystos who have been embodying and engaging in the work of resistance for decades. This listening is integral to the work of multi-generational feminisms. I am listening to Cherríe Moraga, who in her preface to the fourth edition of the pivotal book *This Bridge Called My Back: Writings by Radical Women of Color* shares this perspective: "I was twenty-seven years old when Gloria Anzaldúa and I entered upon the project of *This Bridge Called My Back*. I am now sixty-two. As I age, I watch the divide between generations widen with time and technology. I watch how desperately we need political memory, so that we are not always imagining ourselves the ever-inventors of our revolution; so that we are humbled by the valiant efforts of our foremothers."[15] Returning to Chrystos, to me, means acknowledging her as a foremother and learning from her valiant efforts; it means recognizing that her writing has something important to teach me about how to struggle against colonial and gendered violence. Moraga writes,

> Still, here, in the underbelly of the "first" world, women of color writing is one liberation tool at our disposal. History is always in the making; while women of color and Indigenous peoples remain wordless in the official record. The very *act* of writing then, conjuring/coming to "see," what has yet to be recorded in history is to bring into consciousness what only the body knows to be true. The body—that site which houses the intuitive, the unspoken, the viscera of our being—this is the revolutionary promise of "theory in the flesh"; for it is both the *expression* of evolving political consciousness and the *creator* of consciousness, itself. Seldom recorded

> and hardly honored, our theory *incarnate* provides the most reliable roadmap to liberation.[16]

I see Chrystos's poetry as coming from this place of embodied experience and knowledge, and as providing an urgent portrayal of the systems of violence that need to be undone in order "for our lives to continue in our own Ways."[17] Her writing calls readers to acknowledge that erotic experiences matter, which is a significant understanding to carry forward.

Second, I wish to contribute to the continuing examination of Chrystos's writing in literary and cultural scholarship. Attention to her poetics, politics, and positioning extends from the 1980s up until the present day. In a recent essay, Cheryl Suzack argues that Chrystos's poems in *Not Vanishing* "are crafted deliberately to portray complex circumstances of racialized and sexualized confrontation that elicit various states of sensations, feelings, and expressive energies that the poet's dramatic persona struggles to articulate. These encounters often comprise public personal attacks, sexualized-discriminatory confrontations, and disillusioning public events that stage the failure of political community or the inability of the speaker to move beyond rage, humiliation, resignation, or shame."[18]

It is exactly one of these sexualized-discriminatory confrontations that the poem "Ya Don Wanna Eat Pussy" presents, and I would like to elaborate further upon how this particular poem works to portray a collision of racialized and sexualized verbal violence through the experiences and responses of its speaker.

Third, I insist upon reading Chrystos's poetry again, and continually, because of its personal resonance. I am a queer- and Indigenous-identified woman, a member of the Métis Nation of Alberta, and a dedicated social justice educator who revels in the strong voices of Indigenous, LGBTQ2, and other radical artists. I return repeatedly to Chrystos's writing for its powerful and provocative voice, emerging from her personal, positioned experiences. I had the honour of being part of an audience when Chrystos spoke at a Two-Spirit conference several years ago in Edmonton, and she shared a point that particularly resonated with me. She spoke about Two-Spirit gatherings where she felt she could bring her whole self, or perhaps where her whole self was welcome. This insight resonated with me because, I realized, I do often feel that I am splitting off a portion of who I am in order to participate in certain spaces, conversations, or struggles—for instance speaking as an Indigenous person or as a queer woman, but not both, let alone as a whole being. It is rare that I feel entirely welcome to present my whole self in the contexts I occupy. Part of this discomfort arises from personal interplays of positioning, privilege, resistance, and circumstance. Much of my research and teaching, for instance, focuses on bringing non-Indigenous educators to consider Indigenous perspectives, and I am still learning how to resist the pressure to focus on one urgent issue at a time—a pressure that erodes more nuanced, intersectional analyses in that work. Attending to Chrystos's poetry, then, is a personal act of insistence: while I do not equate my experiences or my positioning with hers, I identify with her writing and feel driven to examine and challenge the forms of violence she portrays. I want to learn from how she articulates and navigates attacks made against the interconnected aspects of who she is.

Taking Offence: Chrystos's Poem and Embodied Conflicts

The poem "Ya Don Wanna Eat Pussy" speaks vividly to the struggles that arise when the complexity of a person's positioning means being targeted from multiple angles. The speaker is a woman identified as Native and lesbian within the text (5, 14),[19] one of two women who are preparing food for a group of men who are there to help with a move. The poem portrays the impact of an offensive remark that occurs in this setting. When I read this poem, I envision the scenario it portrays, elaborating beyond the textual details. I imagine the "men helping to move" (36) as a mixed collection of friends or acquaintances, bonds formed along different lines of identification—Native men who are straight, gay men who are white. I imagine the "two Native women" (5) as a couple, the ones who are moving, somewhat beholden to the men who are helping. I read them as a couple for two reasons. First, the togetherness of the phrase "we're lesbians" (14) and the repeated use of the pronoun "we" throughout the poem (14, 15, 16, 20, 23) suggest to me that the second woman is the speaker's partner. Second, the domestic setting is taken for granted—for example, the poem elides any exposition as to whose house the events are set in or why these two women are there—which to me suggests an intimate familiarity between the women and the home. I imagine that they are either moving into or out of that space.

In my reading, I see how these two women are already in a state of owing something, a vulnerable-making state of needing help to move—one that would be stress-inducing if it involved bringing their disparate (male) friends or acquaintances together in a potentially volatile mix. They are already making the men sandwiches, paying back this debt that originates in circumstances they did not entirely choose: they cannot move everything themselves in the time they have; they need to rely on friends or acquaintances because moving is expensive and a lot of work. This beholden-ness is gendered, already, if there are only men helping, and "six" of them alongside the two women (7). I read all of these extrapolations into the poem as the few details provided refract through my own past experiences—of relying on others to move, of bringing eclectic mixes of people together and seeing discord result. In this kind of situation, I tend to feel bound to be nice, to smooth over any jagged edges that arise out of the conflicting perspectives of the people around me. Perhaps the keenness with which I experience such conflict is what draws me repeatedly to this poem.

The poem begins with "an Indian man's joke" (11): an offensive, sexualized remark—"Ya don wanna eat pussy after eatin hot peppers" (2). The "joke" is articulated at a site that is already permeated by multiple axes of difference—by gender, race, and sexuality—and layered with the complexities of Indigenous-settler relations. The people present in this scene include the (straight) "Chippewa" man who makes the remark, a "white gay man," and "two Native women" who are "lesbians," one of whom is the speaker (1–14). It is this mixture of social locations that shapes the speaker's experience and response. As she assumes, "that Chippewa" likely makes his comment in order to test or provoke the two women, targeting their sexuality: "he probably guessed we're lesbians"—he says it "to see what we'd do" (14–15). The speaker condemns the remark as "crude" (12), which it is, but it also projects her into a space of multiple silences. The comment targets the two women's bodies and sexual practices, drawing their intimacy out for examination. The man making the remark misreads the "white gay man" as a potential co-conspirator, or perhaps targets him, too, seeking to confront him with women's sexuality. The remark reinforces heterosexism, both by missing or invalidating the white man's gayness and by rendering suspect the two women's relationship. The remark, with its painful implications, also threatens the women's bodies. The effects of sexism and heterosexism are tangled up together at this point.

However, the speaker's response is not to resist sexism or homophobia; instead, she anticipates the potential threat of further violence stemming from racism or colonialism. She explains, "Ya don wanna take offense at an Indian man's joke / no matter how crude / in front of a white man" (11–13). I note how, in these lines, the specificity of the men's locations (e.g., Chippewa, gay, let alone their particular identities) is deemphasized, as "Indian man" and "white man" become the most relevant identity categories. I also note the parallelism in the language between the two "Ya don wanna . . ." phrases: this parallelism works together with the image of the "hot peppers" and the pain they cause to compare sexism/homophobia and racism, as is clarified at the end of the poem when the speaker describes her silence as "sharp / & hot" (2, 24–25). That is, she feels compelled, instead of countering the first remark, to defend Indigeneity against a possible subsequent attack from the white man in the room.

As a lesbian and a Native woman, the speaker is forced to split her response, a violent experience for her and one that defies a simplistic analysis that might consider gender or sexuality as isolated variables. She and the other woman say aloud that they are choosing to "ignore" the comment (9–10), but otherwise they "keep on doin what [they] had been doin" (16). This "keep[ing] on" can be read as a silencing, and/or as an act of endurance. I mean endurance in the sense invoked by Erin Wunker, who writes, "We are enduring the effects of rape culture. I am drawn to this language, for like endurance art or endurance sport, it makes room for the long-term work of living a life . . . Endurance also, I think, makes room for agency."[20] For Wunker, the language of endurance resists the victimization of women who experience sexual violence.[21]

I agree with Mark Rifkin that Chrystos's poetry "emphasizes the difficulty of enduring the everyday forms of elision through which indigeneity is seized by non-natives."[22] I find it generative to recognize the endurance of the two women in the poem rather than their silence alone. Chrystos's speaker does not articulate a further response to that remark. Rather, the poem continues to pull the reader into the speaker's awareness of how her own embodied experience might be targeted from multiple angles. The "white gay man," initially, just stops "talking about how much he loved / hot peppers" (17–18); the discomfort of the moment seems to be shared between him and the women, but the speaker is apprehensive about how he might react. While the occasion of the poem is an instance of sexist/homophobic oppression, the text immediately emphasizes the role of racism/colonialism in shaping the speaker's response.

In the instant surrounding the "hot peppers" (2) comment, the speaker is forced to feel fractured, or to feel divided loyalties, as defence along one set of axes (gender/sexuality) comes at the potential expense of defence along another (race/Indigeneity). The situation pits her against herself and her relations. Her assertion that she cannot "take offense . . . in front of a white man" suggests the heft of racism and colonialism as she weighs her options for responding. This assertion suggests that it is dangerous or unacceptable to create divisions between Indigenous people that would invite a reassertion of colonialism. The threat of such oppression is realized later in the poem, when the gay white man calls "that Chippewa a drunk" (22). In this last comment, the racist and colonial threat materializes, turning the verbal violence against "that Chippewa" by invoking the colonial narrative of alcoholism. The comment is a dehumanizing one. The gay white man challenges the man who makes the initial sexist/heterosexist remark, but his reaction brings its own violence, perpetuating racism and colonialism. His response makes a comparable impact: "we both stared at a different floor / in a different silence just as sharp / & hot" (23–25).[23] The poet has crafted a powerful parallel with this ending, comparing the two silences inflicted by the two offensive remarks. The painful experience suggested by the "hot peppers" (2) is also clearly conveyed by the phrase "just as sharp / & hot" (24–25). Again, this comment causes an embodied dilemma, a carnal discomfort, a vulnerability of lived positioning.

Across this brief poem, then, the speaker's embodied positioning as a queer Indigenous woman comes under attack from multiple angles. Any opposition to these inflicted forms of violence must take into account the fullness and complexity of that positioning, as gender, sexuality, and Indigeneity cannot be separated out. She is a whole person, not a bundle of discrete political struggles. What does this complexity mean for shaping feminisms that are responsive to Two-Spirit people's lives?

Expanding Possibilities for Two-Spirit Feminisms

Reading this poem in the spirit of "sovereign erotics,"[24] it is clear that the fullness of such experiences cannot be addressed by any discourse that isolates one aspect of identity, such as gender or sexuality. Such critiques have long shaped understandings of feminisms. As Verna St. Denis (Cree/Métis) explains, "many women of colour have felt excluded from a theory that elevated gender at the expense of race or class identity."[25] Drawing upon the decolonizing frameworks of Linda Tuhiwai Smith (Māori), I see how critiques levelled at the universalizing discourses of Western feminisms over the past decades have challenged "the West's view of itself as the centre of legitimate knowledge, the arbiter of what counts as knowledge and the source of 'civilized' knowledge."[26] Within the relationship between feminisms and Indigeneity, there is potential for both transformation and malignancy, since feminisms challenge the hegemony of Western patriarchal traditions but also threaten to reassert Western ways of understanding.[27] Western feminism has been critiqued for misrepresenting or neglecting Indigenous struggles for cultural revitalization, political self-determination, traditional territory, and resistance to genocide.[28] Shari Huhndorf (Yup'ik) and Cheryl Suzack (Anishinaabe) point out that feminist frameworks have not always been up to the task of representing Indigenous perspectives, since "for Indigenous women, the marginalization of their issues is compounded by the fact that a critical component of colonialism throughout the Americas involved the imposition of Western gender roles and patriarchal social structures."[29] Any feminism that envisions the self-determination of Indigenous people, then, must counter the multiple and simultaneous systems of oppression that undermine the fullness and complexity of Indigenous identities and experiences. This work involves recognizing how colonialism shapes such systems. While "intersectional feminism" has long articulated "the ways in which different oppressive conditions ... are interconnected,"[30] I recognize that understandings of complex Indigenous positionalities remain radical in some contexts, and warrant exploration here in response to Chrystos's poem.

Possibilities for self-determination among Indigenous peoples expand when resistance discourses take into account the intricate interconnections between heteropatriarchal and colonial oppressions. It is vital to attend to this insistence from Driskill: "Homophobia, heterosexism, misogyny, and gender binaries are central to the invasion and occupation of Indigenous lands and the marginalization, genocide, and oppression of Indigenous people. Resistance, then, must centralize gender and sexuality as a central site of radical social transformation."[31] In other words, the well-being of Two-Spirit Indigenous people destabilizes the logics of colonial systems. However, as a cautionary note, social transformation must push beyond the various forms of misrecognition and appropriation that have characterized some problematic interactions with Indigenous understandings of gender and sexuality.[32] That is, problems can occur when people appropriate Two-Spirit experience, or uncritically "seek the primordial bliss of the supposed acceptance or even revered status" of Two-Spirit people.[33] Rather, in acknowledging that contemporary forms of sexism and homophobia are colonial impositions that restrict the self-determination of Indigenous peoples,[34] it is crucial to identify, recognize, sustain, nurture, and learn from existing radical practices of erotic sovereignty.

Continuing in the multi-generational spirit in which I first turned to Chrystos—that is, "humbled by the valiant efforts of our foremothers"[35]—I see how, across her poetic work, Chrystos enacts essential and radical erotic practices. These practices resist the urge to see the erotic as a luxury—as "something which must be earned after, not during, a more primal struggle for physical survival"[36]—and instead see erotic poetics as central to threatening the "alienation" from self[37] and the oppressive discourses that constitute the "status quo" of the nation-state.[38] In so saying, I agree with Rifkin that Chrystos's erotic writing posits "lesbian pleasure as a mode of Indigenous inhabitance"[39] and enacts a way of "refusing settler logics of authenticity as the literal truth of Indigenous peoplehood."[40] The sovereignty or resistance enacted through her erotic poetics is symbolic,[41] but also corporeal—making "theory incarnate"[42] by embodying robust, full, and distinct personal experiences. Chrystos's poems express the erotic as a site of defiance—"I celebrate our outlaw lust"[43]—and as a site of endurance—"Nothing was happening in our bed / as I remembered rape & rape weeping in your arms"[44]—but they also, crucially, express the erotic simply as a site of erotic experience, of pleasure, relationship, and sensuality: "our breasts whisper cloudless blue . . . Your hands keeping me aloft / I fly for you."[45] In this way, her poetry shows how understanding Two-Spirit erotics as sovereign offers necessary insights for Indigenous feminisms. Chrystos's writing opens up space for the whole well-being of Two-Spirit people.

Conclusion: Sovereignties and Solidarities

Chrystos's poem "Ya Don Wanna Eat Pussy" is an indictment of the ways in which oppressions are both perpetuated and compounded at sites where they interlock, and is therefore a call for anti-oppression work that does not counter discursive violence with different discursive violence. Chrystos reflects in her 1993 collection that "Indian country is becoming less homophobic faster than lesbianism is coming to understand Native spirituality and culture."[46] Twenty years later, Scott Lauria Morgensen reflects similarly that "given the lack of commitment to Indigenous decolonization struggles in queer politics, clearly there is work to be done."[47] Recognizing that I am listening to Chrystos's poetry thirty years after it was written magnifies the urgency of the calls made in her writing. My recognition here also points to the importance of carrying understandings forward across generations. Reading Chrystos's poetry calls me to reimagine resistance, to demand relational understandings that honour Indigenous women and trans folks, to celebrate queer experiences, and to validate broader kinships. In dialogue with Chrystos's poem, I denounce the colonial dynamics that target queer intimacies, racialized bodies, and Indigenous self-determination. In defiance of such colonial violence I call for feminisms that honour the erotic as a site of sovereignty.

Notes

1 Chrystos, *Fire Power*, 129–33.
2 Acoose, "'A Vanishing Indian?,'" 52.
3 Chrystos, *Not Vanishing*, 36.
4 Driskill, Justice, et al., "Introduction: Writing in the Present," 3.
5 Driskill, Justice, et al., 3.
6 Rifkin, *The Erotics of Sovereignty*, 266.
7 Driskill, Justice, et al., "Introduction: Writing in the Present," 4.
8 Driskill, Finley, et al., introduction to *Queer Indigenous Studies*, 3.
9 Driskill, Justice, et al., "Introduction: Writing in the Present," 4.
10 Driskill, *Walking with Ghosts*, 85.
11 Razack, *Looking White People in the Eye*, 13.
12 Razack, 13; Razack, "When Place Becomes Race," in *Race, Space, and the Law*, 16.
13 Chrystos, *Not Vanishing*, n.p.
14 Chrystos, n.p.
15 Moraga, "Catching Fire," xix. Some of Chrystos's poetry was published in the first (1981) edition of *This Bridge Called My Back*.
16 Moraga, "Catching Fire," xxiii–xxiv. Italics in original.
17 Chrystos, *Not Vanishing*, n.p.
18 Suzack, "Transitional Justice, Termination Policies, and the Politics of Literary Affect in Chrystos' *Not Vanishing*," 9.
19 Chrystos, *Not Vanishing*, 36. From this point onward, references to this poem will appear as line numbers in parentheses.
20 Wunker, *Notes from a Feminist Killjoy*, 80.
21 Wunker, 80.
22 Rifkin, *Erotics*, 238.
23 I read the pronoun "we" in this passage as referring to the two Native women, as it does in lines 14 and 16, but acknowledge its ambiguity.
24 Driskill, Justice, et al., "Introduction: Writing in the Present," 3.
25 St. Denis, "Feminism Is for Everybody," 48.
26 Smith, *Decolonizing Methodologies*, 2nd ed., 66.
27 See, for instance, Dhruvarajan and Vickers, introduction to *Gender, Race, and Nation*, 11; Mohanty, "Cartographies of Struggle: Third World Women and the Politics of Feminism," 10; Mohanty, "Under Western Eyes," 56–57; Razack, *Looking White People in the Eye*, 13; and Smith, *Decolonizing Methodologies*, 2nd ed., 168–70.
28 See Monture, "Ka-Nin-Geh-Heh-Gah-E-Sa-Nonh-Yah-Gah," 266; Smith, *Decolonizing Methodologies*, 2nd ed., 155; and Sunseri, "Moving beyond the Feminism versus Nationalism Dichotomy," 144.
29 Huhndorf and Suzack, "Indigenous Feminism: Theorizing the Issues," 2.
30 Wunker, *Notes from a Feminist Killjoy*, 37–38.
31 Driskill, *Asegi Stories*, 10–11.
32 Midnight Sun, "Sex/Gender Systems in Native North America."
33 Jacobs, Thomas, and Lang, introduction to *Two-Spirit People*, 5.

34 See, for instance, Allen, *The Sacred Hoop*, 1; Anderson, *A Recognition of Being*, 62–78; LaRocque, "The Colonization of a Native Woman Scholar," 11–12; Midnight Sun, "Sex/Gender Systems in Native North America," 34; and Smith, *Decolonizing Methodologies*, 2nd ed., 151.

35 Moraga, "Catching Fire," xix.

36 Miranda, "Dildos, Hummingbirds, and Driving Her Crazy," 141.

37 Hall, "Writing Selves Home at the Crossroads," 116.

38 Miranda, "Dildos, Hummingbirds, and Driving Her Crazy," 146.

39 Rifkin, *The Erotics of Sovereignty*, 256.

40 Rifkin, 266.

41 Hall, "Writing Selves Home at the Crossroads," 109; Rifkin, *The Erotics of Sovereignty*, 263.

42 Moraga, "Catching Fire," xxiv.

43 Chrystos, *In Her I Am*, 81.

44 Chrystos, *Fire Power*, 39.

45 Chrystos, 51.

46 Chrystos, *In Her I Am*, 7.

47 Morgensen, *Spaces between Us*, 230.

CHAPTER 7

Naawenangweyaabeg Coming In: Intersections of Indigenous Sexuality and Spirituality

CHANTAL FIOLA

Remembering and Seeking Naawenangweyaabeg

Boozhoo nindinawemagunidoog. Zaagaate nindizhinikaaz, biizhew nidoodem, Red River Métis kwe ndaaw. Bezhig mide, Chigaasinipii nidoonjibaa. Greetings, my relatives: My spirit name refers to the sun's rays piercing through an overcast sky. I am Red River Métis, and first-degree Midewiwin.[1] My mother is from the Métis community of St. Laurent, Manitoba, and my father is from Ste. Geneviève, Manitoba—a French Catholic farming community. I am the adopted daughter of Mizhaakwanagiizhik, Grand Chief of the Minweyweywigaan Midewiwin lodge (Roseau River First Nation, Manitoba) and Noodinasimogaabowid, the late Violet Caibaiosai. In 2011, I was initiated into the Three Fires Midewiwin (at Bad River Indian Reservation, Wisconsin) under the guidance of Uncle Bawdwaywidun Binaise, Grand Chief Eddie Benton-Banai.

I identify as an Indigenous feminist and with the terms Two-Spirit, lesbian, gay, queer, and the Anishinaabe concept of naawenangweyaabe: a person who mends; or, from the centre, keeps others together and from wandering; a mediator.[2] Like Nancy Cooper, I wonder: "Where are the Elders who carry the teachings about our [naawenangweyaabeg] roles and responsibilities as important, integral members of our community?"[3] She encourages us "to go in search of our aunties' traplines, watching and learning about all of the ways to survive as Native women, as lesbians and as members of various communities."[4] Here, Cooper reminds me of the Niizhwaswi Ishkodekaan (Seven Fires

Prophecy) among the Anishinaabeg, which predicted European contact and a time when Indigenous people would almost lose our ways, but in the time of the seventh fire, Oshkibimaadiziig (New People) would emerge and retrace the steps of our ancestors to find what was left by the trail so that Indigenous ways would thrive again.[5] Many believe we are currently in the time of the seventh fire and that the work of the Oshkibimaadiziig is occurring;[6] elsewhere, I have discussed Métis participation in this work.[7]

I believe Two-Spirit people also play an important role among the Oshkibimaadiziig: it is our responsibility to search for naawenangweyaabeg traplines, decolonize ourselves, help keep our communities together, and prevent members from wandering off.[8] Like our older Two-Spirit relatives who persisted and helped clear a path for us during a time when colonial forces tried to suppress naawenangweyaabeg, it is important that younger Two-Spirit people take our place alongside our Two-Spirit Elders to ensure this path continues into the future.

This chapter reflects my efforts to pick up this work: to remember the sacredness of naawenangweyaabeg, make space for us, call us back into the sacred circles of our communities. With this in mind, I offered asemaa (tobacco) to four naawenangweyaabeg role models to share their thoughts and experiences regarding sexuality, the importance of Two-Spirit people in Creation, and our responsibilities and gifts; their stories form the foundation of this chapter. Moreover, I encourage other naawenangweyaabeg to participate in our intergenerational resurgence, and urge our heterosexual relatives and community members to decolonize their own homophobic beliefs so that we can hold each other up in pursuit of mino-bimaadiziwin (a good balanced life). Together, our work involves understanding Indigenous conceptions of gender and sexuality as inextricable from spirituality, and the impacts of colonization upon these. I believe our work is also inherently feminist: an Indigenous feminist lens can expose how "tradition" is sometimes used to oppress Indigenous women and naawenangweyaabeg. Two examples are the claims that homosexuality did not exist on Turtle Island before contact, and that Indigenous women's subordination is traditional. As I explain below, both claims are false and are a direct result of the legacy of colonization which took specific aim, in part, at stripping Indigenous women and Two-Spirit people of our sacredness. Today, "skirt shaming" and body sovereignty reflect another site of contention playing out on the bodies of Indigenous women and naawenangweyaabeg, as we will see in the experiences shared by the four Two-Spirit role models below.[9]

Colonial Suppression and Resurgence of Naawenangweyaabeg

In her discussion of erotics as a site of sovereignty in Chapter 6, Aubrey Jean Hanson insists on integrating Two-Spirit perspectives to disrupt colonial violence. This insistence relies on the recognition that gender and sexual diversity were common among Indigenous nations across Turtle Island: "at the point of contact, all Native American societies acknowledged three to five gender roles: female, male, Two Spirit female, Two Spirit male and transgendered."[10] Anthropological research details the widespread extent of such diversity.[11] Many Indigenous nations—whether they were technically patrilineal (clan passing through father to child) or matrilineal (clan passing through mother to child)—were nonetheless egalitarian and understood that all genders and sexualities had important roles to fulfill in keeping our communities balanced.[12] Beliefs about the ethic of non-interference were also widely held across Indigenous nations; for example, "Cree law means an individual does not have the right to interfere in the sacred path of another by using manipulation or coercion. One is not to interfere with the sacred covenant between the Creator and another being or there will be negative consequences."[13]

Indigenous nations that valued gender and sexual diversity posed a significant barrier to the imposition of the colonial project, which included Euro-Christian patriarchy, individualism, private property, and heterosexism;[14] as a result, Indigenous women's and naawenangweyaabeg sacredness were targeted for assimilation. Christian heteropatriarchy was forced upon Indigenous nations via treaty making, the Indian Act, residential schools, and the like.[15] Suppressing Indigenous ceremonies from 1884 to 1951 also devastated gender equity because women and Two-Spirit people played important roles therein.[16]

The colonial project tried eradicating Indigenous beliefs and values, including those regarding the diversity of human genders and sexualities, and replacing them with patriarchy (male domination), and dichotomies of sex, gender, and sexuality (male/female, masculine/feminine, heterosexual/homosexual—with the first of each pairing enjoying dominance).[17] Anthropologists studying Indigenous gender and sexuality ignored Indigenous terms and concepts, and berdache became the favoured term among non-Indigenous "experts." In Arabic, "bardaj or barah meant 'kept boy,' 'male prostitute,' 'catamite [a boy kept for homosexual practices]'"; the word was adapted by the French as "berdache" and referred to "transvestitism (cross-dressing), effeminacy, the carrying out of female tasks and activities, entering into homosexual relationships, and intersexuality,"[18] then applied indiscriminately, and with pejorative connotations, to Indigenous nations. Euro-Canadian government, religious, and medical authorities then took it upon themselves to stamp out such supposedly abhorrent behaviour.

Naawenangweyaabeg were pathologized and suppressed in this way for many generations, and European beliefs and values were internalized by many Indigenous people. For example, many Indigenous men have learned to debase Indigenous women and Two-Spirit people in keeping with the two false claims mentioned above; indeed, even the ethic of non-interference can be co-opted to oppress women and Two-Spirit people.[19] Two-Spirit people and considerations were absent from the Royal Commission on Aboriginal Peoples, the United Nations Declaration on the Rights of Indigenous People, and the Truth and Reconciliation Commission of Canada's 94 Calls to Action.[20] Hopefully, such erasure will lessen following Prime Minister Trudeau's implementation of a Special Advisor on LGBTQ2 issues (Randy Boissonnault) in 2016, the 2017 national apology to 2SLGBTQ[21] Canadians for state-sponsored discrimination based on sexuality, and the inclusion of Two-Spirit people in the National Inquiry into Missing and Murdered Indigenous Women, Girls, and Two-Spirit People (MMIWG2S).

The historic trend of overshadowing Indigenous Two-Spirit concerns in larger lesbian, gay, bisexual, transgender (LGBT) efforts may also be reversing. Egale Canada's "Just Society Report—Grossly Indecent: Confronting the Legacy of State Sponsored Discrimination Against Canada's LGBTQ2SI Communities" by Egale Canada Human Rights Trust offers one recent example.[22] Indigenous LGBTQ and Two-Spirit issues are being studied in their own right, including the impacts of migration, homelessness, and suicide prevention.[23]

Efforts to resist and counter this legacy of colonization have given rise to larger movements of decolonization, reconciliation, and a return to Indigenous sovereignty. I argue that these cannot be achieved as long as some of us (Indigenous women, Métis people, naawenangweyaabeg) remain excluded. I hope to contribute, for example, to the growing body of literature written by Indigenous 2SLGBTQ people, focusing on cultural understandings of sexuality, especially those grounded in spiritual perspectives.[24]

Contextualizing the Term Two-Spirit

The term Two-Spirit was adopted by self-identified queer Indigenous people who sought a term to refer to themselves. In 1990, there was a three-week-long demonstration at the Manitoba Legislative Building in Winnipeg, in solidarity with the Mohawk struggle over land in Oka, Quebec. A woman who was camped on the grounds fasted for fourteen days in a Dakota Sundance tipi; Myra Laramee was her spiritual caregiver there. One night, Myra had a powerful dream about "the two-spirit, and those ones that came and they were man, woman, man, woman, man, woman; their faces, you know that vignette on TV, when people's faces change, it was like that. Seven of them talked to me."[25] This did not mean that people have two spirits—despite the translation from the Anishinaabemowin niizh manidoowag[26]—but rather, the ability to "see things in two ways."[27] Myra shared her dream at the third International Indigenous LGBT gathering that year and it spread like wildfire, and the term is now used internationally: "Two-spirit identity may encompass all aspects of who we are, including our culture, sexuality, gender, spirituality, community, and relationship to the land."[28]

As with other Pan-Indigenous terms, Two-Spirit enables us to dialogue across differences of gender, sexuality, culture, and nation while engaging in our common struggles and celebrations. Terms such as Aboriginal, Indigenous, and Native fall short because they did not come from Spirit, a vision, or an Indigenous language. They are English names given to us by others that risk erasing our beautiful differences and homogenizing or universalizing our identities and realities. To ensure that "Two-Spirit" does not fall prey to the same pattern, we would do well to search out the words in our Indigenous languages that describe people like us—for example, naawenangweyaabeg in Anishinaabemowin. Other examples include:

- Anishinaabe/Ojibwe: Ininiwiijininiwangaa-nooji'aad (gemaa ikwe) (a man who is attracted to or pursues his fellow man), Ikwewiijikwemangaa-nooji'aad (a woman who is attracted to or pursues her fellow woman);[29] Agokwa (man-woman);[30]
- Nêhiyaw/Cree: Aayahkwew (neither man nor woman; man and woman);
- Dakota/Sioux: Winkte (desirous of being woman; would-be woman; hermaphrodite);
- Diné/Navajo: Nadle (being transformed)[31]; and,
- Inuit: Sipiniq (male child who turns into a female shortly before or at birth).[32]

Sometimes terms like these can be found in older anthropological texts; these must be read critically, with an Indigenous feminist lens, to expose Eurocentric, male, and homophobic bias. Such texts can nonetheless be an interesting avenue of research, and we must not "throw the baby out with the bathwater."

Of course, the legacy of colonization and accompanying loss of language, knowledge, and internalization of homophobia make this challenging.

One way of countering this legacy, and avoiding old anthropology texts, begins with seeking out our Elders and language speakers (approaching them with tobacco for those familiar with the protocol) and asking if they know of any terms in our languages that describe Two-Spirit people. Once we learn these terms, it becomes our responsibility to use them (for example, via self-identification) in our daily lives and bring them, and the medicine they carry, back into circulation. In so doing, we demonstrate that our resilience is stronger than colonization and that we actively participate in reclaiming our self-determination, which includes reclaiming our culturally-specific genders and sexualities.

Naawenangweyaabeg Traplines

The four naawenangweyaabeg role models I interviewed for this chapter accepted my asemaa and welcomed me to bear witness to the powerful work they are doing on their traplines to heal our communities; I have permission to share some of this with you. By way of introduction, Dr. Myra Laramee is Anishinaabe/Nêhiyaw (Cree) from Fisher River First Nation, Manitoba, and Albert McLeod is Nêhiyaw from Nisichawayasihk First Nation, Manitoba; they are Two-Spirit Elders and have been trailblazers in the international queer Indigenous movement, participating in the earliest International Two-Spirit Gatherings and helping co-found the Two-Spirited People of Manitoba Inc. Their work has included community, sexual, and mental health education; HIV/AIDS advocacy; and addictions and suicide prevention. Dr. Alex Wilson is Cree from Opaskwayak First Nation, Manitoba, a full professor and director of the Aboriginal Education Research Centre at the University of Saskatchewan, and is also a long-time participant in this movement; she has published extensively on Indigenous sexuality and sovereignty. Ron Indian-Mandamin is Anishinaabe from Shoal Lake First Nation, Ontario, a fluent Anishinaabemowin speaker, fourth-degree Mide, and chief of a Midewiwin lodge that includes naawenangweyaabeg ceremonies.

Sexuality and Self-Identification

I asked each interviewee how they self-identified in terms of sexuality. Albert explained that when he is in a workshop setting, he identifies as "a classic homosexual" attracted to men; and "in terms of the social or spiritual context, I identify as LGBTQ and sometimes two-spirit."[33] Since 1978, Albert has been comfortable using both male and female pronouns: "As my peers have aged, we now refer to each other as aunties and kookums [grandmas]." The grandchildren of a friend refer to Albert as Grandma Albert. Context is also important for Alex; she self-identifies as "two-spirit, lesbian, queer, LGBT, depending on the context and my mood."[34] Despite helping coin the term Two-Spirit, Myra does not often use it to self-identify, explaining that "those labels and titles and things, they are not my identity. My identity is being a strong-hearted woman. I know that Mide Manitou has accepted me from the day I was born."[35] Ron self-identifies as "gay" and dislikes the term Two-Spirit because "every human has a set of spirits . . . up to four guardians. . . . But I'll accept that term because it was shared by way of a dream."[36] Ron is demonstrating the ethic of non-interference and respecting people's personal connection with Spirit.

While discussing her own sexuality and self-identification, Alex shared that there exists another understanding of the origin of the term Two-Spirit. While acknowledging Myra's dream and its contemporary influence, Alex stated, "The term two-spirited originated in Alaska [regarding] bi-racial people; it was used in the psychological literature . . . in the 50s and 60s." She continued, "When we started using it, it really referred to sexuality and I see it changing now to refer more to gender. . . . I personally think it refers to sexuality and sexual orientation connected with land and all the other parts of our identity. Being Cree and being a lesbian, for me, is two-spirit." Alex worries that "Two-Spirit" is being used to entrench a heteropatriarchal world view: "[Two-Spirit] is being used as a third gender . . . so you could have male, female, and now this third group which . . . is homophobic." When two queer Indigenous women in a relationship are said to be "two-spirited, which means they're part male," their relationship is framed in "a heterosexual design" which delegitimizes relationships between female Indigenous lovers. She rejects the belief that historically, two female-identified Indigenous women in a relationship were not considered homosexual because one would have belonged to a third gender. Such relationships did exist, but so did relationships between two female-identified women. Alex insists that "if I exist today, chances are it [relationships between two female-identified women] would've existed two hundred years ago."

Regarding whether non-Indigenous people can self-identify as Two-Spirit, Myra replied, "That's not theirs," explaining that it is "a name that was given to us." Albert added, "Consider it a spirit name. Why would you take someone else's spirit name?" When a trans group in Switzerland asked if they could use the term Two-Spirit for their gathering, Albert said no: "This has history to it.... It came through a vision or a dream ... you don't need to appropriate it from us." Alex has never heard a non-Indigenous person self-identify as Two-Spirit. Initially, Ron didn't want non-Indigenous people co-opting the term but changed his mind after a fasting experience wherein he was reminded that all humans come "from the same life source."

Self-Discovery, Coming In, and Picking Up Our Work

Each of the Two-Spirit role models who accepted my tobacco to share their views on sexuality spoke about coming to know themselves, accepting their gift of being naawenangweyaabe, and committing to bettering the lives of Two-Spirit people. Culture and spirituality played an integral role in their journey of self-discovery and helped them leave the party lifestyle so often associated with "gay culture."

Growing up in Opaskwayak, Alex's development was influenced by a Cree world view and by the church and education system. She shared three defining experiences that taught her how race, gender, and sexual orientation are regulated. When she was around age seven, a friend invited her over but Alex was stopped at the front door by parents who said, "There's no Indians allowed in our house." Around age eleven, Alex was at a dance when a friend told her to "quit dancing like a boy." In high school, "the teacher said I couldn't wear boy skates because people would think I was a dyke." She learned early that "interconnection of these different parts of my identity was some kind of threat to people.... They felt [the need] to take it upon themselves to enforce some kind of law or rule." In her community, such regulation was juxtaposed with "room for me to be grounded in the ceremonial life.... Body sovereignty and the ethic of non-interference is a really central principle in Cree daily life [and] led to me being confident in knowing that I'm okay [with] who I am in my sexuality."

Ron was never closeted: "I was always just myself, my parents accepted that. Well, not my dad, not for a long time but he came [around] before he passed away and said 'never change.'" When Ron left the reserve for work, he noticed partying and promiscuity in gay culture and came to believe that "spirituality was what they need, because people already then were committing suicide even though they were out [of the closet] in the cities [but when they went] back home they were pushed down, teased, beaten, even killed."

Myra also spoke of choosing spiritual communities over partying. Similarly, Alex talked about leaving her reserve and finding racism, homophobia, partying, and suicide, which led her to explore how queer Indigenous people "maintain healthy or empowered identities given the context of ongoing colonial oppression." She explained "coming in" as a final step in "an empowered identity that integrates their sexuality, culture, gender and all other aspects of who they understand themselves to be."[37] She says, "Two-spirit identity is about circling back to where we belong, reclaiming, reinventing, and redefining our beginnings, our roots, our communities, our support systems, and our collective and individual selves."[38] The concept of coming in has also taken on a life of its own, with communities now holding coming in ceremonies.

The interviewees have committed themselves to bettering the lives of Two-Spirit people, and Elders Albert and Myra spoke extensively about their involvement in the international queer Indigenous movement. Recently, Albert helped put forward three requests to the Assembly of First Nations: to create a Two-Spirit council; to educate First Nations about Two-Spirit people; and to support the International Two-Spirit Gathering. "We come to you with our bowl full," he asserts. "We know our gifts, we know our strengths, we have a lot to contribute." Alex has produced an impressive body of published literature dedicated to these issues. Ron freely shares naawenangweyaabeg teachings and ceremonies. Myra was instrumental in having the chief of her Sundance community (David Blacksmith, Sprucewoods Sundance) accept Two-Spirit people in the lodge. At the 2016 Sundance, a ceremony welcomed Two-Spirit people to "their rightful place in the lodge;" they can choose which side (male or female) to dance on. These role models' efforts to heal our communities could fill books; they show us examples of how to decolonize our views on gender and sexuality, and how to reclaim our own culturally specific spiritual beliefs and practices that contribute to our collective efforts at self-determination and sovereignty.

Naawenangweyaabeg Teachings

The importance of seeing naawenangweyaabeg represented in aadisokanag (sacred stories), Creation stories, and ceremonies cannot be overstated. While my focus here is Anishinaabe and Nêhiyaw, such sacred knowledge about the existence of and respect for Two-Spirit people, exists in many (if not most) Indigenous nations.[39] Knowing there have been people like us since time immemorial—that we are a sacred part of Creation—heals the wounds of colonization. Naawenangweyaabeg teachings were targeted for eradication to impose a settler heteropatriarchal order. Colonization tried replacing the spiritualities of conquered nations with Western ones; the global spread of Judeo-Christianity and subordination of women is proof.[40] Yet our resilient ancestors retained some of our languages, ceremonies, and naawenangweyaabeg teachings. Ron, Alex, and Elders Myra and Albert each discussed the existence of Two-Spirit people in our sacred knowledge, and the place of Two-Spirit people in community and ceremony.

During our interview, Ron shared a one-hour naawenangweyaabeg teaching that is part of the Anishinaabe Creation Story.[41] It speaks of a time of early humanoids, when "Ninaniikwe, keeper of all human beings" birthed Nanaboozho. Nanaboozho's poor behaviour frustrated everyone; he was "approached in a dream by the queen of the underworld . . . mishi biizhew, gichi biizhew, the giant lynx, the water lynx," who warned that his descendants would act like him. When Nanaboozho's children (humans) began to treat each other poorly, Ninaniikwe sent an oshkabewis (helper) from anangokwan (sky realm) to earth to find those who could bring healing. Eventually, oshkabewis noticed some humans were different: "[They] were always pushed down, made fun of, teased; they were given the hardest of the work to do. They were entrusted to that hard work; they were waakaan, slaves. . . . They are correcting things as they go. They are making things better, watching children; they are doing things that this person should be doing, or that person [should be doing]." Oshkabewis called Ninaniikwe to earth and asked: "Why are they the way they are? They are mistreated yet they do the work that is being asked of them. And they pick it up, and do it without being asked, to make sure that it's done anyways." Ninaniikwe confirmed: "These people are the ones I am seeking. They are going to be the keepers that make sure everything is corrected. . . . They will hold [humans] together. . . . Nanangwewad, people from the centre, using a snare [hoop] to hold it together . . . [to] keep them together so they don't branch off, so they are not stranded anywhere, not walking aimlessly. That will be their job." They would carry out the role "of a mom or dad, they would replace a person that was missing, [or] had been killed in battle . . . [or while] hunting."

Humans started to mature, treat the different ones better, notice their worth: "You that don't have children, can you watch mine while I go out? You that's a better hunter than my husband, you who cooks better than my wife, can you cook [for me]?" Humans began to learn "everlasting love, unconditional love. Zaagidiwin . . . to love everything about everyone in the village. . . . They were being appreciated for the work that they did. . . . All these things gave [those ones] the ability to stand up and be proud of who they were." As society grew, those ones were entrusted to be "keepers of knowledge. . . . They were given dream; they were given insight. These were the first fasters, two-spirited people.... 'Gikendaasowin gichi mashkiiki, science of medicine, gikendaasowin manidookewin, science of spirituality, we give this to you. There will be a time where the world will become sick; we want you to be ready with this knowledge...'" Gizhi Manitokwe and Ninaanikwe entrusted these ones because of how "they thought and planned: it wasn't about themselves. It was about making sure everyone was taken care of... that everything was safely kept so that when that time [came] to move, they all moved together leaving nobody behind."

The general population (other early humans) was not keen on education and knowledge; they were not ready to remember yet. Those ones we now call Two-Spirit were ready: "Their minds evolved differently, they thought differently than the rest of the population, so they became knowledge keepers. They became entrusted to take care of our children... [and] knowledge of the plants, foods, medicines, shelter. They became experts at that." This teaching shared by Ron illustrates how naawenangweyaabeg played, and continue to play, an important role in Creation among the Anishinaabeg. Sacred knowledge of Two-Spirit roles in Creation can also be found in other Indigenous cultures.

For Alex, it took twenty years to piece together her understanding of Wiisagichahk, the trickster/creator figure in Cree cosmology. She explained that in Cree, gidachak is "your spirit" (and star) and in the middle of Wiisagichahk is saagii (or zagii) which means love. She elaborates: "It's built into the cosmology that this character is a representation of ongoing creation... and love is that continual energy of that creation. The fact that Wiisagichahk can shift genders, can be male, female, animal, plant, or all of the above, and highly sexual is, I think, an indication of queerness being continuity of energy that is ongoing creation." She pointed out that Wiisagichahk (like Nanabush/Nanaboozho among the Anishinaabeg) is "always turned into a male" in English.

Alex also discussed challenges in her journey to share what she was learning about sexuality in Cree cosmology. In 1992, Alex's proposal on queer Indigenous issues was accepted at the World Indigenous People's Conference on Education (WIPCE) in Australia, but the organizers "lost" her paperwork and kept her off the agenda. She decided to hold an informal session but "within an hour, we got word back that if the Australian and New Zealand delegates went to this meeting they would be asked to leave [the conference]." She left the building and ended up befriending Elder Jerry Brown (Flathead tribe, Montana). During the closing ceremony, Jerry accepted the

WIPCE bundle on behalf of the United States as the next host country. He addressed the thousands of people in the stadium with a story about how "in his nation, [people] can't exist without the character of the Wiinkte, which is somebody that brought them to this current world that we're in. And so, it was part of their cosmology in the same way that Wiisagichahk is part of our Cree cosmology."

Ron also spoke of colonial homophobia, including the false belief that only heterosexual people should carry ceremony. Spiritual roles were often entrusted specifically to naawenangweyaabeg as "keepers of the peace" who could share without needing payment. The benefit they received was "the beauty of love, the comfort of love . . . unconditional love without restraint, without fear." Myra also discussed the special roles in ceremony and community held by Two-Spirit people historically; roles based on skills and gifts (not gender) and called upon to benefit the community. Myra shared, "There were two women in my mother's community, in Fisher River, who were called when it was Jiibaay, when somebody was going home [dying]. . . . That was the gift that those two women took care of. And, in some communities . . . there was a special dish made for those people and they ate with that Jiibaay spirit so that everybody in the community would be safe." Alex echoed the view that Two-Spirit roles were based on skill and fulfilled community needs, and that this continues: "If you look at our community today, at all the people that are First Nations or Métis and queer, you'll see people that hunt, trap, people that are teachers, people that are hairdressers, people that are mechanics, people that are on welfare, people that are depressed, people that are happy." She gave a reminder to remember the diversity of Two-Spirit roles (not fixating on any one role); otherwise, she joked, people could say that today "all two-spirit lesbians are professors."

A Note on Skirt Shaming

Another issue that came up in my interviews with Myra, Albert, Alex, and Ron was skirt shaming—forcing female-bodied people to wear skirts in ceremony and making them leave if they do not. This issue is directly related to Indigenous conceptions of gender and sexuality, to the impacts of Christianity upon them, and to agency and self-determination. Some argue that Indigenous women wore skirts traditionally and ceremonially before the advent of Christianity, while others argue that shaming women into wearing skirts in ceremony is a contemporary phenomenon influenced by heteropatriarchal Christianity. The following illustrates the tension and complexity of this debate.

In June 2015, the University of Winnipeg held a pipe ceremony and talking circle to discuss the new mandatory Indigenous course requirement. The ceremony was conducted by Elders Myra Laramee and Dan Thomas. In Myra's words, "My nephew said, 'Elder Myra Laramee invites you to respect the protocol [of women wearing a skirt in ceremony].'" In response, a non-Indigenous, feminist professor submitted a piece to a local newspaper calling the "dress code sexist."[42] A well-known Indigenous man published a piece agreeing that it was sexual discrimination.[43] Many have pointed out that it is not the place of non-Indigenous women or Indigenous men to comment on skirt shaming.[44]

In Myra's view, that non-Indigenous professor "doesn't understand that Indigenous feminism is different than Eurocentric feminism." Myra shared a teaching about the first skirt that was given to Anishinaabeg: the one that wraps around the tipi and was originally made from hide. She spoke of the tipi as a representation of women, linking the doorway to the fire with the doorway where children are born: "That's why we wear skirts, because that was our first dress. And we were responsible for that fire." Myra and Albert emphasized honouring women in childbearing years. Myra explained that historically, once a woman was past her menstruating years, there was a ceremony where "you were adopted into that open world of being able to do ceremonies anytime.... You didn't have the sanctity of that moontime." She also spoke about Two-Spirit people with male bodies being welcome to wear women's clothing and dance on the women's side of the Sundance lodge, and being adopted by the women as such (and vice versa). Myra has also made a skirt for a straight Indigenous male who wanted to wear one while firekeeping women's ceremonies; when that man went home to the Spirit World, his skirt went with him. Myra did not say that women should be banned from ceremony for not wearing a skirt.

For Alex, no matter the traditional teachings, "it's the impact of imposing those teachings on another person that most concerns." She believes skirt shaming arose because women who refuse to wear skirts in ceremony are "upsetting hetero-patriarchy."[45] She again brought up the ethic of non-interference, not "interfer[ing] with somebody else's body sovereignty." In her words, "Indigenous feminism, from a Cree world view, aligns very well [with body sovereignty] because there's an understanding that there's a place for everybody within the circle.... That's what feminism and Indigenous feminism are doing; understanding so that we can address ... power dynamics and power structures." Adding to this, Ron said there are "pictures in the early 1800s [of] our own women completely covered, hiding themselves" in the hope of escaping the rise in violent alcohol-related abuse. He reminds us of how the changing social context impacts regulation of women's clothing and bodies.

It is easy to find pro–body sovereignty/anti–skirt shaming perspectives on the internet; it requires more effort to find individuals with "skirt teachings"—such as those carried by Myra—and offer them asemaa for understanding. How can we know which teachings have been influenced by heteropatriarchal Christianity? What are the consequences of welcoming women (and Two-Spirit people) to wear skirts in ceremony but not turning them away if they choose not to? How can we simultaneously respect teachings and protocol, body sovereignty and gender self-determination, and the ethic of non-interference? The so-called skirt shaming debate is gaining traction, and questions like these are being raised as more and more Indigenous people return to ceremony,[46] especially self-identified Indigenous feminists and Two-Spirit folks who do not identify with the gender binary of male or female.

Creating Hope amid Challenge

Myra, Albert, Ron, and Alex also shared advice for Two-Spirit people who may be struggling. Albert reminded us that when we "articulate [our] needs or intentions, like through prayer or ceremony, they begin that momentum. Now, the skill is to recognize when you receive what you've asked for. Because you need to recognize that you've received, appreciate what that means, and then share that with the community." Putting this into practice, Alex explained, "It's important for them to see people that are out and so I always talk about being Two-Spirited, or being lesbian, or being queer. I think it is important to find people that they can be completely safe with and that's up to us to do. . . . So many are isolated and if they feel uncomfortable in a situation, ceremonial or [in a] classroom they have the right to leave."

Ron had this to offer: "Never give up, find your purpose in life. Sometimes you may find it in a church, in a lodge, but ultimately, it's with nature you'll find yourself. . . . Know that God created you . . . for a divine purpose." He included Two-Spirit people in the work of the Oshkibimaadiziig of the seventh fire: "The old people say that the new people are going to pick up the pieces and they're going to put them together; they're going to safekeep that knowledge and they're going to carry it with them. I believe that's our role [as naawenangweyaabeg]." Myra agreed: "We are the New People, and it is time to pick up what was left by the trail." Ron also shared that when humans begin to lose their way, Ninaanikwe "will always send somebody to someone who is willing to listen. . . . Spirit has summoned you to be there, to do that work."

While we can take comfort in knowing that Spirit is guiding us, ultimately, we must choose to pick up this work. I encourage Two-Spirit people (especially in positions of authority) to honour our gift, come out (or come in, to use Alex's concept), live openly; in Myra's mother's words, "Don't be afraid to love." Be the role model you wish you had. Find naawenangweyaabeg teachings in your communities.

Hanson insists that Indigenous sovereignty depends on the well-being of Two-Spirit peoples, and I would add that we must not be afraid to ask the leaders in our communities what they are doing to promote Two-Spirit empowerment; the same goes for leadership in our ceremonies and spiritual lodges—we can approach them respectfully (again with asemaa [tobacco] when appropriate) and ask questions. Is this lodge and leadership accepting of Two-Spirit and LGBTQ people? Are there any Two-Spirit people in leadership positions here? Can you point me toward specific knowledge holders who carry Two-Spirit teachings? If seating in the ceremony/lodge is divided by male and female gender, where are Two-Spirit people welcome to sit?[47] If clothing or regalia is divided by gender, what are Two-Spirit people welcome to wear? Are there certain roles and duties in the ceremony/lodge that Two-Spirit people are specifically encouraged to undertake given our gifts? If a teaching is given that seems to focus solely on heterosexual males and females, consider approaching the knowledge holder (when it is respectful to do so, and with asemaa) and ask where Two-Spirit people exist within that teaching. Offer suggestions to leadership about how to use your gifts to strengthen the spiritual community.

At this point, I would like to offer a cautionary note: not all leaders and knowledge holders will be open to your questions. Indeed, some may feel threatened or afraid and attempt to silence or shame you. We must remember that our leaders, knowledge holders, and Elders have also been impacted by colonization and have sometimes internalized patriarchal, sexist, and homophobic or transphobic beliefs that did not previously exist in our cultures. Consider your own personal safety when approaching people and asking questions or offering to help in ways that promote Two-Spirit empowerment—perhaps bring a friend with you, or communicate your concerns and questions to a trusted confidant of the knowledge holder who can create a safe space for you to approach this person. You may come across those who say that it is wrong, or not traditional, to question leadership or ceremony conductors. Where do such beliefs come from and whom do they protect? Does this marginalize and silence certain people or groups? Of course, it would be rude to interrupt a teaching while the lodge is in session, but once the "doors are open," you can approach the helpers and leaders with humility and respect (as opposed to confrontationally or aggressively) and ask your question. If you are silenced or shamed, you don't have to keep attending that ceremony or lodge. Don't give up; you will find another ceremony conductor or lodge where you are welcomed and feel comfortable. For example, in the lodges I belong to (Three Fires Midewiwin, Minweyweywigaan Midewiwin, Shoal Lake Midewiwin, Spruce Woods Sundance Lodge), questions are encouraged. In fact, among the Midewiwin, we are reminded that our great uncle Nanaboozho (the figure in the Creation Story Ron shared above) questioned everything and everyone; we are encouraged to do the same![48]

This Helps Us Learn Our Place in Creation

Alex, Ron, Myra, and Albert are Two-Spirit role models because they were not afraid to question the status quo, even when it made others feel uncomfortable, even when they themselves risked being shunned, and Spirit led them to those teachings and people who understand and value naawenangweyaabeg (Two-Spirit people) in Creation. I recognize them as among the Oshkibimaadiziig (New People) spoken of in the Niizhwaswi Ishkodekaan (Seven Fires Prophecy). I invite other Two-Spirit people, especially those from younger generations, to carry on the important work of our naawenangweyaabeg ancestors and contemporary Two-Spirit Elders. Once you find some of the teachings, because you will, share them so that we can carry out our important spiritual work of keeping our communities together and ensuring nobody is left behind to wander aimlessly. Then let us watch our self-love grow, and the suicide rate fall. There are others like us who are coming—let us clear a wider path for them so they can enjoy mino-bimaadiziwin (good, balanced life). Our collective efforts toward mino-bimaadiziwin will be heightened if we work together: naawenangweyaabeg, Indigenous feminists, straight Indigenous allies (especially those in positions of authority, leadership, Elders, ceremony conductors), and non-Indigenous LGBTQ, straight, feminist and non-feminist allies. The healing of our communities will benefit from everyone's efforts; indeed, everyone will benefit from the healing of our communities, including our spiritual communities.

Gitchi-miigwetch—thank you very much.

Notes

1 Midewiwin refers to the ancestral spiritual way of life among the Anishinaabeg and other Indigenous peoples.

2 Ron (Indian-Mandamin), personal communication with author, 11 October 2016.

3 Cooper, "Learning to Skin the Beaver," 42.

4 Cooper.

5 Benton-Banai, *The Mishomis Book.*

6 Simpson, *Lighting the Eighth Fire*; Benton-Banai, *The Mishomis Book.*

7 Fiola, *Rekindling the Sacred Fire.*

8 The suicide rate among First Nations people is double the national average in Canada (National Aboriginal Health Organization [NAHO], "Suicide Prevention and Two-Spirited People") and ten times higher among Two-Spirit youth (Wilson, "Two-Spirit People, Body Sovereignty, and Gender Self-Determination").

9 Wilson, "Two-Spirit People, Body Sovereignty, and Gender Self-Determination."

10 Brayboy, "Two-Spirits, One Heart, Five Genders."

11 Lang, *Men as Women, Women as Men*; Roscoe, *Changing Ones*; Thomas, "Navajo Cultural Constructions of Gender and Sexuality."

12 Suzack et al., *Indigenous Women and Feminism.*

13 Anderson, *Life Stages and Native Women*, 68.

14 Morgensen, "Cutting to the Roots of Colonial Masculinity."

15 Fiola, *Rekindling the Sacred Fire*; Lawrence, *'Real' Indians and Others*; Anderson, *A Recognition of Being.*

16 Pettipas, *Severing the Ties That Bind.*

17 Morgensen, "Cutting to the Roots of Colonial Masculinity."

18 Angelino and Shedd, quoted in Lang, *Men as Women, Women as Men*, 6–7.

19 McGuire, "Wisaakodewikwe Anishinaabekwe Diabaajimotaw Nipigon Zaaga'igan," 219.

20 Royal Commission on Aboriginal Peoples, Final Report; United Nations General Assembly, Declaration on the Rights of Indigenous Peoples (UNDRIP); Truth and Reconciliation Commission of Canada (TRC), *Calls to Action.*

21 Two-spirit folks have been encouraging others to begin the LGBTQ acronym with "2S" (instead of placing it at the end) out of respect for the fact that Indigenous people were on these lands first, and to avoid the familiar (and unhelpful) "add Indigenous and stir" tactic; it is an act of reconciliation and decolonization.

22 Egale Canada, "Just Society Report—Grossly Indecent."

23 Ristock, "Aboriginal Two-Spirit and LGBTQ Migration, Mobility, and Health Research Project"; Passante, "Aboriginal Two-Spirit and LGBTQ Mobility"; National Aboriginal Health Organization (NAHO), "Suicide Prevention and Two-Spirited People."

24 Little Thunder, *One Bead at a Time*; Chacaby, *A Two-Spirit Journey*; Wilson, "N'tacimowin inna nah': Our Coming In Stories; Wilson, "Two-Spirit People, Body Sovereignty, and Gender Self-Determination."

25 Myra Laramee, personal communication with the author, 12 October 2016.

26 Vowel, "Language, Culture, and Two-Spirit Identity."

27 Myra Laramee, personal communication with the author, 12 October 2016.

28 Wilson, "N'tacimowin inna nah': Our Coming In Stories," 193.

29 NAHO, "Suicide Prevention and Two-Spirited People," 3.

30 Lang, *Men as Women, Women as Men*, 249.

31 With the exception of the first and last bullets, this information can be found in an extensive list of terms in Indigenous languages differentiated by nation compiled by Dr. Sabine Lang (1998) in *Men as Women, Women as Men*, 248–51.

32 Ekho and Ottokie, *Childrearing Practices*, 135.

33 Albert McLeod, personal communication with the author, 12 October 2016.

34 Alex Wilson, personal communication with the author, 14 October 2016.

35 Myra Laramee, personal communication with the author, 12 October 2016.

36 Ron Indian-Mandamin, personal communication with the author, 11 October 2016.

37 Wilson, "N'tacimowin inna nah': Our Coming In Stories," 197.

38 Wilson, 198.

39 Brayboy, "Two-Spirits, One Heart, Five Genders"; NAHO, "Suicide Prevention and Two-Spirited People"; Vowel, "Language, Culture, and Two-Spirit Identity"; Lang, *Men as Women, Women as Men*; Roscoe, *Changing Ones*; Jacobs, Thomas, and Lang, *Two-Spirit People*.

40 Eisler, *The Chalice and the Blade*; Stone, *When God Was a Woman*.

41 We followed protocol: *asemaa*, feasting, a spirit dish for *nookomis mitigwaa'akik* (grandmother waterdrum), smudging, smoking the pipe, and songs. Miigwetch to everyone for contributing a dish, including Amanda Smart. Miigwetch to Jason Bone for recording and transcribing the teaching, and to Sylvie Wiens and Sita Hajzler for transcribing.

42 Boucher, "Dress-Code Message at U of W Sexist."

43 Taylor, "The Shame of Skirt Shaming."

44 Hopkins, "On Skirt Shaming—Another Perspective"; Lee, "'Skirting the Issue'"; Paul, "Pipe Ceremony Dress Code 'Uncalled For.'"

45 Wilson, "Two-Spirit People, Body Sovereignty, and Gender Self-Determination."

46 Fiola, *Rekindling the Sacred Fire*.

47 At a later stage in writing this chapter, I became aware of a Sundance Lodge (Nookomis) where Two-Spirit people dance in the centre, at the point where the male and female dancers connect (rather than having to sit on the "male side" or "female side"). Changes such as these are very encouraging.

48 Gitchi-miigwetch to Ron Indian-Mandamin, Chief of the Midewiwin Lodge in Shoal Lake, Ontario, for reminding me of this.

CHAPTER 8

Morning Star, Sun, and Moon Share the Sky: (Re)membering Two-Spirit Identity through Culture-Centred HIV Prevention Curriculum for Indigenous Youth

RAMONA BELTRÁN, ANTONIA R.G. ALVAREZ, AND MIRIAM M. PUGA

We Begin with Ceremony: A Collaborative Poetic Narrative

Thirteen days before our ceremony, blood moon filled the sky. We don't need to say that this is significant, but it is.

> All around the fire, our beautiful beloved Two-Spirit relatives prayed with love in their hearts for the lives of our children. And then it happened. Maybe it was well intentioned or even coming from a place of care. It hurt, nonetheless.
>
> "Same-sex relationships are against our natural laws."
>
> Medicine flew through the air in slow motion and danced on hot coals.
>
> My comadre and I exited the teocalli (ceremonial house) to help prepare the morning foods.
>
> "Lo siento, hermana." (I'm sorry, sister.)
>
> The cold autumn air chilled my tears. I was shaking.
>
> "No llores, estoy acostumbrada." (Don't cry, I'm used to it.)

As we lined up the sacred foods, we looked up into the sky. There we saw the bright morning star, and the sun and moon as they were passing each other to transition into dawn. It's rare in our modern lives to see these moments of slow and peaceful transition. They were so still and bright, the three of them together. Just in the distance, we heard early morning traffic and saw power lines, flickering streetlights, and man-made water canals.

I thought to myself, "If all of this can co-exist, how is it that we struggle with the complexity of gender, love, and creation in our communities?"

"This can be a really holy moment if we time it just right."

(Re)Membering Two-Spirit[1]

As demonstrated in the poetic narrative above and by Chantal Fiola in Chapter 7, the remnants of colonial heteropatriarchy and resulting homophobia and transphobia are experienced in even our most sacred ceremonial spaces and are sometimes imposed by our sacred people. In one moment, a string of misguided words can shift the transcendent healing properties of a ceremony into properties of harm. Heteronormative policing of gender and sexuality within Indigenous communities recreates settler-colonial oppression strategies and serves to further marginalize members of our community who do not fall into limited Western constructions of gender and sexuality. Although complex gender identities existed and were honoured in many Indigenous communities prior to colonization, many lesbian, gay, bisexual, transgender, queer, and Two-Spirit (LGBTQ2S)[2] people today are targeted by acts of violence related to homophobia and transphobia from both outside and within their own cultural communities.[3] The term Two-Spirit was adapted from the Algonquin concept niizh manidoowag (two spirits), which refers to cultural, gender, and spiritual roles rather than sexual orientation or behaviours.[4] As a Pan-Indigenous term, Two-Spirit signifies diverse experiences of gender identity and sexual orientation and acts as a contemporary Indigenous concept for an old idea—that both feminine and masculine expressions can be complexly embodied.[5] While many Indigenous groups favour tribally specific terms, Two-Spirit is generally understood as a decolonizing term that allows Indigenous LGBTQ people to reject the limited colonial binary of Western/Christian definitions of gender and sexuality.[6] The prolific and profound effects of colonization through

Christianity condemned traditional ceremonial roles of Two-Spirit people, relegating them to the furthest margins of society.[7]

Additionally, legacies of the sexual abuse that occurred in boarding schools have created a culture of silence around sex and sexuality in many Indigenous communities.[8] This has led to shame, discipline, and stigma related to gender, sex, and sexuality among Indigenous communities and has far-reaching impacts today, including an increase in HIV health-risk behaviours and outcomes in Two-Spirit communities.[9]

Indigenous feminism provides critical responses not only to colonial heteropatriarchy[10] and its resulting racism and sexism but also to the ways that internalized colonial heteropatriarchy further marginalizes notions of gender and gendered bodies in Indigenous communities.[11] Disruptions to matriarchal tribal societies and complex understandings of gender roles, adoption of Christian/Western values, demonizing non-heterosexual and gender non-conforming individuals, and cultures of silence related to sex and sexuality are all part of settler-colonialist efforts to control and maintain dominance over Indigenous peoples. Some Native scholars have called for challenges to heteronormativity as a decolonizing imperative and for inclusion of queer theory principles into liberatory Indigenous theoretical frameworks as a way to create more open, queer-inclusive, and sex-positive discussions of gender, sex, and sexuality within a decolonizing Indigenous cultural context.[12]

Discussing the connections between gender, sexuality, and colonization exposes "heteronormative discourses of colonial violence directed at Native communities."[13] Rather than arguing for an uncritical return to "tradition," this queer and decolonizing lens challenges the oppressive discourses that are occurring in some Indigenous communities today.[14] Even the heterosexualization of the land that recurs in colonial contexts, including conceptualizations of the land as penetrable sites of conquest and/or possessions, must be explicated and challenged.[15] Further, it is our assertion that making the discussions energetic, lively, and humorous helps to bring "sexy back" into discussions about liberation and health.[16]

In this chapter, we focus on identity experiences of Two-Spirit and/or LGBTQ-identified Indigenous youth[17] who participated in a culture-centred HIV prevention program. The Indigenous Youth RiseUp! (IYR) curriculum was developed and implemented using an Indigenous feminist framework integrating queer theory principles, with attention to concrete decolonization practices in sexual health knowledge. We begin by describing the increased HIV risks associated with historical trauma, substance use, and violence to illustrate the need for culture-centred, sex- and body-positive HIV prevention curricula for Two-Spirit Indigenous youth. We then describe the IYR curriculum and present a qualitative exploration of Two-Spirit identity experiences described by youth who participated in the curriculum. Findings from the Two-Spirit youth who participated in the program reveal three main themes related to changes in gender and sexual identity: strengthening queer identity, Indigenizing queer identity, and building intersectional queer community. All of these themes can be understood as contributing to increased senses of self-esteem, cultural pride, and the development of community—mechanisms that buffer the impact of historical trauma on health outcomes in Indigenous communities.[18]

We bookend this chapter with a collaborative poetic narrative emerging from multiple shared experiences in ceremony where expressions of homophobia were described as "traditional." Poetic narrative allows for the illustration of the internalized colonial heteropatriarchal subjugation of Two-Spirit bodies. It also is a vehicle for imagining the hope of decolonizing our cultural teachings to (re)member our Two-Spirit youth and broader community.

Historical Trauma, Substance Abuse, Violence: The HIV "Triangle of Risk"

In the United States, American Indian and Alaska Natives (AIAN) who are diagnosed with AIDS have shorter survival times than whites, Asian and Pacific Islanders, and Hispanics. While the most recent national estimates of new HIV diagnoses are reported to be proportionate to the population, AIAN Two-Spirit community members are at greater risk.[19] For example, from 2005 to 2014, rates of infections increased by 19 percent in the overall AIAN community while increasing 63 percent in gay or bisexual AIAN men.[20] Over the last several decades, Indigenous scholars have linked historical trauma[21] to health-risk behaviours in AIAN communities.[22] Some of the individual and collective responses resulting from historical trauma include high rates of anxiety and depression, substance abuse, suicidality, as well as other forms of somatization.[23] American Indian gay and bisexual males (youth and adults) report higher lifetime experiences of sexual and physical abuse when compared with heterosexual AIANs.[24]

Indigenous scholars suggest the combination of historical trauma, alcohol and substance abuse, and interpersonal violence creates an HIV "triangle of risk."[25] Although existing research is limited, Two-Spirit youth may face even greater obstacles related to their status as sexual minorities, which is compounded by experiences of historical trauma, higher rates of violence, and substance use. For example, Teengs and Travers interviewed thirteen Two-Spirit youth fleeing homophobic violence in their reservations and small towns to seek the safety and acceptance perceived to exist in big cities.[26] Teengs and Travers found that in addition to drug and alcohol use, previous and current violence, and ongoing racial and sexual discrimination, Two-Spirit youth who migrate to the city face additional challenges related to housing stability, access to employment and income, food security, and safety. The authors of this study suggested further research is necessary to understand the complex factors impacting Two-Spirit youth vulnerability to HIV, and stressed that immediate attention should be focused on developing "culturally-appropriate" prevention programs.[27] This recommendation for prevention programs focusing on culture aligns with Indigenous health models that describe the importance of various aspects of culture and enculturation in mitigating the impacts of historical trauma and life stressors on health outcomes.

In their development of the Indigenist Stress Coping Model, Walters and Simoni suggest that "identity attitudes (the extent to which one internalizes or externalizes attitudes toward oneself and one's group) are important in enhancing self-esteem, coping with psychological distress, and avoiding depression."[28] Enculturation has also been found to mitigate negative impacts of life stressors on health outcomes and has been empirically supported in studies examining the role of culture and cultural identity development in improving educational health outcomes and reducing health (including mental health) burdens in Indigenous youth.[29] Accordingly, our research team worked to develop a curriculum that addressed the multiple prongs of HIV health-risk behaviours, the manifestations of homophobia, transphobia, and heteronormativity via internalized colonial heteropatriarchy while focusing on supporting positive social and cultural identity development. We describe the research project and process of developing the curriculum below.

Indigenous Youth Rise Up!: A Culture-Centred HIV Prevention Program

In 2015, our research team collaborated with five community organizations serving Indigenous communities to design, implement, and evaluate a culture-centred HIV prevention program for Indigenous youth in the Colorado/Rocky Mountain Region. The program lasted four days (two weekends in a single month) and included experiential modules on historical trauma, alcohol and other drug use, interpersonal violence and healthy relationships, and HIV and sexually transmitted infections.

Our curriculum development team, which was led by three Indigenous/Latinx womyn (one identifies as Two-Spirit), drew on multiple sources for preparing a comprehensive module that would honour both traditional and contemporary Indigenous understandings of gender, sex, and sexuality. In our review of established HIV-prevention curricula for Indigenous youth, it became clear that educational content related to gender and sexuality was most often limited to male/female bodies and emphasized heterosexual roles and relationships. While there was no explicit condemnation of non-binary or gender-queer bodies and sexual relationships within the curricula we reviewed, the omission reveals the implicit bias toward colonial constructions of gender and sexuality that is a function of heteropatriarchy. Aubrey Jean Hanson's and Chantal Fiola's work in Chapters 6 and 7 likewise points to the need for recognition of and kindness toward Indigenous LGBTQ2S peoples as a foundation for decolonization and sovereignty. Guided by queer and Indigenous feminist theories, we wove together the educational material and activities with a commitment to illuminate the narrow definitions and discourse available in mainstream Western education related to gender, sex, and sexuality, and to provide concrete examples and role models that embodied the expansive nature of these identities and experiences. This approach is rooted in Indigenous ways of being and knowing and is illustrated by the brief example from the module on sex and sexuality in the following section.

Decolonizing Gender and Sexuality for Sexual Health

Decolonizing strategies focus on liberating Indigenous ideas of gender, sex, and sexuality and challenge systems of colonial dominance through providing counter-narratives and centring Indigenous knowledge rather than relying on cultural additive approaches to mainstream Western (colonial) education. This fosters and encourages critical consciousness through concrete actions and tools for developing new language and thoughts. Activities in the module on sex and sexuality included watching videos with historical information on the role of Two-Spirit people in traditional Indigenous cultures, current Two-Spirit identity and experiences, and examples of non-binary identities (e.g., transgender and intersex youth). Other activities were interactive; for example, an exercise in which various illustrations of sexual anatomy were posted around the room had participants correctly apply the anatomical names from a list they were given. One of the aims of this exercise was to depict sexual anatomy in the absence of ascribed gender in order to encourage discussion about the multiple ways that gender identity can exist within male/female and in gender-non-binary bodies. A takeaway that emerged during group discussion is how little is taught about the forms and functions of sexual anatomy, regardless of gender and sexuality. Participants were shocked to learn they did not know where various anatomical parts were located (in their own bodies) and how they worked. During the debrief, we asked critical questions about the omission of these lessons in general education and described body parts in ways that did not ascribe them to a gendered body. For example, we used phrases like "bodies that have a uterus" or "bodies that menstruate" to discuss body functions without assigning a gender role.

We also discussed the differences between gender identity, gender expression, gender roles, and sexual orientation using ourselves (facilitators) as examples as we infused teachings about various tribal understandings described by Indigenous Elders, leaders, and writers (e.g., Muxes in Mexico). Highlighting and exploring Indigenous concepts of non-binary or non-heterosexual examples of gender and sexuality allowed participants to see clear examples of lives that reflected some of their experiences and also encouraged them to imagine beyond the limited examples provided by mainstream Western definitions and education. As such, the youth were able to more openly get to know their bodies, destigmatize their sexual anatomy, and understand the complex functions of reproduction and pleasure. Learning pre-colonial (or decolonized) Indigenous understandings of gender, sex, and sexuality opened the door for more questions and pointed them in the direction of learning for liberation. The curriculum was created for and by young people, and emphasized sex and sexual identity as topics to be discussed on their own terms.[30] As we focused on integrating cultural beliefs, customs, and practices into each educational module, participants were encouraged to make connections back to their own established or emerging identity.

At the conclusion of the curriculum, we conducted surveys and in-depth interviews with the twenty-three youth who participated. Of the participants, three identified as Two-Spirit and two identified as LGBTQ and are represented in the findings. In our analysis of the interviews, we found important themes related to changes in gender and sexual identity that demonstrate emerging and active embodiment of decolonizing strategies; these themes are detailed below.[31]

Findings: (Re)Membering

dykes remind me of indians
like indian dykes
are supposed to die out...

they don't
because the moon remembers
because so does the sun
because so do the stars
remember
and the persistent stubborn
grass
of the earth.[32]

Indigenous Two-Spirit identities are harmed, erased, dismantled, and purposely forgotten (dis-membered) through the social, structural, spiritual, and emotional violence of colonial heteropatriarchy. Racism, patriarchy, hetero- and cis-normativity, and even the re-enactment of "traditional" male/female binary gender roles in modern-day Indigenous communities impact the health and well-being of Indigenous youth of all genders and sexualities. The data gathered throughout the IYR program speak not only to the harm done by colonial violence, but also to the potential for hope and healing that can be reached with the intentional intervention shaped by Indigenous feminism and queer theoretical principles.

For the Two-Spirit youth who participated in the IYR curriculum, three main themes emerged around changes in identity: strengthening queer identity, Indigenizing queer identity, and building intersectional queer community. These themes are consistent with several decolonizing strategies articulated by Indigenous feminist scholars, including deconstructing or problematizing intersectional settler colonialism, acknowledging and centring Indigenous ways of knowing, and moving beyond discourse into embodiment and action.[33]

Deconstructing and Healing: Strengthening Queer Identity

The internalized racism, homophobia, and transphobia that are "logics of colonialism" must be fought through the "reimagining of the queer Native body."[34] The young people who identified as queer, LGBT, or Two-Spirit during the IYR curriculum used language in the post-test survey and interview that was stronger, clearer, and more empowered than it had been at the onset of the program. They spoke with determination, demonstrating authority over their own identities and the potential to heal from historical trauma. Desi (minor, female) wrote in the pretest that their[35] gender identity was a "handsome person," which is significantly different from the way they articulated their gender identity after participating in the program. In the follow-up interview, Desi described themself in this way: "I see myself as a manly person, and I'm a girl. But I'm a girl; so I'm a dyke. That's how everybody describes me. And I describe myself like that you know . . . a dyke. I'm a strong dyke. [laughs] I use 'they' and 'she.'" Interestingly, the phrase "manly hearted woman" has been used in the past among the Sioux and Blackfoot people,[36] and the term "dyke" was reclaimed historically by some Native American women who identified as lesbians or third or fourth genders.[37]

Another youth discussed the importance of intergenerational support for queer Indigenous visibility and the role that she felt she needed to play. Sasasui, who identified as a "queer two-spirit" female, said, "I think that the biggest thing that I learned was that I need to be more visible about my identity so that younger people could do that too. And that I want Elders to be visible with their identity for me." This indicates Sasasui's recognition of her dual role as both mentor and mentee. The importance of identity visibility in both Two-Spirit Elders and young people speaks to the need for modelling and healing from the erasure of queer Indigenous identities in communities.

Amara, a gender-fluid female, described feeling more confident, certain, and able to talk about her queer sexual identity. "I think I just left feeling a lot more comfortable with my sexual identity. I think it's really hard for people to figure out their sexual identity, and I had already been trying to figure it out, but just going over some of those different sexual identities reassured me like, yeah . . . this is how I identify." This emerging confidence illustrates the possibilities and promise of curricula that provide reflections of Indigenous experiences of gender and sexuality in ways that are de-stigmatized and represented concretely via real-life examples and the presence of Indigenous mentors and role models.[38]

Reclaiming: Indigenizing Queer Identity

The act of decolonizing through Indigenization allows the integration of Indigenous histories (or alter-Native) and knowledges to be centred within youth definitions of self.[39] Here the young person's queer or gender-fluid identity is reclaimed or articulated as inseparable from their Native or Indigenous identity. Galena (minor) entered as a self-identified member of the LGBTQ community, identifying as a "cis-gender female" in the pretest, which demonstrated potential awareness of the Two-Spirit/transgender community but did not specify an Indigenous identity. In the follow-up interview, her identity had been Indigenized. Galena said: "I'm a 'two-spirit' myself; and it's just . . . mostly the thing that has been the hardest, I guess, is just putting the name on it. Like at first you get the label that's like, 'You're gay,' 'You're lesbian,' whatever . . . and they didn't quite fit for me; so then when I heard 'two-spirit,' I was like, 'Yeah, that's me.' It just felt like so Native and it just felt right. I didn't use the term before the workshop." Understanding the term Two-Spirit, and feeling like it resonated with her better than any other words from the queer identity spectrum, enabled Galena to claim her queer, Indigenous identity.

Javi (male) described a similar experience: "That [Two-Spirit] was like a better way for me to explain it, 'cause I like always explained it another way; so when I heard them talk about it, the explanation was just absorbed by me, because I understood theirs better, and I felt like I could help other people understand it better the way they explained it." In his pretest survey, Javi described his gender identity as follows: "I view this question as completely complex. I view my gender identity as something I have no control over or would want control over. I haven't exactly pinned it down or figured it out but I know who I am as a person and I'm very satisfied with that." In his post-test, Javi simply explained, "I am two-spirited. I would say I'm masculine but also feminine." Through the Indigenization of his identity, Javi developed a clear and also nuanced understanding of his experiences with gender that demonstrates the control and intentionality of reclaiming.

Sasasui (female) entered the program with a queer Indigenous identity, but after the program was able to describe the ways that her queer Indigenous identity is integrated in everything that she does: "[I express] my Indigenous identity through a lot of ways, 'cause I feel like it intersects a lot with, well, everything. Because I'm not just Indigenous every day. Like [not] only Indigenous. I'm also queer, I'm also two-spirit, everything else; and so it plays into like everything that I do. Everything from identifying as two-spirit to the food that I cook and the food that I grow and eat and feed myself—the food that was traditional for our ancestors and things like that." Sasasui did not differentiate between her queer, Two-Spirit, and Indigenous identities but instead understood that they all impact and are impacted by the ways she lives and acts in the world. For her, even the act of growing traditional Indigenous foods was an act of Two-Spirit identity and part of the fundamental Indigenous way of knowing that all things are connected.

Taking Action: Building Intersectional Indigenous Queer Community

As Indigenous epistemologies understand the interconnectedness of all things and processes, youth stories of emerging identity development are connected to the ways they enact those identities and corresponding values in the world. D'Augelli's model of LGBTQ adolescent identity development posits "entering community" as the final identity process.[40] The stories from these young people indicate that entering community is not necessarily the final identity process but rather an ongoing deepening and fluid process of self-awareness and identity that requires a commitment to decolonized understanding of queer intersectional identity. The act of having, seeking, or living in intersectional queer community as described by several young people, is a strategy of resistance and liberation. For example, Sasasui described her experience on the first day of the program when she immediately encountered queer, Indigenous community: "The coolest thing that I saw the first day that I went in was one of the young people also identified as two-spirit, and we were able to make that connection, and she was able to come up to me after and be like, 'I really like want to like continue this relationship with you.' It was really cool. And so I think that visibility of two-spirit and transgender and gender non-conforming and queer people of colour is like super important, especially in these spaces where it's normally your race or normally like put on the back burner." For youth who came in with a less-articulated queer identity, the experiences of building community and being around others with queer or Two-Spirit Indigenous identities gave them more knowledge and understanding. Amara, a lesbian, gender-fluid female, explained:

> Meeting some people that identified as queer and what it meant to them was something that I learned that was new. Like when it comes to "queer," I think it means a lot of different things. I think that's the whole thing of the word, is that it doesn't mean one thing or one specific identity; it's kind of an identity that doesn't fit into the box, so it's just kind of like an umbrella term for people that don't feel like they identify with just one certain identity, or whatever. I never really met anybody that identified as queer; so it kind of gave me like more of a visual and like a better understanding of it.

Providing Two-Spirit youth with multiple opportunities to engage with other Indigenous community members who embody diverse genders and sexual orientations creates space for hope, visioning, and looking forward to a future. This kind of "queer world-making" is part of healing from historical and colonial trauma, and helps the youth to envision something new for themselves and their communities.[41]

Conclusion

As described throughout this chapter, decolonizing strategies articulated by Indigenous feminist scholars must respond to colonial heteropatriarchy to reimagine Indigenous identities and sexual health. That is, we must challenge the limited definitions of gender, sex, and sexuality provided by colonization and understand them as a mechanism by which settler colonialism asserts and maintains dominance and control over Indigenous bodies. As such, we can imagine, define, and enact our own ideas of what gender, sex, and sexuality is and can be for Indigenous peoples. The youth who participated in the project demonstrated elements of the vision of (re)membering—through strengthening and Indigenizing queer identity, and through involvement in queer community building. These elements are consistent with emerging Indigenous scholarship highlighting the role of culture and community in improving health outcomes in Indigenous communities.

When given the opportunity and educational tools, Indigenous youth conceptualize and enact gender and sexuality in ways that can make a powerful contribution to reducing HIV-risk behaviours in Two-Spirit communities, destigmatizing gender, sex, and sexuality, and to healing the wounds of colonial heteropatriarchy in broader Indigenous communities. This study presents a brief exploration into the possibilities of an HIV-prevention program rooted in Indigenous feminism and queer theories in order to begin the process of decolonization and liberation among Indigenous youth. The data discussed demonstrate positive cultural identity development and contribute to emerging scholarship that shows the potential of culture in interrupting legacies of trauma and improving health outcomes in Indigenous communities. Additional research is needed to explore the relevance of these themes among other Indigenous communities, and to further test the IYR curriculum as a liberatory intervention and HIV-prevention model. We are humbled to have witnessed, participated in, and co-created this journey, and we know that the contributions of all gender and sexual identities reflect the complexity and beauty of the true natural world and its laws.

We End with Ceremony: A Collaborative Poetic Narrative

As we walked around the teocalli, I watched my breath billow into the cold and prayed to the morning star for the right words. It's not my place to correct an Elder.

"Prayer is not the right place for politics."

I felt my belly fill with love for my Two-Spirit relatives. I felt all that love for my Elder too.

My comadre and I hugged each other in quiet knowing. Our eyes had seen the same sky.

The flap opened and the fire called us back.

Love is the truth. The medicine knows that. The ceremonies know that.

Notes

1 We use this specific spelling of "(re)membering" to describe the process of both remembering cultural knowledge and re-membering, or putting back together (queering), the bodies, minds, and spirits of our Two-Spirit/queer relatives in a way that reflects our current needs and contexts.

2 Throughout this paper, we will most often refer to LGBTQ2S as "Two-Spirit." While the term itself is not always used to indicate gender identity or sexual orientation, we are using it here as a tool of inclusivity that refers to all Indigenous lesbian, gay, bisexual, transgender, queer, intersex, and/or gender non-conforming folks. We honour the fact that many Indigenous peoples have tribally specific terms to identify their gender identity and sexual orientation, and are using the term Two-Spirit to describe a common community experience related to complex colonial oppression of gender identity and sexual orientation.

3 Fieland, Walters, and Simoni, "Determinants of Health."

4 Walters, Horwath, and Simoni, "Sexual Orientation Bias Experiences."

5 Balsam et al., "Culture, Trauma, and Wellness"; Fieland, Walters, and Simoni, "Determinants of Health."

6 Balsam et al., "Culture, Trauma, and Wellness"; Lehavot, Walters, and Simoni, "Abuse, Mastery, and Health."

7 Tinker, *Missionary Conquest*; Walters et al., "'My Spirit in My Heart.'"

8 Finley, "Decolonizing the Queer Native Body."

9 Finley; Walters et al., "'My Spirit in My Heart.'"

10 Heteropatriarchy is social structure that perceives patriarchy and heterosexuality as natural and correct. See Arvin, Tuck, and Morrill, "Decolonizing Feminism."

11 Green, "Introduction: From Symposium to Book," in *Making Space for Indigenous Feminism*, 1st ed.; Smith and Kauanui, "Native Feminisms Engage American Studies"; Smith, "Heteropatriarchy and the Three Pillars of White Supremacy."

12 See, for example, Smith, "Heteropatriarchy and the Three Pillars of White Supremacy"; Finley, "Decolonizing the Queer Native Body"; Driskill et al., *Queer Indigenous Studies*.

13 Finley, "Decolonizing the Queer Native Body," 33.

14 Denetdale, "Chairmen, Presidents, and Princesses"; Denetdale, "Securing Navajo National Boundaries."

15 Driskill et al., "The Revolution Is for Everyone."

16 Finley, "Decolonizing the Queer Native Body."

17 The Indigenous Youth RiseUp! curriculum participants included youth who identified as cis-gender, heterosexual, and male/female, as well as youth who identified as LGBTQ or Two-Spirit. The analysis in this chapter focuses on data from interviews with the LGBTQ/Two-Spirit youth.

18 Walters and Simoni, "Reconceptualizing Native Women's Health."

19 Centers for Disease Control, "HIV Among American Indians and Alaska Natives."

20 Centers for Disease Control.

21 Historical trauma is defined as a collective and cumulative trauma experienced and transmitted across generations, resulting from devastating events targeting a community (e.g., Indian boarding schools, forced relocation, massacres); effects are felt both personally and collectively. See Brave Heart and DeBruyn, "The American Indian Holocaust"; Evans-Campbell and Walters, "Catching Our Breath"; Evans-Campbell, "Historical Trauma in American Indian/Native Alaska Communities."

22 Duran et al., "Healing the American Indian Soul Wound"; Evans-Campbell, "Historical Trauma in American Indian/Native Alaska Communities"; Evans-Campbell et al., "Interpersonal Violence in the Lives of Urban American Indian and Alaska Native Women."

23 Evans-Campbell and Walters, "Catching Our Breath"; Evans-Campbell et al., "Interpersonal Violence in the Lives of Urban American Indian and Alaska Native Women."

24 Walters et al., "'My Spirit in my Heart'"; Simoni et al., "Victimization Substance Use, and HIV Risk Behaviors."

25 Walters et al., "Keeping Our Hearts from Touching the Ground."

26 Teengs and Travers, "'River of Life, Rapids of Change.'"

27 Teengs and Travers.

28 Walters and Simoni, "Reconceptualizing Native Women's Health."

29 Walters and Simoni; Zimmerman et al., "The Enculturation Hypothesis"; Whitbeck et al., "Traditional Culture and Academic Success among American Indian Children"; Bals et al., "The Relationship between Internalizing and Externalizing Symptoms and Cultural Resilience Factors."

30 Finley, "Decolonizing the Queer Native Body."

31 Excerpts from participant interviews have been edited for clarity and flow, and pseudonyms are used to protect confidentiality, along with a "minor" designation when the participant was under eighteen.

32 Allen, "Some Like Indians Endure," 9.

33 Arvin, Tuck, and Morrill, "Decolonizing Feminism."

34 Finley, "Decolonizing the Queer Native Body," 33, 41.

35 Consistent with Desi's articulated gender pronouns, we use "they/them" to describe their identity story and in our analysis.

36 Lewis, "The Manly Hearted Women among the North Piegan"; Allen, "Lesbians in American Indian Cultures."

37 Allen, "Lesbians in American Indian Cultures"; Jacobs, Thomas, and Lang, *Two-Spirit People*, 5.

38 It is important to note that all of the IYR curriculum developers, facilitators, and research team identified as Indigenous or Latinx/Indigenous.

39 Trinidad, "Toward Kuleana (Responsibility)"; Smith, *Decolonizing Methodologies*, 1st ed.

40 D'Augelli, "Identity Development and Sexual Orientation," 319.

41 Yep, "The Violence of Heteronormativity in Communication Studies"; Muñoz, "Introduction: Feeling Utopia."

Part III
Multi-Generational Feminisms and Kinship

CHAPTER 9

Honouring Our Great-Grandmothers: An Ode to Caroline LaFramboise, Twentieth-Century Métis Matriarch

ZOE TODD

This chapter is an exploration of the multi-generational Métis feminisms instilled in my family by a celebrated matriarch many of my relations hold in deep regard: my Cree/Métis great-grandmother Caroline Todd (née LaFramboise). As a daughter born to a Métis dad and a settler mom, I have done a lot of work to explore what it means to situate my work ethically within the context of my settler, Métis, and Métis-Cree relations. In thinking through what Caroline's life and stories mean to me, I draw inspiration from Kim TallBear, who reflects on the role that her mom, LeeAnn TallBear, played in shaping her intellectual life as she was growing up, calling her mother one of her "formative theorists."[1] In many ways, one of the most enduring theorists in my life is my great-grandmother Caroline, whose life and legacy continue to shape my family's dynamic understanding of who we are and how we relate to the world as Métis people. My dad, Garry Todd, reminded me in 2013 that his grandparents' world view was shaped through kinship: "Their world was full of who was related to who, and how." As I illustrate in this chapter, both kinship and refusal were two of the most enduring forms of praxis that my great-grandmother enacted in her life and movements through prairie worlds in the twentieth century.

I grew up in an urban context in the same prairie city in which my Métis dad and his siblings grew up in the mid-twentieth century. My dad spent much of his early childhood in the 1950s sitting around the kitchen table at his grandparents' home in the Rossdale Flats in inner-city Edmonton, listening to women tell stories. Many of our family stories are stories that my dad, the eldest of eight children in his immediate family, remembers from this time. These stories are shared here in this chapter with his permission.

The twentieth-century Todd family revolved around the matriarchal figure of Caroline Todd. Caroline was born in 1885 to Louis LaFramboise—a Métis man who was born in Assumption (Pembina) in Black Mud River, North Dakota, in 1851—and Isabelle Cardinal—his Cree/Métis wife, born in what is today known as Whitefish (Goodfish) Lake First Nation in 1859.[2] Caroline Todd continues to exist in stories that my dad, aunties, and a broad array of second cousins and distant cousins share with me over cups of coffee, plates of fries, and stolen moments when I'm able to set up short visits with family across western Canada.

There was a period from the time I was fourteen to twenty-three years old that I did not see my dad. He had moved to the West Coast, while my little sister and I continued to live in Edmonton, Alberta, with our mom. Though very connected to our family in my earlier life, I spent my adolescence mostly disconnected from my Todd (Métis) family. But kinship has a powerful way of continuing to asserting itself across time and space. Though I was formally estranged from my dad for nine years, his stories and teachings from my early life continued to shape how I understood my presence in Edmonton and the Prairies. My early university undergraduate classes were a place where my family's presence firmly re-entered my life even before I formally reconciled with my dad. When I enrolled in courses on Indigenous issues in my third year at the University of Alberta (after nearly failing out of the biology program), a non-Indigenous professor who worked with residential school survivors arched her eyebrows when she saw my last name. She immediately asked me if I was related to so-and-so and so-and-so. My eyes widened in surprise. "Yes!" I exclaimed. She nodded knowingly. From there, she took me under her wing, encouraging me to soften into my relationship to my family's history and stories, reassuring me that my place in the constellation[3] of prairie Métis relations mattered within that cold prairie university. This was the first of many moments where my otipemisiwak (Métis) kinship relations preceded me in prairie colonial spaces, making space for me in an academe that is otherwise impossibly hostile and sterile and devoid of any recognition of Indigenous life-worlds. Those first university courses on Indigenous issues were life-saving for me. That professor recognized my family in ways that most scholars would never be able to. And in that moment, I became more legible as a Métis person with reciprocal responsibilities within amiskwaciwaskahikan (Edmonton) and beyond.

A few years later, while completing my master's degree at the University of Alberta, I was introduced to noted historical geographer Frank Tough. Again, when he heard my last name, he asked, "Are you related to the Todds descended from Dr. William Todd in Red River?" Indeed! I explained that I am a descendant of Dr. William Todd and his Métis wife (the records disagree as to whether we're directly descended from his wife Isabella or from Marianne; that's a whole other Indigenous feminist conversation for another day). A few days later, Tough dropped off an article about my ancestor, written by his mentor Arthur "Skip" Ray. Again, I was excited to find evidence of my kinship relations celebrated and acknowledged within the academy, in unexpected and surprising ways.

The Todd side of my family history has always been present and accessible to me. However, I know a lot less about my LaFramboise connections, given that my great-grandmother passed away in the 1960s. Initially, I only knew her through my dad's and aunties' stories about her. Several years later, in the winter of 2017, I heard Métis historian Brenda Macdougall recount her most recent work on Métis kinscapes at a conference on Métis historical and contemporary legal-political relationships.[4] In her talk, she outlined the political significance of the LaFramboise family—specifically LaFramboise women—in bringing various actors together in Métis fur trade relations across the prairies in what is now Canada. In outlining the relationality of Métis leader Louis Riel within significant webs of Métis families across the plains, Macdougall explained the importance of LaFramboise women: "LaFramboise women for the Plains Métis are like the lynchpin of almost every family. They are embedded somewhere in a lot of those historical relationships, and Louise [LaFramboise] is just one example of that."[5]

Macdougall went on to describe the co-constitutive nature of Métis kinscapes across the plains and the political actions that tied Métis together throughout the nineteenth century. As she explains, if we take an explicitly relational view toward how Métis families worked across their kinship responsibilities and entanglements, we gain a stronger understanding of how and why particular Métis political actions came to be. Politics for the Métis are deeply entangled in who we are related to and what obligations, laws, and urgencies flow from our family connections across time and space. As Macdougall points out in discussing the Métis political trajectories between the Battle of Seven Oaks in 1816 to the first Métis (Riel) Resistance in 1869 and the North-West Resistance of 1885: "These are not isolated events. It's not as if families in Red

River did something that families in Batoche did differently. This is all part of one long political action that spreads itself across the 19th century."[6]

This work by Macdougall helps me to situate the political exigencies and actions of my own Métis family within broader Métis legal traditions and assertions of Métis self-determination in the face of violent settler-colonial dispossession across the plains in the nineteenth and twentieth centuries. Macdougall's explicit attention to the political power of the women of the LaFramboise family also enables me to examine the leadership and legal traditions enacted by my great-grandmother as she moved through the difficult period for Métis on the plains following the North-West Resistance of 1885. In this way, I can situate my family's experience within the "one long political action" that Macdougall references.

I know the relationality and political leadership of LaFramboise women, viscerally, from the stories my family shares about my great-grandmother Caroline LaFramboise and her steely-eyed determination as the matriarch of the Todd family throughout the early half of the twentieth century. It is this story—of my links to Caroline and to the kind of insistent and persistent Métis feminism she manifested—that grounds my legal-ethical responsibilities as a Métis iskwew (Métis woman) today. I think here of the ways in which her ethical orientation to the world, as told and re-told by my family members, anchors us to the specific prairie temporalities and territories that my family is bound to and borne of. In Caroline's movements through lands and temporalities I find a modality for living, one bound up with prairie wild roses, misaskwatomina, rivers, fish, grasses, and—to gesture to the work of Mohawk political theorist Audra Simpson[7]—to the persistent socio-political refusal enacted by prairie Métis women who were navigating a heavily colonial, white supremacist, and settler-patriarchal prairie socio-scape after the 1869 and 1885 Métis resistances. Though I never met Caroline, her life (along with the lives of my non-Indigenous grandmothers) fuels my ongoing work to tend to prairie worlds and cosmologies with care.

In the following section, I explore Caroline's political commitments through the lens of Mohawk scholar Audra Simpson's work on refusal and the Cree legal-ethical principle of wahkohtowin, which I come to through the work of Brenda Macdougall.

Caroline LaFramboise: Refusal and Wahkohtowin in Twentieth-Century Prairie Life

My great-grandmother was a matriarch. In the spring of 2014, while we gathered at my sister and brother-in-law's home after my dad's wedding to his long-term partner, our stories turned to family. My dad began by sharing stories about growing up in the prairies. He wove together accounts of odd jobs Métis men took to make ends meet in early twentieth-century Alberta with funny anecdotes about his younger siblings getting up to trouble in downtown Edmonton in the 1950s. I asked my dad, "What was Great-grandma Caroline like?" He paused and thought for a moment. "Oh, she was always present in the background, running everything from behind the scenes." This notion of Métis women in my family working insistently in the background to shape and determine how relationships unfolded across kinship entanglements is very real and visceral for me. I come from a family of strong women who are unafraid to vocalize their views and to challenge the status quo. I take great pride in belonging to this web of insistent and steadfast women and the powerful ways they shaped and continue to shape community. Though not every family necessarily reflects the same dynamics as mine, I view my family—with its ties to LaFramboise, Cardinal, Gladue, Laboucane, Desjarlais, and Dennet families—as a matriarchal one. Caroline LaFramboise was fiercely central to the running of the Todd family in the twentieth century.

There is a foundational story that shapes not only how I view my family's historical ties to the lands of central Alberta but also how I view my ongoing responsibilities to Métis political-legal action and feminist formulations. This story, about Caroline and the horses, has been shared in various iterations over the last decade by my dad, my auntie, my cousins, and myself. The first time I heard the story about Caroline and the horses was when my dad shared it as a formal oral history at my cousin's wedding in 2006. This version or telling of the story revolves around Caroline LaFramboise refusing the enclosure and dispossession of common pasture lands that my family shared with other Métis families they farmed with in the early twentieth century.

The details of the story are complex and nuanced, with various tellings by different actors within my family offering different details. Some versions place it in or around the St. Paul des Métis settlement in the early twentieth century, where Caroline married her husband, James Todd, in 1903. In 1900, James had appeared before the North-West Half-Breed Claims Commission in Egg Lake, Northwest Territories. When he applied for scrip, James indicated he was living in St. Paul, at that time a Métis settlement north of present-day

Edmonton and adjacent to Saddle Lake First Nation.[8] James and Caroline farmed in the lands around the settlement in the first two decades of the twentieth century. They lived and farmed alongside many other Métis families who held land in the townships set aside by the Oblates for the Métis, including Caroline's parents, Louis LaFramboise Jr. and Isabelle Cardinal.[9] Caroline and James later moved to South Cooking Lake, where they would farm until their retirement in 1954, at which time they moved to the Rossdale Flats.

While I cannot pin down exactly which farm the story took place at (and it appears that Caroline and James moved frequently in the area around St. Paul des Métis through the period between 1900 and 1921, because they list numerous different farm addresses in the 1906, 1911, 1916, and 1921 censuses), what is important is that Caroline and James lived and farmed in the area around the St. Paul des Métis settlement for nearly a decade. They were part of a web of Métis families living in the region during a brief period prior to the opening of St. Paul des Métis to French Canadian settlers in 1909.[10]

The St. Paul des Métis settlement was established by the Catholic missionary order of the Oblates of Mary Immaculate in 1895, at the direct instruction of Father Albert Lacombe.[11] The settlement was envisioned as a "utopia" by Father Albert Lacombe, a kind of Métis reserve meant to buffer Métis from the supposed corrupting influences of white settler culture.[12] All was not well within the settlement, however, as it became quickly evident that Métis were unruly and resistant subjects. A well-documented act of refusal at the settlement took place in 1905, when children forced to attend the Catholic day school in St. Paul des Métis burned down the school.[13] Given the discord between Métis who had moved to the settlement and the Oblates who struggled to discipline and govern the settlement, it is not surprising that Lacombe's "utopia" evaporated. St. Paul des Métis was officially opened to French Canadian settlers in April 1909,[14] and within a few short years, many of the Métis families at the settlement had relocated elsewhere.[15]

Returning to Macdougall's kinscapes and her arguments regarding the ways in which Métis kinship shapes political action, it is plausible to consider the entanglements of Caroline LaFramboise, her husband, children, and extended family within the broader network of Métis families farming in the area around St. Paul in the early 1900s. With the history of Métis life in the region shaped deeply by the political struggles at the settlement, it is important to understand how Caroline's actions reaffirm the refusals of the people in the settlement proper. However, given the paucity of details about the year or the exact location where the story of Caroline and the horses took place, I want to focus on the substantive actions within the story and how they deeply inform my own Métis feminist pedagogy and praxis.

As the story goes, the other Métis families who farmed alongside my great-grandparents tended to a common pasture where they collectively looked after one another's livestock. One day, these animals were removed from the common pasture and locked up by a non-Métis actor. In the version of the story that I have been told, the perpetrator is a nameless settler who locked up the Métis livestock, as it was an affront to a settler-capitalist and individualist farming ethos.

I am primarily interested in how my family responded. The men in the community were reportedly scared to challenge this move to lock up the animals. The community was in crisis: their mode of governance depended on the collective labour of common pastures and shared care of the livestock. To have the animals locked up meant that principles of private property, enclosure, and settler-colonial domination over lands and animals were imposed upon the community's own formulations of shared labour across kin ties and space. In the tellings of this story shared by my father and my aunt, it was Caroline LaFramboise who organized the women in the community to collectively refuse this imposition upon their social-temporal formations. Caroline rallied the women together in a midnight raid, where together they let the livestock back into the common pasture, to be tended to collectively once again.

The story, as told within my immediate family, revolves around how Caroline and the women of the community let the horses back into the commons. The account challenges many formations of settler understandings of Indigenous political action, given that (a) the protagonists were women; and (b) the action took place on Métis farms. Nonetheless, I read Caroline's work as an extended expression of Métis legal principles that centre relationality, kinship, and care across time and space—principles that she would later enact in her elder years in urban Edmonton.

In both formulations of this story, when told within our family, the focus of the narrative is on Caroline's heroism, collective labour, and her refusal of settler domination. This is what we celebrate as a family. But what is also important is the collective will and refusal of the Métis women in the community when faced with a settler-colonial violation of Métis legal traditions. Eschewing the fear that the men in the community expressed toward possible punishments from settler-colonial agents, my great-grandmother and the women of the community fearlessly organized to return the order of the farming community to one that embodied Métis kinship ties and principles of collective labour and tenderness. I read the act of letting the horses back into common pasture as an embodiment of two Cree legal principles that also animate Métis lives and laws in central Alberta: wahkohtowin (kinship/relatedness)[16] and wicihitowin (the principle of working together).[17] Brenda Macdougall explains wahkohtowin in the following terms in her own research: "The metis family structure that emerged in the northwest and at Sakitawak was rooted in the history and culture of Cree and Dene progenitors, and therefore is a worldview that privileged relatedness to land, people (living, ancestral and those to come), the spirit world, and creatures inhabiting the space. In short, this worldview, wahkootowin, is predicated upon a specific Aboriginal notion and definition of family as a broadly conceived sense of relatedness of all beings, human and non-human, living and dead, physical and spiritual."[18] Through their refusal to adhere to settler-colonial formulations of family, space, more-than-human relations, and land, Caroline and the women she worked with enacted instead an insistently Métis ethical orientation to the land, animals, and families they co-existed with. And through this orientation, they insisted on honouring human and non-human relations before adhering to colonial impositions.

Notions of settler-colonial private property and enclosure would play a big role in the mis-recognitions of Métis women's political labour in my family in twentieth-century Alberta. When Caroline and James retired from farming, it was to a small clapboard home in the Rossdale Flats in central Edmonton that, according to my dad, their grandson had bought for them with his earnings as a soldier in World War Two. This is where they lived out their retirement, in the heart of the burgeoning prairie city, within the floodplains of the kisisaskiwacini-sipiy (North Saskatchewan River).

At the very end of their lives, James and Caroline faced another egregious act of settler-colonial dispossession. This time, it was in the name of modernizing the burgeoning prairie urban utopia. Their home was expropriated by the City of Edmonton to make way for the James MacDonald bridge, a mid-twentieth-century traffic infrastructure that tellingly chose to cut through an impoverished community where many Métis families like my own lived. The story shared with me by second cousins is that the city did not allow my family much time to collect their belongings. My family was never compensated for the loss of their home, a home that was a central gathering place, a hearth, for Caroline and James' children, grandchildren, and great-grandchildren.

While Caroline and other women in her farming community enacted powerful assertions of Métis law for the betterment of their community and polity, the kind of political refusal of women like my great-grandmother is not recognized as worthy of care or attention by the formulations of the Canadian nation-state. When I was very young, my dad drove my little sister and me down to Rossdale one afternoon. He parked the car in a gravel parking lot and we got out and walked over to an empty field next to the James MacDonald bridge. He pointed to the land around us: "My grandparents lived here," he said. I did not fully understand the importance of this memory work he was performing with us until adulthood, when he shared more of his stories about Caroline with us. Now, when he tells his stories about Caroline, I feel the Rossdale grass beneath my feet, and I see the sightlines of the downtown rising above us and the river stretching out behind us as it did on that day nearly thirty years ago when he took us back to where the Todd house once stood. Today, in the place where Caroline's home was located, is an embankment covered in cement, over which cars speed through the river valley day and night. Sometimes when I am back in Edmonton, I visit this place to bear witness to the concrete and cold prairie settler erasure of Caroline and her tenderness and fiery refusals of colonial order.

In a particularly galling example of white supremacist settler Canadian feminism, urban prairie planners enacted a further ironic intervention into Caroline's life and legacy. It was not enough to tear down her home without compensation. The city also decided to memorialize a noted eugenicist just metres away from where Caroline had once tended to her kin, shared stories, offered tea, admonished grandchildren, gardened, laughed, and died. Across the road from where Caroline's home stood is a small urban parkette dedicated to a member of the Famous Five, recognized eugenicist and first woman cabinet minister in the British Empire, Irene Parlby.[19] The Famous Five were white women who are celebrated within Canadian history for fighting for the vote for white women in the early twentieth century.[20] Around the time that my great-grandmother was fighting alongside other Métis women for recognition of Métis self-determination on their prairie farms, a group of well-heeled white suffragettes in Alberta were seeking white women's right to vote and also fighting for eugenicist legislation that was quite explicitly white supremacist.[21] While there is no monument to Caroline and the women she collaborated with to refuse the enclosure of Métis lands and life, Irene Parlby is memorialized with a park that stands opposite to Caroline's erstwhile home and centre of my family's matriarchal liveliness. I like to imagine my great-grandmother in eternal refusal of the white woman who is celebrated at her doorstep, turning her back to Parlby and tending instead to the legacies and memories of other Métis and First Nations families of the Rossdale Flats who have been erased from Edmonton's official history.

In my new home of Ottawa, the nation's capital in unceded and unsurrendered Algonquin territory, there is a monument to the Famous Five on Parliament Hill. Bronze casts of the five haughty White Anglo-Saxon Protestants (WASPs) who secured the vote for white women sit at a bronze table, bronze teacups set out politely at their disposal. I contemplate, often, chipping some of the cement from that hulking entombed Edmonton embankment where Caroline once told her stories. I imagine myself bringing this artifact from the concretized prairie tomb of my family's former home as an offering/threat to the bronze Ottawa effigy of Irene Parlby. If my great-grandmother was robbed, over and over again, of the collective space to share her tender and visceral kinship and legal-ethical ground with the people she loved and laboured alongside, then I suppose it is up to me to enact a contemporary refusal of sorts in Irene's teacup-adorned playground in Ottawa.

So, put the kettle on to boil, ladies. A great-granddaughter is coming to speak back to the racist settler state formations that her great-grandmother fearlessly refused.

Conclusion

In ending this essay, I want to wrap up by underscoring how deeply Caroline shapes me even today, more than fifty years since she passed away.[22] Even though she lived more than a lifetime away from me, her commitments to Métis resistance continue to guide me today. I'm thankful to have her body of work as something I can turn to as I do my best to enact meaningful refusals and tenderness in the face of ongoing colonial incursions today. The other day, just before Halloween, I stood by the Rideau River, which runs alongside the university I work at. I was surrounded by maples, oaks, and beech trees turning in the late autumn afternoon. The sky was steely grey and the orange, yellow, and red leaves clinging to the tree branches stood out, a shock of unapologetic colour against the muted backdrop of the river and clouds. For a moment, I was transported back to the edge of the North Saskatchewan River back home in Edmonton. This little patch of forest next to the Rideau River was not that different from the river's edge my great-grandparents' home once stood next to. For reasons that are inexplicable in western universalist or colonial empirical terms, I suddenly could feel Caroline's presence there. Fleetingly. And I knew she was speaking her truth and power across planes I cannot even fathom in my current human form. To say she is foundational to who I am is an understatement. Her guidance is eternal, and her political formations unshakeable. I am doing my best to carry her life and legacy forward, however haltingly I can, in my own life. And I draw inspiration from her throughout everything that I do. For this, I am grateful.

Notes

1 Kim TallBear (@KimTallBear), Twitter, 25 October 2016, https://twitter.com/KimTallBear/status/791146068603990017.

2 Family genealogical data consulted for this article were compiled by my aunt, Carol Howell-Jones, who maintains a family genealogical website at https://todd-genealogy.ca. I also consulted a comprehensive genealogy prepared by genealogist Stanley Hulme for my cousin in 2006, as well as doing independent archival research through Library and Archives Canada.

3 I draw on the idea of "constellations" from the work of Cree scholar Karyn Recollet, who employs "kinstillatory" thinking in her examinations and explorations of movement through dance and kin-making processes in her own communities of praxis. This is recently explored in her article "Kin-dling and other radical relationalities," co-authored with Emily Johnson in *Movement Research* (2019).

4 Macdougall, "Wahkootowin as Methodology."

5 Macdougall.

6 Macdougall.

7 Simpson, *Mohawk Interruptus*; see also Simpson, "Consent's Revenge."

8 Library and Archives Canada (LAC), Scrip document form E. number 1346, scrip claim number 2014. Accessed via Library and Archives Canada, Online MIKAN no. 1515411; former reference number RG15-D-II-8-c.

9 LAC, 1906 Census document, Item Number 732947, Reference: RG31, Statistics Canada, Microfilm: T-18362, Page Number: 3, Family Number: 20.

10 Devine, *The People Who Own Themselves*.

11 Devine, 183.

12 So described in Galka, "Father Lacombe OMI."

13 Olshefsky, "Revisionist History: St Paul Des Métis"; see also Devine, *The People Who Own Themselves*.

14 Devine, *The People Who Own Themselves*, 184.

15 Devine, 184.

16 For a comprehensive discussion of the mobilization of the Cree legal-ethical principle of wahkohtowin in Métis kinscapes, see Brenda Macdougall's writing on wahkohtowin (wahkootowin) in Macdougall, *One of the Family*.

17 Dorion, "Opikinawasowin: The Life-Long Process of Growing Cree and Métis Children," 113.

18 Macdougall, *One of the Family*, 3.

19 Cavanaugh and Mcleod, "Irene Parlby."

20 Cavanaugh and Mcleod.

21 Kurbegovic, "The Famous Five."

22 Simpson, *Mohawk Interruptus*; Simpson, "Consent's Revenge."

CHAPTER 10

on anishinaabe parental kinship with black girl life: twenty-first-century ([de]colonial) turtle island

WAASEYAA'SIN CHRISTINE SY WITH AJA SY

the foothills of ŁAU,WELNEW, 2016

wcs: [Stands at bedroom doorway, late on a Friday evening.] Hey, Aje. Are you busy?

as: [Hanging over the bed, scrolling on her phone.] Yea, why?

w: Do you wanna listen to this story I told you about? The one about us—me as anishinaabe feminist parent and you as daughter of?

a: [Keeps scrolling.] No.

[silent pause]

a: Okay, fine.

w: Awesome! Scooch over so I can be close to you while I read it.

a: [Scooches over. Keeps scrolling on her phone.]

w: Okay, when I'm reading it think about what you like and don't like.

a: 'K.

w: Are you gonna put the phone down?

a: No.

[silent pause]

w: Okay, fine. [Takes a deep breath with long exhale, pauses, and begins reading.]

w: [Stops reading. Looks at daughter.] giizis. Do you know that word?

a: Yes. [Still scrolling through phone.]

w: What does it mean?

a: The sun.

w: [Smiles, relieved. Starts reading again, from the top.]

giizis dwells in black ahhfreeka

everyone believes giizis lives in the sky, rises in the east, and sets in the west. my maternal people, the anishinaabeg of the great lake region of turtle island believe this. my paternal, white-canadian family, does too. what i know to be true, based on my anishinaabe ways of knowing through dreaming, is that the sun dwells in black ahhfreeka.

the sun dwells here and it's the children born from mixed-race love and raised up through indigenous philosophies, with indigenous interests, that rise and set across landscapes. moving life forward through the generations. starting anew and again—maadjiimaadiziwin. rising and setting pushing, contracting creation echoing a pulse. a primordial echoing (im)pulse.

and, all life knows this. we only have to go outside at night and gaze up at jiibay miikaana to experience billions of years of reverberations across landscapes.

bawating, sault ste. marie, 2001

giizis set herself in my anishinaabe womb beside a flow of water at bawating, by the river. now tamed by white men and their locks, this river—once falling and rumbling—was known as the rapids. i felt giizis two weeks after she set; i suddenly became round. now, she rises in anishinaabewaki + coast salish territory. each does its part of growing her up. i'm teaching her to do her part, too. before all this though, a dream:

> She is there, a little girl standing brilliantly in her smile. She seems to be watching how it lands on me, watching it travel through all the ethereal veils of time and space. Her skin, glowing earth—a blackbrown glow—and her smile. Star-eyes, Milky Way teeth, and apple-cheeks explode n'ode making a new galaxy.

Who is she?

Against the humble, ochre landscape of flat, dry, dust, she is vibrant. She reminds me of mokijiiwanibiish, water coming up from earth. This and a libation in the middle of a drought; a compass amidst the unfamiliar. She is content to be here, as though a work of manidooyag.

But who is she? This girl embraced by expansive land stretching into nothing and everything at once. A disorienting sight for anishinaabe eyes accustomed to greetings from rolling hills of hyperboreal[1] forests held upright by massive stretches of dark grey cliffs and nurtured through sopping wet freshwater pools and intricate, flowing trails. Landscapes marked with bridges, etched with forever-winding asphalt highways, and secondary dirt roads eking through the bush. Snow, and frost.

Here, in this dream, the vastness is speckled with markers of identity: a few gangly trees; seven skinny cows; meandering wooden fences; and, a doctor in crisp, white cotton. This doctor is a man and this man's energy is kind, warm, welcoming. He's proud of all this, all this vast nothing and everything. And she standing away from both of us—this little girl is alight. She wears a bright, shimmering orange cloth fashioned over her hair.

Or maybe, that's what sunbeams look like woven together.

a: [Laughs.]

w: What?

a: This part here. [Points to the line about the cloth on her head.]. Cringe.

edmonton, 1996

it's 1996 and late autumn in western canada. i wake, lying on my mattress, my mattress lies on the floor. the dull expanse of a murky, undulating sky beyond my curtain-less bedroom window and a familiar tug in my belly greets me: broke and alone-ish, still. it's unnerving looking for work in a city that seems to dislike aboriginal women in a way that is more hostile than the other cities i've looked for work in. this place, now, in the fall, is cold. harsh cold. this is a moment in post-undergraduate life where a different kind of no money lives:

hard settler stares on streets + from brown "sisters" in bars where my rural-small-town self witnesses a new kind of hustle—another kind of keeping the lifeline going. i have pasta belly which is fine because i love pasta, i love my sisterfriend who i live with, and i love her home which keeps us warm. i also get scars on my lungs from heaving in bitter november air while looking for work. i get heartbreak. i live long waning waiting days that wax into nothing where everything is sun-filled, child-filled, and resource stretched. economic poverty is as harsh as the climate and attitudes. lying here on my mattress on the other side of learning about colonization, patriarchy, and native dignity, i realize that the source of happiness is inside my body. it does not come from outside and it certainly does not come from people. i learn canada is sick. i learn how it made me hate myself for being indian. made me feel uncomfortable around other indians. made me think of myself as an opaque nothing called indian instead of human being, a good being, anishinaabe. colonization made me forget i'm anishinaabe. it made me forget that i forgot. made me forget that i live in the lands of my ancestors thousands of years over. where it turned those who made me forget into heroes, western feminism turned them into sheroes. both guilty of glorifying the system that enforced this amnesia and reconstruction-without-consent. indigenous political analysis, cultural knowledges, and feminism become the lifelines that lead me through the rest of my life to now. none of them are wholly adequate unto themselves but together they powerfully change the white, settler-colonial, patriarchal, and misogynist world i live(d) in.

i'm so tired and let my eyes drift shut. don't be lazy. open: blinkblink. i stare at a tiny ball of purple lint on the industrial brown rug used to carpet the native housing floors of my sisterfriend's beautiful home. poor-bored in the city is a whole other ball game. i shift my attention to the worn little grey balls on the thin top sheet. feel them beneath my fingertips. sensation.

a tug.

a girl-tug. a little girl in a dream tug. a bright, shining girl in a dream. that smile!

she pulls me from the white noise and static. electric jolts jumpstart my brain, a flicker moves in my belly. i curl up fetal just so i can keep these embers bundled up close—this bit of new life bubbling and coursing through my body pushing out the hopeless flash-forward of the day. i close my eyes and meander through the details, sensations, colours. it smells hot-dry. i hold on to her, that heat, and that sunshine. i doze back off in thought: who is she? is this africa? why africa? there's been nothing on the news ...

montreal, 2000 and tekane

"... and there were these skinny cows, a doctor, lots of flat, dry land ..."

"mm. that's my father's farm and one of my brothers back home in ah-hfreeka. the farm is in tekane and my brother is a doctor." the vibrations of a deep, sure voice resonate inside me.

a: [Points to the line above.] That's definitely how Papa sounds.

a dance floor; dreams of waterfalls and snow; stories of stars, death, and an old, beloved grandmother who offered water every morning to the hard desert just outside the door of her home in the village. a libation. peppermint and green tea ceremonies on the floor with friends, storytelling hands, and later, just long bodies ...

bawating, near the river, 2002

a piece of her fur is buried beneath nokomis giizhigaatigoog in the blended tradition of her parents. it was buried there in frozen earth with friends and family as witnesses. only a piece of her fur though. i would not allow all of it to be shaved off. muslim tradition would have to compromise. she was born in a den with brown and white and shifting-identity women. all of us nestled in a snowy night. after a magical and much-needed effacing of my stubborn cervix, she emerged. the smell of a particular kind of mashkiki emanated from a particular spot on her body. i asked my midwife, "did you use __________ to help her move out of me?" she responded, "no."

the morning she was born, the sun sparkled off the fresh snow. i recall seeing it through the tall windows of the old place where we lived in downtown-ish bawating. i remember how it weighed down the mighty boughs of the magnificent spruce trees that bordered the yard of our rental. i see her father's eyes darting around the bedroom, searching for something. finding it, he confirms, "this way is east, yes?" looking at me and gently picking her up from my chest. his eyes are bloodshot. sisterfriend told me he was a wreck throughout the night. in early talks he said he wanted me to go the hospital. i said i wanted to have our baby at home with the women. i realized in that moment that not being in the hospital created a lot of stress for him and wondered when it was that we stopped trusting and valuing ourselves, our bodies, our ways. he turns and raises her up high and away from him; raises her up toward waabanong—the east. i hear word rhythms in a language i don't know. held out to the universe like that, in her brand-new self, she looks distant from each of us, from all of us.

she looks like she is unto herself and unto life itself. autonomous + connected. he looks like he knows this and wants creation to know he understands. i think of my teachings, and Kahlil Gibran.

a: [Laughs]

w: What?

a: It sounds like Lion King.

w: [Chuckles]. Haha. Yes, it does. But this is real and true, girly.

a: I like this line here. [Points to last line.]

w: The one about my teachings and Kahlil Gibran?

a: Yep.

it doesn't take long for life in the den to become punctured by reality. the first breathtaking and startling truth arriving while she was in my womb: she will be born into a patriarchal world despite (my) feminism—a world that teaches her to value her being and her life based on her relationships with boys and men. after the midwifery, the burying of her hair, and my own private ceremonial burning of a million journals that focused on love and men, her first birthday saw many cultural teachings about the first seven years of life, The Good Life.

i put down my tobacco for the people who love anishinaabe life and who have, up until this point, taught me. Jules Casselman was my teacher and friend and she helped me start my daughter's life with anishinaabe teachings. she was also the first woman to ever look me in the eyes and say these words: "what do you think about this, Christine . . . ?" i was in my late 20s and we were cleaning cedar at her kitchen table.

island lake home, fall, 2004

when i was able to, i ceremonied her and our connection back to aki with her placenta. up until this time it rested, in frozen incubation through various moves. we do what we have to and we do what we can, when we can.

in overcoming my shame for not being able to ceremony her placenta in the way some of the traditionalists indicate, i honoured the circumstances of my own life. i consider that traditionalists often do not likely speak from a place of recognition of the fact that many indigenous women live diverse, complicated, and difficult lives with variable access to nurturing relationships, valuable knowledges, land, and financial and material resources. add to the mix feminist-thinking indigenous women, and you get another layer of disconnection.

when the time was right, my relationship with the lands i grew up in, and memories of some of those women teachers, brought me to ceremony. i returned her placenta to the land and spirits in the forest that was my childhood yard. despite being alone and afraid, in the middle of that ceremony, aki, manidooyag, ininaatig, and mashkiki assured me that everything would be fine: i was not alone; the land would take care of us. walking back down the hill from beneath the halo of that crimson maple tree, i was newly filled with the courage to face my biggest fear: being a single mother.

white supremacy, the place, 2006+

"mom, why is everybody here white?" she says to me, once, after daycare.

surprised by her four-year-old observation i think she is too young for the truth. i tell her anyways.

years later, "mom, you're not brown. you're white, too, like everyone else."

i look at my skin. "yep." it's the first time i'm ever told this, always being the other in a white world. "and?"

"i don't know. i get lonely. papa's the only one with skin like me and his skin is not even the same brown."

"i'm sorry, my girl. i know it must be hard. how do you feel about me being white?"

"it doesn't matter. you're my mom."

bell hooks becomes our best friend, our bestbookfriend.

> a: [Laughs.] I like this part, a lot. [Points to the line, "It doesn't matter. You're my mom."]
>
> w: Really? What do you like about it?
>
> a: Well, it's like, "Oh. Okay. I'm over it now."

TinTin, and the male francophone teacher who teaches it, are not our bestbookfriend. we learn again that in canada, when you call out racism sometimes you get an incredible story—une histoire incroyable—about being here for a few hundred years, being victimized by the english, and how violent the sun is in his classroom.

the sun is taken out of school a month early that year for her safety because the systemic structure of white male bosses does absolutely nothing.

at the same age, there was also the white father who accosted her on the schoolground in front of white friends and a white female schoolyard supervisor who did nothing to stop him. he said she made his daughter cry and he made my daughter cry. swift intervention on our part as parents and the principal, too, however here's something interesting: the father apologized to the principal for violating a rule which remains vague but never once humbled himself before the sun. the principal, when challenged by me to compel the parent to apologize for his behaviour, refused. here is the moment when white male ally to indigenous women and girls of colour departs to keep himself centred in the hierarchical, institutionalized structures and systems of white settler-colonial, male patriarchal power. there would be no apology for anything. i leave the office grateful to be able to name his particular brand of allyship as false generosity. i see the poster for restorative justice is still on the bulletin board outside his office and laugh.

earlier, at seven, a racist joke about how nobody likes the black jellybeans and five years later an aggressive verbal attack from said girl's mother. to this day, i remain open to creation providing an opportunity to respond to this woman in a profound way. something to do in the way of powerful, like (no) eye-contact; a diplomatic word or two said in passing. something that lingers. a haunting. spirit work.

> a: Mom! This—"something that lingers. a haunting. spirit work."
> [Looks at me and smiles.] I like this, a lot.

and, "mom, how come everyone in my class knows about the holocaust but i don't?"

"because you need to know about your own holocausts as fulani, walof, anishinaabe."

silence.

"why are they teaching you this and not the atrocities here on the turtle?"

"good question."

and,

"mom, we're learning how to be good canadian citizens."

"oh really? does that include how to be a good treaty person?"

"no. but i asked about that."

and, later,

"mom, my friends think i'm bad for always asking the teachers why they don't talk about colonization. i'm getting a reputation."

"mom, mr(s). ______ said the word 'anishinaabe' today over the p.a. system. and there is a medicine wheel on the bulletin board in the main hall. there's a map of all the first nations in ontario up now, too."

"mom, they brought in this indigenous performance group from toronto and mr(s). ________ was very clear to the students about having to be respectful to the performers. the whole school is going to the pow-wow in june and they're circulating a survey to see who wants to learn anishinaabemowin."

"mom, i really like mr(s). __________, the student teacher. they're black and i never get to have teachers who have the same colour of skin as me. and, they're not afraid to use the word colonization or talk about it happening here."

"it's okay, mom. i'll be safe."

i'm here, laid up from a pulled sciatica and can hardly move. she is seven and ready to walk to the bus stop by herself.

"okay. but here's the plan."

she is happy. new freedom! and, at eleven, "mom, can i ride my bike to the school and meet my friends?"

jezus christ. my heart beats faster. i do not want to deal with this.

"okay. here are the rules . . . ."

i take a deep breath, smudge, put my asemaa down.

i just let my daughter go bike riding in this white town.

what was i thinking?

i was thinking great kind mystery. i was thinking pawaamanag. i was thinking she's a tween who wants to go

hang with her friends.

> a: [Laughs.] Ha, Mom. I remember this. You literally followed me in the car with check-in points along the way.

"mom, i can't not ride the city bus because we live in a white city! i'm sure there are many black girls that ride buses in cities and i'm sure nothing bad ever happens to them."

and then the hot summer day came: "mom. today, me and —— were riding our bikes down the river trail and these guys in a truck went by and yelled out 'effing n-word.'" i can see she is disturbed, unsettled, sad, confused. i rage at the violence inflicted and the danger she was in; the danger her friend would have been in had he intervened, even if he was able. it seems hopeless. we process. we plan for safety. we smudge and we locate this squarely back on that truck, those men. we blame the city.

> a: I remember this. We were biking away from home on the trail and I remember the sun was setting.

and then it's late spring and she is free. really free. she has bus fare and a bank card. she hangs with her friends in the mall and makes a stop at a store in the neighbourhood on her way back home. we touch base and i hear joy in her voice, "no, i'll walk home from there, mom. it's a nice day." a little while later, a call: "hi mom. can you come get me?" i'm a bit surprised by this change in plan and think i hear something in her voice that's a bit off.

i see her on the corner of the street. she has a bouquet of flowers and i remember it's mother's day. i smile. that kid! i wonder why she's waiting there when she could have kept walking toward home. she gets in and i sense her energy is off. after checking in with her she tells me that as she was walking down the street, some young womxn in a car yelled out the n-word at her: "mom, i didn't realize at first what happened but then i did realize. that woman literally leaned over from her driver's side to call me that out the passenger window."

i am always at a loss for what to say to her at times like this. "i'm sorry, my girl" seems weak, meek, puny. i say it anyways. i do my best to be empowering—do you want to talk about it? now? later? do you want to share details? i ask her if i can ask her details. i don't know why they are important. we know that violence can be emitted by anyone but i guess the details give me something to sink my teeth into, assess. try to understand. but in a white supremacist society, there is no understanding. there is just coping, surviving, and creating relationships of people who love you and will be there for you when you experience violence and are hurting.

"mom, it felt dehumanizing."

i'm struck at her use of this word. i'm grateful she has it and the power of language to describe how she feels, what she thinks, and how she has been impacted.

"well my girl, it felt dehumanizing because that's what that word, in that context, is intended to do. that's what those womxn were up to when they did that to you."

and suddenly, as though this alchemy of language, naming, and validation created the perfect medicine, the energy shifts. i see the weight on her spirit lift with the slight shift in her body language. and, just like that she is back to herself. i'm awed by her magic and will to be free.

later, i drive down the street, trying to see what those womxn saw: a young, vibrant, strong, brown body with a confident step and a bouncy ponytail pushing ecstatically at the day. they saw a beautiful, black girl on a beautiful spring day carrying a beautiful bouquet of spring flowers and they wanted to make that stop.

and, it's on them.

there are anti-black attitudes among indigenous peoples, too. in her world, indigenous womxn—elderly and middle-aged—have admonished her in her girlhood playfulness, have been harsh to her in her kindness, shown preferential treatment to the not-black indigenous kids (including those who have white privilege for many reasons including because they are white passing). in some cases, she has been erased from publicized versions of community land-based and ceremonial stories she was a part of—stories of anti-anishinaabe racism and anishinaabe "resurgence." and, she has been deeply hurt by indigenous men who've uplifted and rewarded young boys who did not contribute while simultaneously diminishing her hefty contributions. she raises an eyebrow to it all. all these truths are in her bundle. i have no idea if she'll ever give voice to these things beyond the mother-daughter intimacy that exists between us and this, our/her/my testimony.

sidney-by-the-sea, summer, 2016

a: Mom, all the people here are old and white.

w: I know.

a: They stare at me.

w: I know. I've seen them. I don't like it.

a: It's like they've never seen a Black person before.

w: Well, they probably haven't seen someone so beautiful before but I know that's not the point. I get that it's rude, about power, and invasive.

a: It's rude!

w: I'm with you, child. I get it.

a: I'm learning how to stare back.

w: [Laughs.] Really?!

a: Yep. If they're going to stare at me, I'm learning to stare right back at them. It works too! I mean they eventually look away. I like how it feels to be able to do that.

w: You still have to be careful. White people are allowed to stare at Black people but when you do the same thing back it will be considered aggressive.

a: I know. It feels good though to learn how to start using eye contact with them. And to get them to stop staring. I see some of them staring at you too and I'm like, "'Boy! Or, 'Yo, lady, we're together!'"

w: [Laughs.] My little protector.

the foothills of ŁAU,WELNEW, 2016

as she grows into herself and negotiates her world, i often think of where she's going and where life will take her. a few years ago, she posed a hesitant question:

"mom, will you be angry with me if i don't practise anishinaabe ways?"

i smile because i knew this was coming. i'm touched by her consideration. also, i feel a slight tugging in my heart.

"no, my girl. your life is your own." i pause. "but, you do know that you don't get to choose being anishinaabe, right? how you honour and recognize the gifts and responsibilities that come with that though is up to you."

"yea. i know." she pauses. "you know i still talk to gizhe manidoo and my protectors a lot, right?"

"do you?" my heart leaps. that's half the battle right there—recognizing there is something greater than ourselves that is kind and that we also have protectors to help us with much of the work of being here in this physical world.

w: [Standing at the kitchen counter reviewing this paper.] I had this same feeling when you read your leadership camp application to me.

a: Really?

w. Yep. When they asked you what you would do if you were ruler of the world and you said the first thing you would do would be to make Canada get right with Indigenous peoples? [Smiles a big smile.] That made my heart just swell up.

a: Hmmm. [Smiles. Nods her head as if saying "Ah yes."] So, do you wanna see me dab to Frank Sinatra, Mom?

w: [Laughs.] Um, yea!!

a: [Scrolls through her phone, plugs into the speakers, "Girl from Ipanema" starts playing. As she dabs, her curly, take-up space hair with the mahogany-reddish remnants of an old dye job shimmers and bounces beneath the kitchen lights here in our den located in the damp, wet foothills of a mountain.]

Glossary

aki – popularly translated as land
anishinaabe'aadiziwin – culture
asemaa – tobacco as medicine; used to make offerings or requests
bimaadiziwin – life; the process or art of living life
ininaatig(oog) – maple tree(s); sugar maple
jiibay miikaana – spirit trail; the Milky Way; Anishinaabe believe that our spirits return to this trail when our spirits leave this world
ŁAU, WELNEW – place of refuge in the SENĆOTEN language of the WSÁNEĆ people on Vancouver Island, BC. it is the place name of their mountain, also known to the settlers as Mt. Newton.
manidooyag – spirits
mashkiki – medicine
mokijiwanibiish – water coming up out of the earth; spring water
nibi – water
n'ode – my heart
nokomis giizhigaatig – grandmother cedar
pawaamin(aag) – dream; protectors
waabanong – the east; where the spirit of the east lives

Notes

1 This description of forests in anishnnaabewaki is found in Liz Howard, *Infinite Citizen of the Shaking Tent*.

CHAPTER 11

Toward an Indigenous Relational Aesthetics: Making Native Love, Still

LINDSAY NIXON

As someone with an academic background in feminist thought, I came to theorizations of love through the field of feminist ethics. I have pored over pages of feminist ethicists the likes of Card, Gilligan, and Friedman, considering how the revolution isn't just grandiose statements of anti-state action but informed by the way we care for one another throughout revolutionary states.[1] White feminism rightly asserts that ethical love ontologies require reciprocity and equality, denouncing colonial conceptions of love that constrain through obligation and ownership, uncorrupt love (as Hardt and Negri might say)[2] does not succumb to subject/object binaries or inflict personal will on others.[3]

But even in my early readings of the white feminist ethics of care and love, I noticed a mirroring of lifeways found within communities of colour: relational (and ethical) ways of being, grounded in responsibilities to communities of origin—a "being through love," as bell hooks described.[4] Ethical love is a pedagogy of relationality taught to Indigenous peoples by their kin—siblings, aunties, grandparents, and other individuals of influence—and activated, its animated self, through attentiveness to kinship responsibilities.[5] Ethical love, being in a good way with all Creation, is something that is learned by feeling, doing, being, building, and even destroying—by enacting relations with one's self and the surrounding world.[6] Perhaps this is why the ethics of love emerged so organically from women of colour feminisms (like those of Simpson and hooks): because they mirror networks of care that already existed within communities of colour. White feminism's ethics of love seem somehow cerebral, lacking the same heart, in comparison.

As I argue in this chapter, Indigenous creators and cultural workers unleash Indigenous Relational Aesthetics (IRA) on settler-dominated arts institutions and within their own communities to transform histories of unethical relationality—imagining revolutionary futures for Indigenous peoples contending with settler-colonial presents by enacting Indigenous IRA to inform feminist change. Practitioners of IRA hold that Indigenous feminist revolution is achieved by positively transforming our relationships to be more ethical, both within and without our communities, and by healing our connectedness to all Creation. Not to be confused with Nicolas Bourriaud's philosophical writing and art criticism about relational aesthetics,[7] IRA is a reappropriation of the term to describe relational ways of making art encoded within Indigenous epistemologies.[8] Though art critics have begun to appeal to relational philosophies to account for the artist's place within a web of spaces and communities associated with art industries, relational aesthetics mirror Indigenous kinship ontologies that have existed in Indigenous communities since time immemorial, and can only be appropriated, observed, and described by non-Indigenous critics (much like the feminist ethics of care).

Drawing from interviews with former members of Nation to Nation (N2N), an arts collective founded by Skawennati,[9] Ryan Rice,[10] and Eric Robertson,[11] along with archival items provided Rice, I posit that N2N's late-1990s touring exhibition *Native Love* exemplifies how Indigenous peoples ground curatorial and creative practices in IRA to enact feminist change within art museums, the dominant arts community, and the Indigenous art community itself. In this chapter, I will discuss *Native Love* and the curatorial efforts of N2N as a case study for the essential qualities of IRA: creating, curating, and facilitating aesthetics of (Indigenous) love that inadvertently address intra-community differentiation within Indigenous art communities; forging new pathways in community-engaged curation that break away from Canada's institutional arts and culture sectors, thereby activating the communities where one stands; and disrupting colonial understandings of material cultures—ontologies that Kim TallBear has called (Indigenous) new materialisms—and thereby expressing an aliveness extended to art itself. I will conclude this chapter with a brief consideration of what it might entail to identify as a relational critic and to embed IRA throughout one's art criticism.

Love Aesthetics

In settler discourse, we see a plethora of distortions that portray a homogenous Indigenous sexuality, and one that is often hypersexualized and fetishized in order to legitimate the settler-colonial project and mark Indigenous bodies as violable and consumable, thereby promoting sexual violence perpetrated against Indigenous peoples.[12] Paradoxically, Indigenous life is considered extinct, of the past, disappearing, incapable of achieving the sexual modernity of settlers, and made a battleground for the naturalization of colonialism vis-à-vis hetero- and cis-normativity.[13] The settler-colonial project functions to supplant Indigenous peoples with the Europatriarchal family structure—a neo-liberal ideology meant to uphold the values of the settler nation by infiltrating our domestic lives.[14]

An ethnographic approach derived from settler anthropology and popular museology might reduce Indigenous love to primitive sexualities that serve colonial domination. Voyeuristic representations of "Two-Spirit" position multiple Indigenous genders as a curiosity of the past (think of We'wha at the Smithsonian,[15] or George Catlin's *Dance to the Berdash*).[16] Alternatively, Indigenous sexualities in the museum may be hypersexualized: from Jan van der Straet's *Allegory of America* utilizing Indigenous women's bodies to visually reference the penetrable Americas,[17] reinforcing the concept of *terra nullius* in sixteenth- and seventeenth-century Europe, to Gauguin's fetishistic paintings of the women of Tahiti that maintained visualities of sexual and territorial conquest in the contemporary.[18] Indeed, Indigenous relationalities, in their many manifestations, have been encroached upon by the settler-colonial project, become a source of frequent misrepresentation, and been made a location for colonial-capitalist biopolitical regulation. How then can we begin to conceptualize a return to Indigenous notions of relationality using methodologies that do not force us to appeal to the same colonial logic that sought to control our love in the first place?

For *Native Love*, N2N drew from their Indigenous teachings to articulate and reclaim an aesthetics of Indigenous love, free of colonial voyeurism or objectification. Mary Anne Barkhouse, Florene Belmore, and Michael Belmore's installation *Lick, Kill, Frolic* (1995) playfully engaged themes from the Bondage, Discipline, Sadism, and Masochism (BDSM) community by positioning a set of mirrors opposite a lineup of dog collars: when viewers looked into the mirrors they became the sub in a puppy-play kink dynamic. A bold exploration of consensual sex play, *Lick, Kill, Frolic* confronts the viewer with colonial power dynamics entrenched within sexual relationships, asking the viewer to interact with the work and consider their relatedness to submission, to being dominated, using BDSM as a consensual sex-positive space to work through colonial affect.

Arguably the standout artwork from the show was *COSMOSQUAW* (1996) by Lori Blondeau and Bradley LaRocque. LaRocque, who photographed Blondeau, is well known for the iconic photo taken of him during the Oka Crisis as the camouflage-clad warrior who went face to face with a Canadian military officer. With its tongue-in-cheek portrayal of Blondeau's hypersexualized body and correlate stereotypes of Native womanhood, *COSMOSQUAW* grapples with complex issues of gender, sexuality, and representation as played out on Native women's bodies.

Audra Simpson's catalogue text for *Native Love* argues that the curators, writers, and artists who participated in the exhibit were desperately seeking representations of the unique intimacies they saw flowing throughout Indigenous communities, intimacies consistently misrepresented when perceived through settler aesthetics. Simpson writes, "This is an exhibition that contemplates our experiences, that represents ourselves, our lives and what is important to us. Love is an emotion, a gesture and a contradiction. Love gives structure to our lives and at the same time seems shapeless, ephemeral and strong. The artists participating in this project recognize the importance of Love, in its many forms to all of us—they recognize that Love matters to us as Indian people in these moments, in the beautiful present of our lives."[19] Simpson's text reads like a love manifesto, written with the same sense of urgency and community-based movement-building apparent throughout the DIY exhibition.[20] Simpson and N2N were giving voice to early Indigenous feminist and queer perspectives on issues of love, sex, and sexuality within art, and in doing so exposed intra-community differentiation within the Indigenous art canon of the time.

The marginalization of feminist perspectives within Indigenous art has persisted until recently because of its predominantly masculinist and male-dominated composition, culture, and canon, and because its existence as a microcosm community flattens difference.[21] Institutional critique has been plentiful within Indigenous art, from admonishing institution-led attempts at reconciliation[22] to expressing the need for decolonization of thought about Indigenous peoples.[23] But the Indigenous art community itself requires Indigenous feminist intervention, and more thorough consideration of unethical relationality within its own mechanisms, communities, and spaces. As art historian Richard Hill has written, we are living in an era of Indigenous art defined by identity politics and a culture of silence that stifles dissent, thereby halting transformative critique of one another as Indigenous cultural workers.[24]

N2N wanted to present art about bodies, gender, sex, love, relationality, care, and intimacy that portrayed their communities with as much aliveness as they truly contained, in a post-Oka climate wherein gallerists and curators only wanted masculinist work about "machine guns and razor wire."[25] N2N did not want to limit themselves to traditional or contemporary methods that predominated in the gallery, preferring instead to subvert that binary by integrating themes like love and sex with traditional practices, and including new media, inventive materials, and performance throughout their activations.[26] Ahasiw Maskegon-Iskwew accurately predicted the importance of N2N's work in a 1996 piece on *Native Love* for *FUSE*, calling the exhibition "the child of a new generation."[27] N2N was part of a generation of Indigenous creators and cultural workers imagining a new and ethical future for their communities through IRA, and in doing so made space for voices and themes that had been previously pushed out of the contemporary Indigenous art canon.

Activating Community

Canada's art industry is host to complex racial and gendered inequalities in need of untangling. As artist Deanna Bowen discusses in her recent interview with art writer Amy Fung, racism and sexism manifest as affect within arts administrations that reify hierarchies of difference, a culture of toxic whiteness and masculinity upheld by a "deadly silence of the masses."[28] Fung reflects on the fact that many senior-level positions in the arts are held by white men, and Bowen on the reality that people of colour are still being forced to create from a space of defence and institutional critique in the face of a white normative Canadian art industry.[29]

Indigenous cultural workers have the unique experience of working toward equitable relationships with Canada's art industries within territories upon which settler-colonial arts institutions interrupt their cultural sovereignty. Museums, in particular, has fraught, decades-old relationships with Indigenous communities. One could argue that archival museums have always been a space for showcasing Western dominance, where hordes of Indigenous objects are displayed for the settler gaze, populated through the pillaging and robbing of Indigenous gravesites.[30] Around the time *Native Love* was organized, the infamous Task Force Report on Museums and First Peoples, a partnership between the Canadian Museums Association and the Assembly of First Nations, was born out of the controversy over the Lubicon Lake First Nation's boycott of

The Spirit Sings at the Glenbow Museum in Calgary.[31] Lubicon was opposed to the portrayal of Indigenous culture because the exhibit was sponsored by Shell Oil, with whom Lubicon was in a court battle over land claims.[32]

Native Love was brought to life entirely outside of the gallery and its settler actors—a space where N2N did not see themselves represented—at a time when Indigenous art was increasingly tied up in arts bureaucracy and monopolized by organizations like the Society of Canadian Artists of Native Ancestry (SCANA).[33] There was a divide between older generations of Indigenous artists, defined by SCANA, and a younger generation who sought to carve out a space for themselves within Indigenous art.

Skawennati and Rice remember piling into Rice's car—without a map—certain that they would eventually make it to Halifax, where SCANA was holding its last conference in 1993.[34] They did make it, only to have their community-based art actions belittled and called "student art" by SCANA artists, which N2N felt reconstituted colonial values within the Indigenous art community.[35] But the remnants of SCANA's crumbling infrastructure were forewarnings to N2N, who rejected the institutionalization and insular nature of SCANA, which they saw as ultimately leading to the organization's downfall.[36]

In the *Native Love* archive I found an artist's contract drafted in 1996 that mentions N2N had submitted a grant application to the Canada Council for the Arts for a *Native Love* publication.[37] Skawennati and Rice confirmed that the Canada Council denied their application.[38] In a curator's talk written for *Native Love*, Rice reflected on N2N's inability to access support from both granting institutions and the contemporary Indigenous art community. "I wasn't part of any particular artist community and felt very out of touch," said Rice.[39] "We decided that we shouldn't and can't wait for opportunity to be knocking at our doors, because in the real world it was just not happening."[40] As Skawennati put it, this was a generation of Indigenous artists ready to "force their way in."[41]

Without having the Western frameworks to describe the relational praxes at the core of their work (Western relational aesthetics in art theory would not emerge until 1998),[42] N2N began organizing art actions at a time when Indigenous art was just starting to find its way into the white cubes of contemporary art galleries.[43] *Native Love* also came about before independent curation was prevalent, when curators were a few specialized peoples who worked within galleries—"before everyone was a curator," as Ryan Rice observed.[44] This stands in contrast to today, where there is a wide array of curators working at various levels within and without art galleries—an era of curationism, as David Balzer coined it.[45] Skawennati reflected on arriving for what she thought was an artist's talk to promote *Native Love*, and the gallery manager asked her if she was the curator: "I didn't even think of myself as a curator, until then."[46]

The loft used for the inaugural show in Montreal, lent to N2N by a local arts collective, had wall-to-wall windows and no walls—to display the art, organizers improvised with bookshelves that had been left in the space.[47] At sundown, they realized there were no lights and rushed out to buy a dozen desk lamps from Canadian Tire, which would promptly be taken back the next day.[48] Artists and writers collaborated on artworks for *Native Love*, and many participants ended up working with family members in respect of kinship that already existed within the communities from which the work derived. What resulted was a DIY, multidisciplinary curation that represented all facets of Indigenous life regardless of celebrity or tenure, thereby bypassing and refusing recognition from the institutions that had kept them out for so long.[49]

From the modest inaugural event in Montreal and the webs of intimacy it created, *Native Love* became a series of shows across Canada. As the exhibition moved, local artists would join the quickly expanding roster, which by the end included George Littlechild, Mary Longman, Paul Chaat Smith, Thirza and Ruth Cuthand, Bradlee Laroque, Lori Blondeau, Shelley Niro, Daniel David Moses, Cheryl L'Hirondelle, and others. *Native Love* would be installed in spaces in Peterborough, Saskatoon, Winnipeg, Brantford, and Victoria—cities across Turtle Island with expansive Indigenous populations within or surrounding them—continuing its community-based intentionality by showing only in artist-run centres.

In an exhibition proposal for *Native Love*, N2N described their work as a "dialogue between peoples" and a "movement"—a constantly mutating collective that moves nomadically from space to space, city to city, and nation to nation.[50] N2N considered themselves community organizers who facilitated collaboration between Indigenous creators, and activated their communities through art.[51] In lieu of funding and institutional supports, and breaking away from the art industrial complex they saw as pacifying generations of Indigenous artists before them, N2N created new pathways for Indigenous arts organizing, pathways grounded in IRA. Considering themselves facilitators of spaces wherein the resulting social relations at the core of their projects were the central focus of the work,[52] N2N suggested that creating a space for togetherness, ceremony, and collaboration is in itself art, life, and love.

Indigenous Materialities

Indigenous artists and curators have always had a unique vantage point for the consideration of material animacy, relationality, and philosophies because of their continued animation of material objects like beading and quillwork. Jolene Rickard has considered how wampum represents the political, social, and cultural order of Haudenosaunee society, constituting a multi-sensory Indigenous technology that activates traditional knowledges.[53] The Indigenous relational artist or curator questions the confines of settler materialities—such as space-time, language, and written law—opting instead to examine Indigenous nonlinear narrative form, which exists in multiple physical and spatial realms, from our dream visions to our waking lives.[54]

For *Native Love*, Rose Spahan and Jeannette Armstrong (who is often credited as being the first Indigenous woman in Canada to have a published novel in Canada)[55] collaborated on a work entitled *Indians After Sex* (1995). Armstrong and Spahan contest the notion of a disappearing North American Indian at the level of Indigenous sexuality, by reanimating Indigenous materialities that are presumed dead, ancient, and sterile through sexual intimacy. Two Northwest Coast–style masks lie in bed together, as one smokes a post-coital cigarette. Far from the anthropological representations of Indigenous materialities found in museums, the masks are sexual and agential beings. Scribbled words are visible all over the blanket, another object used in ceremony among West Coast nations, some words easier to make out than others. One section of the blanket appears adorned with a conversation shared between the two masks—a love ceremony, perhaps:

> "I'm really in love with you."
>
> "I know, I love you too."

Paul Chaat Smith worked with his sister Diane Chaat Smith on a piece called *Awl and Case* (1999). *Awl and Case* features an awl (a tool made out of bone, meant to poke holes in animal hides), displayed on a table alongside a beaded and fringed suede case. The accompanying text written by Paul Chaat Smith makes apparent that Diane Chaat Smith made the case: "Last night [Diane] told me about the ghost dance shirts she and Jake make. The shirts are decorated with the sun and the moon, and a man in Louisiana who works on the oil rigs buys them sometimes. . . . Diane explains ghost dance is about the love of the earth and the buffalo, and 'you know everything I make is with all the love in my heart.'"

Paul Chaat Smith admits he teared up after hearing his sister's words, having thought she had been somewhat listless throughout her life. When Diane Chaat Smith described preparing the ghost shirts to her brother—any variation of material processes depending on the creator, which could include beading, fringe, and designs made from traditional dye compounds—the power shifted in their relationship. Ghost shirts are imbued with spiritual essence, alive and capable of guarding the wearer against external harm—a spiritual force that Diane Chaat Smith lovingly stitches into her shirts, bringing the garments into relation with herself and those she gifts the shirts to. In awe of his sister's "magnificent and mysterious strength," Paul Chaat Smith criticizes himself for having underestimated her when she is such a strong force of love and kinship.

Fine art museums house imperial ideology in the form of curated sacred Indigenous objects presented as "craft," and colonial-era art by white peoples that comprises a visual mythology about the imaginary Indian. The disappearing Indian is a visual catalogue constructed through settler history that portrays Indigenous peoples as dying out and ultimately of the past,[56] thereby discursively preserving the removal of Indigenous life from land and a continuation of settler-colonial occupation.[57] But the work in *Native Love* understands that Indigenous materialities, such as beadwork on an awl or ghost dance shirts, are sacred, susceptible to corruption and bad medicine, and considered within ontologies like kinship to be forms of animate life.

It is as academic Kim TallBear has described in her research on (Indigenous) new materialisms: to Indigenous peoples specific "objects" and "forces," like stones and shells used for wampum, are considered agential beings, alive and containing a soul.[58] IRA makes space for materialist feminist considerations within curatorial and creative practices, resisting a sole focus of human-to-human relationalities within extended kinship networks and a limited understanding of material relations as enacted primarily between bodies and bodies. Materialities, objects like beading and quillwork, can love, be loved, and instill love, relating to the communities from which they derive.

Thinking beyond Criticism

I want to conclude with a brief discussion of how IRA methodologies can be extended to art criticism. To be a relational critic is to extend principles of ethical relationality, kinship, and love in order to promote feminist change within the art industries through one's writing. For me, representation has been an important aspect of grounding my criticism in IRA methodologies. It was my relationships with artists, made through community-based art actions, that made me consider arts writing because from what I could see, there was little coverage of Indigenous feminist and LGBTQ art within the Indigenous art canon, which I viewed as being masculinist in its history and contemporary affect.

Further, the practice of IRA within the field of art criticism hinges on making kin beyond the limits of production and the industry, and on finding new ways to grow capacity, community, resources, and mutual respect, ensuring the industries we work in are more equitable by enacting a positive relationality with one another. In real time, this means my arts writing derives from my relationships. I have remained unconcerned with writing about art that is trending inside the white box. Instead, my work has focused on relationship-building projects that draw from the strength of positive connections throughout the community, and not just between people within the machine of "Indigenous art" in Canada, either—extending kinship to other racialized communities and centring black solidarity, for instance.

I work with individuals with whom I can build long-term creative kinship, artists who have been historically marginalized within the Indigenous art canon, whom I can help with access to resources and whose work represents the love that I know Indigenous art is capable of embodying. I write from the heart, and from the communities who show me love—a direct homage to earlier generations like Nation to Nation. Indigenous relational criticism is a fostering of mutually supportive relations, principles passed down from generations before us, and from their ancestors before them, and so forth, in cyclical connection all the way back to the ancestors.

Notes

1 Card, "Caring and Evil"; Gilligan, "Resisting Injustice"; Friedman, "Liberating Care."

2 Hardt and Negri, "De Singularitate 1: Of Love Possessed."

3 Beauvoir, *The Ethics of Ambiguity*, 66–85.

4 hooks, "Love as the Practice of Freedom," in *Outlaw Culture*.

5 Simpson, "'I See Your Light': Reciprocal Recognition and Generative Refusal," "Embodied Resurgent Practice and Coded Disruption," "Constellations of Coresistence," chaps. 10–12 in *As We Have Always Done*.

6 Simpson, *Dancing on Our Turtle's Back*, 144.

7 Bourriaud, *Relational Aesthetics*.

8 Simpson, *Islands of Decolonial Love*.

9 Skawennati is an independent artist and co-director of AbTeC at Concordia University.

10 Ryan Rice is curator and chair of the Indigenous arts program at the Ontario College of Art and Design.

11 Eric Robertson is an independent artist.

12 Smith, *Conquest*.

13 Morgensen, *Spaces between Us*.

14 Smith, "Heteropatriarchy and the Three Pillars of White Supremacy."

15 Roscoe, *The Zuni Man-Woman*.

16 George Catlin, *Dance to the Berdash*, 1835–37, oil on canvas, Smithsonian American Art Museum, Washington, DC, https://americanart.si.edu/artwork/dance-berdash-4023/.

17 Jan van der Straet, *Discovery of America: Vespucci Landing in America*, 1587–89, pen and brown ink, brown wash, heightened with white, over black chalk, The Met, New York, https://www.metmuseum.org/art/collection/search/343845.

18 Paul Gauguin, *Delightful Land (Te Nave Nave Fenua)*, 1892, oil on canvas, Ohara Museum of Art, Japan, http://www.ohara.or.jp/en/gallery/te-nave-nave-fenua/#; Paul Gauguin, *Nevermore*, 1897, oil on canvas, The Courtauld Gallery, London, https://courtauld.ac.uk/gallery/collection/impressionism-post-impressionism/paul-gauguin-nevermore.

19 Simpson, "Making Native Love."

20 Simpson.

21 Nixon, "Making Space in Indigenous Art for Bull Dykes and Gender Weirdos."

22 Garneau, "Imaginary Spaces of Conciliation and Reconciliation."

23 Smith, *Decolonizing Methodologies*.

24 Nixon, "Making Space in Indigenous Art for Bull Dykes and Gender Weirdos."

25 Ryan Rice and Skawennati, interview by Lindsay Nixon, 25 February 2017, Montreal, QC, audio recording.

26 Rice and Skawennati.

27 Maskegon-Iskwew, "Native Love."

28 Fung, "The Past, The Present, and The Same."

29 Fung.

30 Garneau, presentation at the 2nd Annual Symposium on the Future Imaginary.

31 Task Force Report on Museums and First Peoples, *Turning the Page*.

32 Dibbelt, "Nations Gather to Protest Glenbow's Spirit Sings Display," 2.

33 Ryan Rice and Skawennati, interview by Lindsay Nixon, 25 February 2017, Montreal, QC, audio recording.

34 Rice and Skawennati.

35 Rice and Skawennati.

36 Rice and Skawennati.

37 Nation to Nation, artist's contract for shows at artist-run centres Artspace and AKA, March 1996, personal records of Ryan Rice.

38 Ryan Rice and Skawennati, interview by Lindsay Nixon, 25 February 2017, Montreal, QC, audio recording.

39 Ryan Rice, curator's talk, no date, handwritten on loose-leaf, personal records of Ryan Rice.

40 Rice.

41 Ryan Rice and Skawennati, interview by Lindsay Nixon, 25 February 2017, Montreal, QC, audio recording.

42 Bourriaud, *Relational Aesthetics*.

43 Ryan Rice and Skawennati, interview by Lindsay Nixon, 25 February 2017, Montreal, QC, audio recording.

44 Rice and Skawennati.

45 Balzer, *Curationism*.

46 Ryan Rice and Skawennati, interview by Lindsay Nixon, 25 February 2017, Montreal, QC, audio recording.

47 Rice and Skawennati.

48 Rice and Skawennati

49 Rice and Skawennati.

50 Nation to Nation, "Native Love: Exhibition Proposal," typed document, personal archive of Ryan Rice and Skawenatti.

51 Ryan Rice and Skawennati, interview by Lindsay Nixon, 25 February 2017, Montreal, QC, audio recording.

52 Rice and Skawennati.

53 Rickard, "Considering Traditional Practices of 'Seeing' as Future."

54 Rickard.

55 Jeannette Armstrong's novel *Slash* was published in 1985.

56 Francis, *The Imaginary Indian*.

57 Tuck and Yang, "Decolonization Is Not a Metaphor."

58 Muñoz, et al., "Theorizing Queer Inhumanisms," 234.

CHAPTER 12

Conversations on Indigenous Feminism

OMEASOO WĀHPĀSIW AND LOUISE HALFE

Miyo kesikaw

The cry is not so far away, just a few steps downward
to the guest room, he hasn't slept very long
short intervals of sleep so afraid he will miss out.
His small hands thump whatever is in his reach
as if he was conducting the house of parliament
he demands that we pay attention.

This evening I walked through rain-soaked grass
stole eighteen eggs right from the grackle's
beady eyes. She scolded me as if I was ripping
her heart out. But
the song birds are missing though the occasional
Baltimore oriole sings from the trees.
I miss the chortling harmony from the wild.

He sings to his mother's breast
hiccup songs of anticipation as the flow of
translucent white flows from the nipples.
It gushes as he sucks, so greedy with want.
He lets go, bends backward to survey the room
lifts his trunkish body, grabs his mother's chest
small mouth plastered against her frontier.

Figure 12.1. Louise Halfe with Miyo Kesikaw, 2017. Photo: Omeasoo Wāhpāsiw.

I should, I suppose, mourn for the unborn
chicks but I rationalize the prairie is dry
without the symphony of the song birds.
His little chortling, the pick-me-up cry
is harnessed to my heart,
my grandson, he is my prairie melody.

We are existing, side by side, mother and mother, in my father's house. In October 2016, I was pregnant with the baby, Miyo Kesikaw, who would come in November 2016. The Patriarchy constantly grated at me as a young woman, but not until I became pregnant (and gave birth) did it come crashing down around me. I think perhaps at its core Patriarchy is not a bad way to support families, or so I have been told. Unfortunately, most societies do not live by their ideals. The twisted Patriarchy we are left with had me feeling as if I was not important as a pregnant woman, or worse, as if I was a vulnerable sexual object. As a new mother, when I asked for support I was led to believe I was a whining child rather than a woman in need. In the comfort of my parents' house, surrounded by a different kind of Patriarchy, perhaps closer to its ideals, I rest with my baby, with my own mother, and plan, imagine a world where children are the centre. In this house, we are. I dream of the Matriarchy, where women make decisions for the best of the community—communal living, extended maternity leave, child care, and importantly, human-centred alternatives to capitalism.

In October, before the baby came, I wanted to know: How do women exist in the Patriarchy today? What does the Matriarchy look like from here? What can we do to transform our world to reflect back to us what we believe in, and is it possible for Indigenous women to grasp this vision? What is the vision? What is the past? How do women succeed and attain fulfillment when the roads to fulfillment offered are along Patriarchal, capitalist paths? Are these antithetical to the vision?

The following interview between myself and my mom, poet Louise Halfe, is what resulted from these thoughts. It could have taken place anywhere; we considered the warmth and comfort of her house near St. Denis, a straw-bale house full of artwork, the deep burnt-orange floor and walls of windows looking out over scrubby prairie, swept with snow. Instead, we met with our helper, Marnie Howlett, at the university, in a fishbowl-style room where we sat on hard plastic chairs and shared a meal of Vietnamese rolls and noodles. Either location could tell the story that is reiterated here, in these words: a story of privilege and reflection, resistance and entrenched accommodation. There are tensions in Indigenous feminism that demonstrate the even greater diversity and, some would say, lack of unity or consciousness that being radically feminist or racially Indigenous could empower. Andrea Landry tells Indigenous mothers to embrace a new reality, to "raise your iskwesis with love in her heart, fire in her spirit, and truth in her soul so that she may be unapologetically, wildly and ruthlessly free."[1] Kim TallBear describes a personal history of being uncomfortable organizing with women of colour feminists because she is a land-based woman who does not believe Indigenous women should be defined in relation to white men. TallBear said, "I come from a people . . . and I want to relate to others as coming from a people . . . not a category that centres white power."[2] Likewise, in Chapter 10, waaseyaa'sin considers motherhood and feminism from within the powerful grip of Patriarchy and multiple layers of racism—particularly the dual layers her daughter faces as a black Anishinaabe girl. These powerful indictments of colonial capitalism question and sometimes alienate Indigenous women who embrace a feminism that reflects what might be termed neocolonial trappings of success. The popular hashtags of 2016, #notyourmascot and #notyourstereotype, were often unapologetic proclamations of these trappings, including art gallery shows, publishing deals, philanthropy, tax paying, university advancement, and even light skin. These assertions demonstrate Indigenous complexity, including that many Indigenous people are or aspire to be a part of the middle and upper-middle classes.

At the same time, Indigenous peoples across Turtle Island have proclaimed commitment to our lands and drawn attention to the particular destruction that colonialism has to mostly matriarchal societies. Land-based Indigenous feminism is more diverse and complex than any tribe in North America, each with its own peculiar mixture of governance, society, economies, family dynamics, and history. Colonial destruction is in fact why many Indigenous peoples aim for neocolonial success; for some of our families, including mine (at least for my mother, myself, my brother, and our children), this is what saved us. My mother's work tells stories of what she escaped—alcoholism, physical and sexual violence—when she met my earnest, Canadian (white, Norwegian and British ancestry, two to four generations in the country) father, who by the time I was born was a family physician. And so, circularly, "as long as capitalism is alive and well we will struggle,"[3] and yet we all understand and acknowledge that to be Indigenous, and alive and kicking, is in itself an incredible act of survivance, commitment, and resistance. In what follows, tension is apparent.

How do we be Indigenous women, revive or believe in a Matriarchy for ourselves, and continue to exist and survive in the world we have been given?

Interview between Omeasoo Wāhpāsiw and Louise Halfe

1. The first series of questions establishes what we think of ourselves as feminists. The discussion is primarily focused on activism, which is in itself interesting. Does being a feminist necessarily demand activism? Is this even further required of Indigenous women?

Omeasoo: How do you see yourself engaging with the politics of feminism?

Louise: Oh boy.

Omeasoo: In your day-to-day life, even in your work? Or in any situation you find yourself?

Louise: Well, I think that I've always—I haven't belonged to a political organization per se—but I've always done my own thing as a feminist (as an iskwew). I need and want to clarify that word . . . feminism . . . I don't think that word belongs to me as a nêhiýaw iskwew. Nêhiýaw iskwew translate to a Cree Fire Woman. Hence, I am a womb-an-is, aware of my womb and her strength. In essence womb-an carry the fire within as well as being water carriers. We are creators and yes, can be destroyers. I am a survivor of many events in my life.

Omeasoo: What is that "own thing"?

Louise: Whatever is in front of me, I do it without social pressures, hopefully. For example, my career as a writer is on my own, essentially. And what I believe in, in terms of what I write about, has to do with all of humanity, and and it's coming from a feminist (womb-an-is) perspective, I suppose. One of my poems is about date rape, or the other one I can think of off hand is the losing of a child, and during mid-pregnancy. And having to deal with that from my perspective, from a woman's perspective, without any guidance from anybody, and having to work through that and recover from that.

Omeasoo: From an Indigenous woman's perspective, what do you think made that a particularly feminist experience?

Louise: It's a topic that most people don't talk about. It's a hush-hush topic. And I write about it so that it'll open the gates to anybody, regardless of whether they are Native or non-Native, to talk about the loss of a child in a healthy way.

Omeasoo: Right now, I'm lucky because my work is as a policy analyst with a Women's Commission. So, I get to research for them and provide them with support. And those are all really feminist issues. Outside of work I guess my main hobby right now is this kind of thing, academics. It's a very expensive hobby. I had the opportunity to go speak in my friend's class. And, did I tell you that I went to Katie's class?[4] It was really meaningful to me because one reason we do things in our life is for the next generations, and some of the Indigenous young people in the class came up to me afterwards. So, you can see that they are connecting with Indigenous professors. Given that Katie is not Indigenous—and she still is an amazing professor—I think it had a lot of meaning to them to be able to say, "Oh, you know, you're also Indigenous, I'm Indigenous, you know, tell me more about this, tell me more about that. And this is really exciting and interesting to me because you are an Indigenous person like me." I try to be engaged socially as much as I possibly can be in Take Back the Night March, Sisters in Spirit. You went to Sisters in Spirit.[5]

Louise: Yes. Yeah.

Omeasoo: So, what was your motivation to go?

Louise: That it was women supporting women. And because of the potential violence that Nêhiýaw women are subjected to. You know, I grew up watching my mother being violated in so many different ways, and that was something I swore that would never happen to me or my children.

Omeasoo: And for my part, when I participate, because I grew up with safety, thanks to you and thanks to Dad, and for other reasons, you know, our middle-class lifestyle. I think often that it's my white skin, so I feel safe a lot of the time. It's a huge privilege to feel that safe. But the reason I go to those marches is partly for the women themselves who have passed on, so their spirits know that our spirits are remembering them, and thinking about them, and providing support to them, wherever they are. And the other reason is that I've heard that sometimes the impact of those marches is that the men who have committed the crimes have a harder time with their consciences when they realize that these women are valued. And that conscience is the public coming forward and saying that this is not okay.

2. The next set of questions have to do with our role—in our families, communities, and the nation. This is an important part of the discussion, since I was raised to "honour the Creator by honouring my gifts and blessings." How do we each honour our own gifts and blessings? How do we discover what these are when we are distracted by other needs in our families and communities? Or are the roles we play in our families and communities in fact our gifts and blessings, in and of themselves?[6]

Omeasoo: What do you understand as your role as a woman in your family, community, and the nation?

Louise: Well, there's no doubt that in my family, in our family of origin, that I am a matriarch. I'm not saying my life around you revolves around me, but that our little unit, your dad and I, is a stabilizing influence, and we are always there and we are always together. And I think that as a family, that's really important to be there for our children, regardless of how far away they are. And so I see my role as a wife and a mother, and as a grandmother, as really important.

In terms of community, my understanding is that I have a good reputation in this community and that's good to know. I've been told that. I am also regarded as an Elder, which is a real honour, although I don't feel I'm deserving of it. But I also want to say that my community is really large, so I guess I'll answer the next question, [about my role] in the nation. Because that's my community as well; I have an idea that my community is quite universal, because of my role as a writer. I am reaching a lot of people.

Omeasoo: What do you think makes you a role model?

Louise: Oh, many different things, in terms of behaviour. I'm a non-drinker, I don't smoke, so that reinforces good role modelling. I try to achieve as much as I can, I'm always striving for a little bit more than I can, although that doesn't seem like that most the time, but that is my goal.

Being Indigenous in this country is really important and I represent it. Whether I like it or not, I represent nêhiýaw people, and so my behaviour is really important because people scrutinize that. Like I don't run around, I don't smoke, I don't drink, and people do scrutinize that. Not only for my community, the Aboriginal community, but also the non-Native community here. They're henpecking us to death as it is, so they're looking for ways to drag us down, and say "See, we told you all the time that you were just drunk and lazy Indians," you know.

I don't put myself in that position, but I am aware that I am being put in that position. It's a given.

How do you see your role, Omeasoo?

Omeasoo: I'm still learning about my role as a woman in my family. Like you mentioned, our little family unit has seemed really small because we live far away from both sides of our family. So my responsibilities seem really limited, I guess, in that way. Because I haven't had to help raise other kids, or be involved with any family member's kids. But then the family that I am starting, I am still struggling with, and I am sure I will struggle with this for the rest of my life. My partner likes to tell me how strong I am. Once he said, You have so much love to give. You know, he was right. I have so much love to give. We were probably talking about how many kids we might have or something and I was saying, I don't want to go into this as if all of this weight is on my shoulders.

There are a lot of single mothers, a lot of women raising their kids on their own. And I have been told to just have kids on my own, and I am not interested in that. Nope, never have been, never will be. I see this as a partnership. And I think that's probably going to cause me some heartache, as I struggle to get the support that I need from my partner. But I think that's what I signed up for. I signed up for equality; I didn't sign up for anything less.[7]

I think sometimes about the narrative of a strong, Indigenous woman who can do it all by herself. I don't even want to buy into that narrative, because sure, I can [do it], but it doesn't mean that I want to.[8]

I don't want to. And I don't want anybody to expect me to. So, what if I am strong? What if I'm full of love? I am buying into this for equality. I don't know if that is crazy, or if it is too much to expect, or what. But that's what I want. That's what I want for myself.

And so, sometimes I do think that there are lessons in a lot of our teachings about being pitiful. About how we are given spiritual gifts because we are so pitiful and need help. Maybe that's where some of these lessons lie; I am not sure.

I feel that people have gone out of their way to be mentors to me. And so even though I am young, it is important to me to provide mentorship to young women, too, and support them, so that they feel strong to do what they want to do in the future. Because I think that there's more than enough beautiful life to go around. We should all be contributing with our own gifts and blessings and never underselling ourselves. It just takes too much; it takes too long in life to build the confidence that we need to move forward. So if we—I—try to support people to uncover their confidence before they need it, they are immediately building themselves up and they don't have to struggle, even though we will all struggle.

So I just try and pass that on as much as I can, I guess. And I wonder what will happen and how I will be needed. And I don't know what that means. Who's going to need me, where I'm going to be needed, what my role is—I don't know.

3. This exchange highlights how despite the positive ways that we want to see the world, there are a lot of overwhelmingly negative experiences that have pushed us, both my mom and me—and women at large—into a defence mode. These experiences include family violence and sexual violence, both real and in public imagery.

Louise: I think Kokom was a womb-an-is—a nêhiýaw iskwew through and through. She was—even though she was caught in this violent relationship—she was an incredibly strong woman and was always trying to think of ways to improve herself. She was artistic, she was a dancer, she was a storyteller, and a homemaker. But she strived to really work hard at those roles. Moosom tried to kill her spirit, but it was never, never killed; it persevered. I suppose [her spirit] was severely injured, because she was bitter in her older age, so no doubt it had left its mark.

Omeasoo: What role do you think the community plays in your belief system about being a woman?

Louise: There was no term "feminism" when I was growing up. I didn't really hear about it until probably in my late thirties. And then I didn't belong to a group, per se, but my actions were quite feminist and [your] Dad allowed that, for me to dream and to persevere and to move on. And he still encourages me to move beyond where I'm at. Except sometimes, I too feel constrained because I'm in a relationship, and to me, my relationship is much more important than pursuing some of my dreams, for example. I want to go to Santa Fe to go be an artist, right? He's waiting to retire to let me do that. And I don't want to leave the relationship to pursue that dream, because to me, that's not possible at the moment. I don't know if that answers any questions, dear.

But the community is good. The community is good to me. Like you, [I feel that] if they can utilize me, and if I can use them as an avenue to spread the good work on emotional healing, for example, I'm right there. I'm going to go for it—and attempt to role model that or give people the tools, if they want them. Not because I'm forcing anybody to use these tools, but if I'm invited, I share them willingly.

What informs your beliefs?

Omeasoo: I don't know. Obviously the way that I was raised with my parents is really fundamental. I remember when you and Dad had invited that man to have a sweat lodge on our land. I remember that. I remember going in the cold streams naked, when we were skinny-dipping on our mini camping trips, my favourite thing to do. And I remember spending so many hours outside in Meadow Lake. I know that I had that close connection to being outside all the time when I was little.

In terms of my role as a woman, I know I have spent my whole life watching you. And I have incorporated many beliefs, most of them good, some of them not so good, about how to be a woman from my own mom. And I think that's normal. I spend a lot of time thinking about that, and I don't know if other people do. But I think it's a good thing to reflect on. How have I learned how to be a woman, and what does that mean? Because not everything that you have chosen do I agree with. I think it's important to be self-reflective: What are the patterns that I have learned? What are the patterns that I appreciate? What are the patterns that I want to be slightly different in my own life?

You spoke a lot about the things that I learned from you already. I literally had a chat with myself about whether I wanted to give up my freedom. Because I really liked my single life; I was pretty happy. Did I want to give all of that up? And for women, it means health, wealth, and happiness—literally. Sociologists have shown that's what women give up for a relationship.

Do I want to give up my own health, wealth, and happiness for the opportunity to have a family with this man? This was a very early on conversation in my head. I decided that I did, because I felt that through that relationship I would have an opportunity to experience having my own family, and through the relationship with him, I felt that would give both of us an opportunity to grow emotionally and spiritually in a way that I couldn't do in any other way. And with someone that I really respected and valued. So I did make that choice. Pretty clearly in my head. Although I have heard that we humans just pretend that we are rational. So probably, I just liked him.

I think that when you spoke about your relationship and how much you value it, that probably was something that I felt brought a lot of meaning to your and Dad's life. And something that I wanted to experience for myself.

When I think about "the community," I think about the things that make me mad about society at large. I think about the messages that women are given on a daily basis—from people near and far, from media, from the way things work in general. Just the other day, our family members posted an article about the casual sexual harassment that women experience every day. I think that that's why the women who Trump assaulted stayed quiet, because we literally all experience something all the time.[9] You just forget about it. I myself haven't had too many experiences, but you don't bring them forward because they're just happening. And so now when the conversation started, [the women who were assaulted] said, Yeah, that did happen; I remember, I try not to think about it, but one of the many instances that I experienced sexual harassment happened to be at the hands of Donald Trump. That's what I think about the larger North American community and I think that they are pushing a lot of negativity toward women who are claiming their voices. In downplaying harassment, society at large is trying to undermine the strength of women. I think that's just because it's scary. I think that women are very, very scary. And I don't know what makes us so scary.

For example, I just read an article about how pockets are sexually and politically motivated as a fashion item. It was the history of pockets. And basically, male designers didn't want women to have pockets because they could conceal things in them. It's yet another example of men trying to have control and us being [considered] dangerous. But who knows what makes us so scary, I'm not scared, are you?

Louise: Men are frightened by the strength of our sexuality. They are because we control that. We are supposed to, anyways.

Omeasoo: They are supposed to control their own. It is everybody's job to control their own sexuality.

Louise: Exactly, exactly. That's the bottom line.

Omeasoo: How have women in your community experienced and been shaped by violence?

Louise: Well, let's put it this way. When my mother was in a relationship with your Moosom, there was no interval house on a reserve, there was no place for safety, and even off the reserve, there was no place for her to go as a nêhiýaw iskwew. So that shaped my life. I refused to be—well, I was a victim of violence as well, being raped on different occasions. But not coming forth because of the shame associated with being a "loose" woman. Because back then, the women were blamed. I didn't step forth to disclose to the police or anything like that.

But in this community now and at this age, I am aware of the violence against women through the missing and murdered women inquiry; I hear the stories of those community members, and I also hear the stories through OPIK.[10] I am aware of what's going on in that community with the kids and the partners of some of these women. That depresses me; I have to really work hard at not allowing that to oppress me as well. I suppose in a way that has shaped my writing. Because in telling my story, I am hoping to open up the can of worms, so people can heal and move forward.

We definitely need education, but it's not only women learning some sort of self-defence, but preparing our girls and how to help them with the signs and bring them up in a safe environment. And teaching them about the ceremonies, about puberty rites ceremonies, and respect for self and whatnot. It is important for young men to be taught those same things as well. We can't just focus on the females' safety. The men need to be taught to take responsibility for their own bodies and to be respectful of others as well. There is a lot of work that needs to be done—on bullying, for example. When I am teaching as a poet, I am talking about those situations head on. I don't beat around the bush about family violence or sexual abuse, or any of that stuff; I am always educating.

Omeasoo: Some people are really open about the violence they have experienced. Like I said, I have been really, really lucky in terms of experiencing violence. I don't have those stories of my own. For that, I am lucky and blessed and really fortunate. I feel really hopeful that I won't have to [experience it], because I haven't yet. That is what I hope for.

But as I was saying, every woman has at least one story, if not more, of casual sexual harassment. I think that trauma has something to do with this. I was reading an article and listening to a radio show about how trauma can really undermine a person's ability to have boundaries. And so if you experienced trauma as a child, as you grow up, you are more and more likely to be victimized again. Partially because you literally don't recognize danger. It's staring you right in the face, but because you have had that dangerous experience before, this is normal. And the next thing you know, you've been victimized again.

I can see that happening with some young women. I don't notice it as much in young men, but with young women, you can kind of see when their boundaries are loose, and they might not have an appreciation for where their boundaries are. And I do think that they get blamed a lot for that. It's not their fault. It's the perpetrator's fault.

I know that people have experienced violence. Most people don't talk about it a lot. Recently, when one of these young women that I'm referring to spoke about her violent situation in a public way, people didn't respond well. Again, it was her fault, according to them. There is no past, it's not it used to be the women's fault, it is still the woman's fault, when these things happen.

It hasn't stopped, people are still experiencing it. Really, at the moment, the only thing I can think about in terms of the violence that I've experienced is this one time I was on the subway. I could tell this man beside me was a creep. And he was snuggling up close to me, and I could tell that he was trying to put his gross, little, nasty elbows on my breasts. So, I put my elbows way out like this. And I just sat like that the whole time because I wasn't going to let him know that I knew, I was just going to protect myself, you know. And when I got off the subway, some woman screamed. So, I think he probably groped someone on his way out.

These kinds of things happen—that's just something small, but it's still so casual. How often do I tell that story? Almost never. How important is it? Not very. Because everybody else, or one in four, or whatever, has an experience of sexual assault, has an experience of date rape, has an experience of some kind of sexual violence. That's why we don't talk about it, because it's so prevalent.

I think that the community response is getting better because more people talk about this kind of violence and how casual it is. People try to dismiss it and minimize it constantly, like Trump calling it locker-room talk or men calling it a compliment.[11] But it allows those greater acts of violence to happen, and also allows the perpetuation of violence against women in the media, policy, and legislation, as well as [the perpetuation of] emotional violence.

To change patterns of behaviour and violence, you talked about it: men are part of the solution. I think it's a really complicated issue and I don't want to leave anyone behind, because we are all in this together. But we need to examine those deep-rooted problems we have. Like men being afraid of women's sexuality. Okay. So what are we going to do about that? How are we going to let people own their own sexuality? How are we going to deal with this context of a high level of sexual violence? I don't know. But I think acknowledging the problem is the first step. That's why it's always good to call out this, call out that, et cetera.

4. An Indigenous feminist is not necessarily an Indigenous woman. We asked ourselves how our own sexuality and gender is formed, and how this might influence our gender politics.

Louise: What journey have you been on in terms of your own gender and sexuality?

I think that I answered that in defining my own sexuality as a teenager. It really defined me in terms of my womb-an-hood.

When I was a teenager—I guess I'm looking at ages seventeen to twenty, I call those my teen years, my adolescent years—I decided, mostly I decided who I was going to sleep with. Most of them were my own choices, some of them weren't. But I defined my own sexuality by making those decisions and was upset and angry when there were double standards imposed on me.

Omeasoo: What were those double standards again?

Louise: That I was a slut and the guys weren't.

Omeasoo: Yep. I just think that's funny—sorry—because when I was those ages, my mom was very particular about how I was behaving sexually. So, she got to sow her wild oats.

Louise: Yeah, but I knew the consequences of sowing my wild oats. You know, there's no self-respect, there's very little self-respect. And that was part of it, really. Because I didn't have any boundaries, or those boundaries were loose. Because I didn't grow up with any examples, nobody taught me what right and wrong was. Because I came from residential schools to total freedom, and how do you handle that? From confinement to displacement. From one displacement to another.

Omeasoo: What else made your journey unique as an Indigenous person?

Louise: It was the confusion of residential school, the lack of role modelling at home, and problem-solving through that stuff, and going into therapy and coming out ahead. But going into therapy was the turning point in my life and meeting your father. And meeting your father was like meeting respect head-on. I wasn't used to that, and I had to learn to reciprocate it and how to love in return. I don't know if that's unique as an Nêhiýaw person. The journey was unique.

Omeasoo: In terms of my own gender and sexuality, I always think it's so funny. Do you remember that, that canoe trip we went on with Barry?

Louise: Barry?

Omeasoo: I don't know. I just know his name was Barry. I was little, somewhere between the ages of three and six. Anyways, Barry was my first crush. So, I pretty much know that I'm straight.

I absolutely believe people who are LGBTQ and know when they are two or three, because I remember my first straight feelings were when I was very, very young.

I remember my first straight crush, so I know I'm straight and that hasn't been too confusing for me. I often wished that the world that I grew up in was more gender and sexually fluid, because I thought that it would be interesting to experiment, but I didn't really. And at the end of the day, it didn't matter, because I'm a pretty straight person. So, that was lucky for me.[12]

For me as an Indigenous person, the journey—it would have been defined by the efforts that you made to help me have these strong boundaries you talk about missing. I feel like I've had very, very strong sexual boundaries that are very clear in my mind, my whole life. I think that maybe emotional boundaries are or have been pushed this way or that, but the boundaries as far as my body goes and my sexuality goes have been very, very clear. So I think that in your efforts, you succeeded in helping to make sure that I had those strong boundaries. I remember the books you gave me when I was nine, and I read those front to back, back to front, all the time, because I was obviously very curious about sexuality and sexual expression. Having all that knowledge at my fingertips and all that support to be my own sexual person meant that I never really felt that my sexual boundaries were loose. And the only time that I had trouble with them was when my emotional boundaries became loose.

And my emotional boundaries became loose, I can think of maybe two times. And one time I was feeling very, very vulnerable. I think that life had just really got me down without me realizing. In particular, my relationships and my many breakups had a cumulative effect of an emotional impact, because each one of those men tried to wound me in some way on their way out, and they managed to. I mean, I stayed outwardly very strong, but I still felt those vulnerabilities build up. And, then when I was my loosest emotionally, it was because I had let those vulnerabilities build up and let myself wallow, I guess. And believe what they said, instead of believing what I know.

So, other than that, I feel that you did such a good job. And if anything, as an Indigenous person that is unique, because what I've heard is that, what, 25 percent of children will experience trauma. So, my brother and I managed, or at least I managed not to. In my mind, that was because of the extreme effort you and Dad took to protect me in many different ways, by arming me with knowledge and arming me with support and love and confidence. And I would expect that came about as the result of your own trauma. So because you experienced trauma through residential school, you made up for it doubly, triply, with how careful you were with me.

Part of that journey was trying to understand this idea of promiscuity. Historically, you know, Europeans always talk about Indigenous peoples as if we are so promiscuous. I have no idea where they are coming up with that. One thing that occurred to me when I was talking to another friend about the teachings—she said that ancient teachings were all about monogamy, and how important sharing sexual energy with only one person is. She was talking about some really, really ancient teachings, and I told her, well, historically, this is what is written in western history books. I kind of have this idea that if someone was going to do a history of Indigenous sexuality, what they might understand is that probably the difference is the diseases. When diseases decimated our communities and we were trying to make our nation strong, we had to take different strategies to make that happen—to bear children and to grow again. If that is taken as promiscuity by these really prudish and really sexually repressed and strange Europeans, then maybe that was their interpretation. But in my mind, it could have been part of a concentrated strategy to make our nation strong again. At a time when diseases happened.

My Elder said the same thing: He said that when people were having big families, they were remembering, back at that time when so many people died.

Louise: That's interesting.

Omeasoo: Yeah. I think that if a study was done that's a possible way to understand the difference between the teachings and the written word of early European visitors.

Louise: I was just thinking about what you just said in terms of the European prudishness. I don't think they were prudish, because they brought syphilis. I don't know that syphilis existed in Aboriginal communities back then; perhaps it did, I don't know. But they brought all those diseases to this country.

Omeasoo: But they figured that they could do anything when they came here. They really thought that they could do anything.

When I went to Japan, I had to hang out with this guy. And he was telling me, oh yeah, the Japanese girls just let you grab them and they giggle. Pretty much the same thing that Trump said. And it's just like white men feeling that they own "other" women's bodies, and that they can do with them what they like.[13]

5. The next series of questions relates to our understandings of Indigenous kinship and laws. These are interrelated concepts because with our kin, including non-human entities, we have responsibilities.

Louise: Wahkotowin[14] actually translates as "I walk with my 'crooked' (not criminal, but bent over) relatives," because we are all crooked in the way we walk. Kinship to me is not just our little nuclear family, but the bigger, extended family as well. But it's been injured. That sense of extended family has been injured. My family is our nuclear family plus your aunty and cousins. That's as far as it goes at the moment, but in the bigger picture, the whole reserve is our extended family because there are so many relatives. In Onion Lake as well.

That's just one aspect of my answer. The other aspect of my answer in terms of kinship is the larger extended family, the international, universal community picture. That's the one that I'm thinking of as well in terms of kinship. The way we've adopted our friend, for example, as your little mama and my little sister. I have many other good friends that I call sisters because they just have become sisters in arms, I suppose. They could become extended family.

Omeasoo: Have you reflected on the kinship laws of our ancestors?

Louise: I don't know about the kinship laws of our ancestors. Somebody would have to tell me what they are. I just know that what I perceive is that kinship laws are [about] not just our human kinships, but also the animal kinships and the earth kinships, and all of that, and the cosmos—that to me is quite large if that is a universal law of our ancestors. And it's just more than just you and I.

That resonates a whole lot when people talk about the land as our mother and the sun as our brother. I don't know if the sun is actually our brother, I just see it as a grandmother or grandfather—I think it's unisex—and the cosmos as well. I think that's the universal law they're talking about in terms of wahkotowin, meaning all my relations, all my relations.

Omeasoo: How have women had an impact on these laws and realities?

Louise: Increasingly, what I have observed through my cousins and through some other friends is that women are taking it upon themselves to learn their genealogy and their genograms, so that they are trying to ensure that people know who their relations are in terms of their kinship. That's one observation. There are also walks to protect the water. That's the other universal law that is in action—tree-huggers, so to speak. The ones that are protecting the environment and the ones that are active at the uranium protests. A lot of women are involved in that.

Omeasoo: I've always enjoyed reading what scholars have to say about kinship, like Brenda Macdougall and Rob Innes. My master's thesis talked a little bit about kinship in those death ceremonies and the practice of how some of those ways of mourning in the 1800s drew people even closer together in kinship. People had to recognize how much they were dependent on each other. And I think that's important to remember. Today we act so independent, but we really need each other. I appreciate that teaching and I think you have shared that with me a lot. When we forced Dad to go to church, even at Christmastime, you said, it's about community, we need each other. And unless we build those relationships, we won't be able to call upon those people when we need them, which I think is really important. We can't forget that we're all going to need someone sometime.

Louise: Wichitowin is helping one another.

Omeasoo: I still find it confusing from the relationships perspective. Mostly because I don't think we have spent a ton of time with our extended family, so I haven't had to deal with the complicated messy relationships that extended family present. I miss those feelings.

I don't know if you've ever noticed, I always run around looking for a new family. Did you notice that?

Louise: No.

Omeasoo: So in Australia, you know, Ian became my dad and Lee took care of me. And then when I go out West, I have a whole new family over there.

And that's really meaningful to me—to create a whole new family everywhere I go. I try to find people that I care about and that care about me everywhere. And I don't know if that's because I haven't had such a complicated experience with an extended family. I don't know. I just know that I really like feeling that they belong to me and I belong to them, even if it's not by blood. And it makes it hard because we've travelled, I've travelled, and you have these people that you love so much and they live in every direction of the wind.

But I do think about how important it is that we need each other. If there's anything I could complain about in this area, it would be the colonial laws. And how the colonial laws have separated our kinship. The ways in which we have been confined to our reserves, which was never how we operated, and how interesting that is as a human phenomenon. That humans are not really as mobile as they used to be, I don't think. They are in the individual sense, but not in the collective sense.

But women do have impact, because with legislation regarding gender discrimination in the Indian Act, it's been women who have been fighting against it. That's what's so interesting, because sometimes that comes up against the bands' interests—the bands want sovereignty, they don't want the Canadian legislation to change their sovereignty. But at the same time, women have been deprived of their rights by that legislation. So what are we supposed to do?

Of course, Indigenous women want sovereignty as much as anybody else. But the reality is this Canadian legislation has completely impacted our lives.

Louise: Legislation has impacted our lives. With Bill C-31, I hate that term [Bill C-31]. As far as I'm concerned, I am a full Indian, and so are you. But that has created conflict and division in our communities as well. As well as division with Métis; it's as if they are not a part of us. But they are very much a part of us.

Omeasoo: You have poem on that, about an inability to tell certain stories about relatives, because of the disruption of residential school particularly. It's a poem about how you wish could tell me all these things, or you wish you could tell somebody all these things.[15] But you can only tell snippets of stories, of family history. That's a good example of a woman passing down what she can about kinship, despite the difficulties.

Louise: There's a sense of isolation and loneliness, too, that has been caused by the legislation. I've experienced that myself within this relationship that I'm in. In a way, I almost sacrifice some of my "Indian-ness" to be with your dad. In terms of ceremony and language, and particularly those things that a Native man has more access to because they are on a reserve, or just because they are Native men and they have access to that. Whereas as a Nêhiýaw woman who is married to a white man, it's as if invisible barriers are there in place for me.

And it is compounded by the fact that your father happens to be a physician. And sometimes he receives more teachings that I do, because "white is right." And so, he gets the teachings rather than me getting them ahead of him, you know. That's an interesting dynamic as well.

Observations that I've made, anyways.

6. In conclusion, my mom remarks upon her relationship with my father.

Louise: I am quite enmeshed with your father; I still have a lot of autonomy. As much autonomy as I want to take in the relationship. There is a lot of safety in my relationship with your father, I think. And to me, he is every woman's dream. We need more men like your father. Kind, respectful, loyal, truthful.

Reflections

We began this chapter with a photo and poem by my mom about her grandson, Miyo Kesikaw/Kopit.[16] We end the discussion with my mom's short tribute to my father. In all ways, Indigenous feminism as we know it is to be in relationship—in relationship to ourselves, other humans, and non-human entities including spirits, and the environment of four-leggeds, winged ones, those that swim, those that crawl, plants, rocks, the wind, water, and fire. Perhaps it is because of this interconnectedness that many Indigenous women refute the term feminist. To give ourselves a word, a name, creates difference where unity is necessary for survival.

Much of this discussion has reflected on violence: violence that is intergenerational, sexual, in words and in deed, political. Unfortunately, most of that violence is generated, formed, and reproduced by patriarchal actors, if not by men themselves. In our opening and closing statements, then, we endeavour to tie men to our hearts—our grandparents, parents, partners, and children—to recognize that violence against women in any form is also violence against men, humanity, and the cosmos.

Not explicit is violence that is linguistic, and while some words here are in Cree-nêhiýaw the vast majority of them are not. What are we missing when we don't discuss these deep issues in our own languages? At the bare minimum, the use of language is a reflection of the colonial history that created most (not all) of this violence.[17]

Our introduction also described the challenges of both capitalism and neocolonialism, and how these twin constructs divide not only Indigenous women but also Indigenous nations. Part of this is acknowledgement of the privilege both my mom and I currently have, ensconced in our big farmhouse, protected and even nurtured in many ways by the hard work and whiteness of my father. Part of it is an acknowledgement of my mother's dedication, her survival instinct, her sakiyoso, or innate love of self, that propelled her to move beyond her own considerable pain and into the skin she inhabits now:

poet, essayist, thinker, mother, Kokom (grandmother), and Elder. And lastly, part of it is an understanding that capitalism and neocolonialism necessarily undermine solidarity among all beings (human and non), and that the most important value that will save us as a species, and as women, is generosity, an opposite to violence.

Notes

1 Andrea Landry, Facebook, 7 March 2016, https://www.facebook.com/andrea.landry.7.

2 Kim TallBear, at TallBear, Anderson, and Simpson, "Indigenous Feminisms Power Panel."

3 Audra Simpson, at TallBear, Anderson, and Simpson, "Indigenous Feminisms Power Panel."

4 "History Matters: The Meaning of Historical Indigenous Architecture" (presentation to Turtle Island: A History of Ancient North America [HIST 152.3], University of Saskatchewan, Saskatoon, 29 October 2016).

5 The Sisters in Spirit Vigils are organized nationally each year through the National Women's Association of Canada. Sisters in Spirit began in 2005 as a research initiative to gather and organize statistical evidence on violence against Indigenous women. Local vigil walks are held to continue this work and raise awareness of the historical and ongoing violence faced by Indigenous women. https://www.nwac.ca/home/policy-areas/violence-prevention-and-safety/sisters-in-spirit/.

6 YES! And also only part of the story. We each have gifts and blessings to offer that are specific to us.

7 And now I am a single mother, still struggling for that elusive equality.

8 To describe this further, I felt that my partner at the time was expecting me to do everything for both of us, because he had seen so many other women who were capable of such immense caregiving. In rejecting this narrative, I hoped that he would see his role as also one of caregiving. As my grandmother said, "A relationship is not two people giving 50/50, it is two people giving 100 percent."

9 During the 2016 American presidential campaign, and following the release of a recording of candidate Donald Trump's lewd comments about women, a number of women came forward with allegations that Trump had forcibly kissed or groped them, all of which Trump denied. See Jamieson, Jeffery, and Puglise, "A Timeline of Donald Trump's Alleged Sexual Misconduct."

10 OPIK is short for opikinawason. It is an Elders' circle that advocates for Saskatoon-area children in care.

11 The American president described his discussion with Billy Bush as "locker-room banter." See Fahrenthold, "Trump Recorded Having Extremely Lewd Conversation about Women in 2005."

12 It is not actually the marginalized who benefit the most when a society becomes more inclusive, although one would hope so. In fact, the most privileged receive more privileges: for example, less inequality means less property crime; greater acceptance

and integration of Indigenous knowledge in universities means non-Indigenous people have greater access to Indigenous knowledge; and in this instance, greater gender diversity and flexibility means straight people have more interesting sexual experiences in addition to other, more profound, world view and emotional benefits.

13 This refers to Donald Trump's words to Billy Bush that came to light in the 2016 election. From the transcript provided by the *New York Times*: "Trump: Yeah, that's her. With the gold. I better use some Tic Tacs just in case I start kissing her. You know, I'm automatically attracted to beautiful—I just start kissing them. It's like a magnet. Just kiss. I don't even wait. And when you're a star, they let you do it. You can do anything. Bush: Whatever you want. Trump: Grab 'em by the pussy. You can do anything." See "Transcript: Donald Trump's Taped Comments About Women."

14 Wahkotowin is both a concept and a teaching that we ought to be in relationship with one another. Not only to our next of kin but everyone.

15 Halfe, "*aniskostew*-connecting," in *Burning in this Midnight Dream*, 2–4.

16 Miyo Kesikaw was originally named Kopit after the honourable and noble beaver, in his father's Mi'kmaw language. He now has the additional name of Miyo Kesikaw, beautiful day or beautiful heavens, in his mother's language, Cree/Nêhiwiyan.

17 Colonialism is its own historical narrative that is all-encompassing of most people in the world today. That does not mean that pre-colonial societies were necessarily devoid of various forms of violence based on gender and/or sexuality.

These Are My Daughters

ANINA MAJOR

It happened the day after a snowstorm. I was carefully walking to the train from my studio and saw a straw doll in the window of an old furniture store for two dollars. "How could this be?" I thought. It was a doll I remembered from my childhood that was created by straw vendors and sold to tourists. Now here the same doll sat in the window of an old furniture store in Brooklyn, New York. The straw doll of my childhood was a product that my grandmother made out of straw, locally known as plait. As an adult, I realized the cultural significance of this souvenir. It embodies my country's natural resources and artistry. Some "curators argue that such objects do not embody indigenous values and are only responses to a foreign market."[1] On the contrary, I believe the doll could be considered a symbol of my country's identity. It is fabricated from dried native palmetto fronds braided into rolls that are then cut into patterns and sewn, a traditional construction technique. Using this method, a series of ceramic dolls were created.

1 Barnet, *A Short Guide to Writing About Art*, 3.

Figures 13.1 and 13.2. *These Are My Daughters*, 2015 (detail). Stone ware, raffia. Each doll is 6 x 6 x 12 inches. Photo: Anina Major.

Acknowledgements

As with most large projects, this one could not have been completed without the generous support and guidance of numerous people. The initial idea for this project came from a panel on Indigenous feminisms at the 2015 annual meeting of the Canadian Historical Association. Encouraged by Jill McConkey (University of Manitoba Press) and Robert Innes (University of Saskatchewan, Indigenous Studies) to turn our panel into an edited collection, we began brainstorming right away. This project has seen many changes over the years, including shifts in the editorial team and contributors, as well as professional and personal developments. Some of our number began this project as students and early-career scholars and/or artists, and have now completed their studies, accepted employment, or have been promoted from their former roles. And just as we have evolved in our positioning towards this collection, so too have our ideas grown and shifted over time. In this sense, the work presented here is a snapshot of our thoughts and ideas over the past few years.

As editors, we are grateful to our dedicated contributors for their long-standing efforts to see this collection through to publication. Special thanks to Jill McConkey and Robert Innes for their original vision and continued support, and to the wonderful team at the University of Manitoba Press, whose keen eyes for detail and design are unmatched. Thank you to Eryk Martin for reading through the introduction and offering insightful comments and questions. Colleagues and friends at the University of Saskatchewan and elsewhere across Canada provided significant support through this process, and we are grateful. An extra special thanks to students in the Department of

Indigenous Studies at the University of Saskatchewan (particularly those in multiple iterations of a graduate/undergraduate class on Indigenous women, feminism, and politics) who saw this work in various stages of development and provided thoughtful analysis that helped to strengthen our ideas immeasurably. Finally, to our families (and for Sarah, especially her daughter Ruby, who arrived just as the final edits were coming together), thank you for providing much-needed balance in our lives.

Bibliography

Aarnes, Helle, and Eirik Husøy. "8.marstoget: Vill jubel for 14-åringenes oppgjør med sexisme i skolegården." *Aftenposten*, 9 March 2019.https://www.aftenposten.no/norge/i/1k1q4W/8-mars-toget-Vill-jubel-for-14-aringenes-oppgjor-med-sexisme-i-skolegarden.

Acoose, Janice. *Iskwewak Kah' Ki Yaw Ni Wahkomakanak: Neither Indian Princesses nor Easy Squaws*. Toronto: Women's Press, 2016.

———. "'A Vanishing Indian? Or Acoose: Woman Standing above Ground?'" In *(Ad) dressing Our Words: Aboriginal Perspectives on Aboriginal Literatures*, edited by Armand Garnet Ruffo, 37–56. Penticton, BC: Theytus Books, 2001.

Allen, Paula Gunn. "Lesbians in American Indian Cultures." *Conditions* 7 (1981): 67–87.

———. *The Sacred Hoop: Recovering the Feminine in American Indian Tradition*. Boston: Beacon Press, 1986.

———. "Some Like Indians Endure." *Journal of Lesbian Studies* 1, no. 1 (1996): 9. Originally published in *Living the Spirit*, co-ordinated by Will Roscoe, 11–13. New York: St. Martin's Press, 1988.

Amnesty International. *Stolen Sisters: A Human Rights Response to Discrimination and Violence against Indigenous Women in Canada*. Amnesty International, October 2004. Available at https://www.amnesty.ca/sites/amnesty/files/amr200032004enstolensisters.pdf.

Andersen, Chris, and Jean M. O'Brien. *Sources and Methods in Indigenous Studies*. New York: Routledge, 2016.

Anderson, Kim. "Affirmations of an Indigenous Feminist." In Suzack, Huhndorf, Perreault, and Barman, *Indigenous Women and Feminism*, 81–91.

———. *Life Stages and Native Women: Memory, Teachings, and Story Medicine*. Winnipeg: University of Manitoba Press, 2011.

———. *A Recognition of Being: Reconstructing Native Womanhood*. Toronto: Second Story Press, 2000.

Anderson, Kim, and Bonita Lawrence, eds. *Strong Women Stories: Native Vision and Community Survival.* 3rd ed. Toronto: Sumach Press, 2006.

Anderson, Mark Cronlund, and Carmen L. Robertson. *Seeing Red: A History of Natives in Canadian Newspapers.* Winnipeg: University of Manitoba Press, 2011.

Arcand, Joi T., and Leena Minifie. *When Raven Becomes Spider*, exhibit. Ottawa: Ottawa Art Gallery, 2017.

Archibald, Jo-Ann/Q'um Q'um Xiiem. *Indigenous Storywork: Educating the Heart, Mind, Body, and Spirit.* Vancouver: UBC Press, 2008.

Archuleta, Elizabeth. "'I Give You Back': Indigenous Women Writing to Survive." *Studies in American Indian Literatures* 18, no. 4 (2006): 88–114.

Arvin, Maile, Eve Tuck, and Angie Morrill. "Decolonizing Feminism: Challenging Connections between Settler Colonialism and Heteropatriarchy." *Feminist Formations* 25, no. 1 (Spring 2013): 8–34.

Bäckman, Louise. "Female—Divine and Human: A Study of the Position of the Woman in Religion and Society in Northern Eurasia." In *The Hunters,* edited by Å. Hultkrantz and Ø. Vorren, 143–62. Tromsø: Universitetsforlaget, 1982.

Bals, M., Anne Lene Turi, Ingunn Skre, and Siv Kvernmo. "The Relationship between Internalizing and Externalizing Symptoms and Cultural Resilience Factors in Indigenous Sami Youth from Arctic Norway." *International Journal of Circumpolar Health* 70, no. 1 (2011): 37–45.

Balsam, Kimberly F., Bu Huang, Karen C. Fieland, Jane M. Simoni, and Karina L. Walters. "Culture, Trauma, and Wellness: A Comparison of Heterosexual and Lesbian, Gay, Bisexual, and Two-Spirit Native Americans." *Cultural Diversity and Ethnic Minority Psychology* 10, no. 3 (2004): 287–301.

Balto, Asta. *Sámisk barneoppdragelse i endring.* Oslo: Ad Notam Gyldendal, 1997.

———. "Traditional Sámi Child-Rearing in Transition: Shaping a New Pedagogical Platform." *AlterNative* 1, no.1 (2005): 85–105.

Balzer, David. *Curationism: How Curating Took Over the Art World and Everything Else.* Toronto: Coach House, 2014.

Barkaskas, Patricia. "The Indian Voice: Centering Women in the Gendered Politics of Indigenous Nationalism in BC, 1969–1984." Master's thesis, University of British Columbia, 2009.

Barker, Joanne, ed. *Critically Sovereign: Indigenous Gender, Sexuality, and Feminist Studies.* Durham, NC: Duke University Press, 2017.

Barker, Joanne. "Gender, Sovereignty, Rights: Native Women's Activism against Social Inequality and Violence in Canada." *American Quarterly* 60, no. 2 (2008): 259–66.

———. *Native Acts: Law, Recognition, and Cultural Authenticity.* Durham, NC: Duke University Press, 2011.

Barnet, Jean. "Taming Aboriginal Sexuality: Gender, Power, and Race in British Columbia, 1850–1900. *BC Studies* 115/116 (1997/98): 237–66.

Barnet, Sylvan. *A Short Guide to Writing About Art.* 11th ed. Toronto: Pearson, 2015.

Barnston, George. "Journal Kept by George Barnston, 1827–8." In *The Fort Langley Journals*, edited by Morag Maclachlan, 28–32. Vancouver: UBC Press, 2000.

Barr, Juliana. *Peace Came in the Form of a Woman: Indians and Spaniards in the Texas Borderlands.* Chapel Hill: University of North Carolina Press, 2007.

Beauvoir, Simone de. *The Ethics of Ambiguity*. New York: Philosophical Library/Open Road, 2011.

Bedard, Ella. "Becoming Xwiyálemot: Traditional Knowledge and Colonial Experiences in the Life of a Stó:lō Elder." Ethnohistory field school report, 2013. Available through the Stó:lō Archives, Sardis, British Columbia, and at www.ethnohist.ca.

Benson, Koni. "When There's Work to Be Done, Our Hands Go Out: Expressions of Power Dynamics and Community Change, Stó:lō Women and Politics. Ethnohistory field school report, 1998. Available through the Stó:lō Archives, Sardis, British Columbia, and online at www.ethnohist.ca.

Benton-Banai, Edward. *The Mishomis Book: The Voice of the Ojibway*. Hayward, WI: Indian Country Communications, 1998.

Bhabha, Homi. *The Location of Culture*. Oxon: Routledge, 1994.

Bierwert, Crisca. *Brushed by Cedar, Living by the River: Coast Salish Figures of Power*. Tucson: University of Arizona Press, 1999.

Blaney, Fay. "Aboriginal Women's Action Network." In *Strong Women Stories: Native Vision and Community Survival*, 3rd edition, edited by Kim Anderson and Bonita Lawrence, 156–70. Toronto: Sumach Press, 2003.

Blaney, Fay, and Sam Gray. "'Empowerment, Revolution and Real Change': An Interview with Fay Blaney." In Green, *Making Space for Indigenous Feminism*, 2nd ed., 234–52.

Bobb, Memxe/Edna, Siyamíya/Amelia Douglas, Siyameltset/Albert Phillips, and Qw'etosiya, eds. *Classified Word List for Upriver Halq'eméylem*. Sardis, BC: Coqualeetza Education Training Centre, 1980.

Bolton, Rena Point. *Xwelíqwiya: The Life of a Stó:lō Matriarch*. Edmonton: University of Alberta Press, 2013.

Bongo, Berit Andersdatter. "'Samer snakker ikke om helse og sykdom.' Sámisk forståelseshorisont og kommunikasjon om helse og sykdom. En kvalitativ undersøkelse i Sámisk kultur." PhD thesis, UiT The Arctic University of Norway, 2012.

Boucher, Joanne. "Dress-Code Message at U of W Sexist." *Winnipeg Free Press*, 17 June 2015. http://www.winnipegfreepress.com/opinion/analysis/dress-code-message--at-u-of-w-sexist-307799831.html.

Bourgeois, Robyn. "Perpetual State of Violence: An Indigenous Feminist Anti-Oppression Inquiry into Missing and Murdered Indigenous Women and Girls." In Green, *Making Space for Indigenous Feminism*, 2nd ed., 253–73.

Bourriaud, Nicolas. *Relational Aesthetics*. Dijon: Les Presses du Reel, 2009.

Bower, Cayley. "From Wanting In to Opting Out: Home Sewing and Fashion Then and Now." *Active History*, 24 May 2018. http://activehistory.ca/2018/05/from-wanting-in-to-opting-out-home-sewing-and-fashion-then-and-now/.

Bradford, Tolly, and Chelsea Horton, eds. *Mixed Blessings: Indigenous Encounters with Christianity in Canada*. Vancouver: UBC Press, 2016.

Brave Heart, M.Y.H., and L.M. DeBruyn. "The American Indian Holocaust: Healing from Historical Grief." *The Journal of American Indian and Alaska Native Mental Health Research* 8, no. 2 (1998): 56–79.

Brayboy, Duane. "Two-Spirits, One Heart, Five Genders." *Indian Country Today Media Network*, 23 January 2016. http://indiancountrytodaymedianetwork.com/2016/01/23/two-spirits-one-heart-five-genders.

Brown, Leslie Allison, and Susan Strega. *Research as Resistance: Critical, Indigenous and Anti-Oppressive Approaches*. Toronto: Canadian Scholars Press, 2005.

Brownlie, Robin Jarvis. "Intimate Surveillance: Indian Affairs, Colonization, and the Regulation of Aboriginal Women's Sexuality." In *Contact Zones: Aboriginal and Settler Women in Canada's Colonial Past*, edited by Katie Pickles and Myra Rutherdale, 160–78. Vancouver: UBC Press, 2005.

Buchanan, Astri, Maureen G. Reed, and Gun Lidestav. "What's Counted As a Reindeer Herder? Gender and the Adaptive Capacity of Sámi Reindeer Herding Communities in Sweden." *Ambio* 45, supplement 3 (December 2016): 352–62. https://doi.org/10.1007/s13280-016-0834-1

Buker, Lolehawk Laura. "Walking Backwards into the Future with Our Stories: The Stó:lō Is a River of Knowledge, Halq'eméylem Is a River of Stories." PhD thesis, Simon Fraser University, 2011.

Canada, Department of Citizenship and Immigration. *Report of Indian Affairs Branch for the Fiscal Year Ending 31 March 1948*.

Canada, Department of Mines and Resources. *Report of Indian Affairs Branch for the Fiscal Year Ending 31 March 1948*.

Card, Claudia. "Caring and Evil." *Hypatia* 5, no. 1 (1990): 101–8.

Carlson, Keith Thor. *The Power of Place, the Problem of Time: Aboriginal Identity and Historical Consciousness in the Cauldron of Colonialism*. Toronto: University of Toronto Press, 2010.

———, ed. *A Stó:lō-Coast Salish Historical Atlas*. Vancouver: Douglas and McIntyre, 2001.

———, ed. *You Are Asked to Witness*. Chilliwack B.C.: Stó:lô Heritage Trust, 1997.

Cavanaugh, Catherine, and Susanna Mcleod. "Irene Parlby." In *The Canadian Encyclopedia*. Historica Canada. Article published 27 October 2009; last edited 3 October 2018. http://www.thecanadianencyclopedia.ca/en/article/mary-irene-parlby/.

Centers for Disease Control. "HIV among American Indians and Alaska Natives." 2016. https://www.cdc.gov/hiv/pdf/group/racialethnic/aian/cdc-hiv-natives.pdf.

Chacaby, Ma-Nee. *A Two-Spirit Journey: The Autobiography of a Lesbian Ojibwe-Cree Elder*. Winnipeg: University of Manitoba Press, 2016.

Child, Brenda. *My Grandfather's Knocking Sticks: Ojibwe Family Life and Labor on the Reservation*. St. Paul: Minnesota Historical Society Press, 2014.

Chrystos. *Fire Power*. Vancouver: Press Gang, 1995.

———. *In Her I Am*. Vancouver: Press Gang, 1993.

———. *Not Vanishing*. Vancouver: Press Gang, 1988.

Cooper, Nancy. "Learning to Skin the Beaver: In Search of Our Aunties' Traplines." In *Me Sexy: An Exploration of Indigenous American Sexuality*, edited by Drew Hayden Taylor, 41–49. Vancouver: Douglas and McIntyre, 2008.

Coqualeetza Cultural Education Centre. "About Us." http://www.coqualeetza.com/page2.html.

Dagsvold, Inger, Snefrid Møllersen, and Vigdis Stordahl, "What Can We Talk About, in Which Language, in What Way and with Whom? Sámi Patients' Experiences of Language Choice and Cultural Norms in Mental Health Treatment." *International Journal of Circumpolar Health*,74, no. 1 (2015). DOI: 10.3402/ijch.v74.26952.

Dankertsen, Astri. "Samisk artikulasjon: Melankoli, tap og forsoning i en (nord)norsk hverdag." PhD-avhandling, Universitetet i Nordland, 2014.

D'Augelli, Anthony R. "Identity Development and Sexual Orientation: Toward a Model of Lesbian, Gay, and Bisexual Development." In *Human Diversity: Perspectives on People in Context*, edited by E.J. Trickett, R.J. Watts and D. Birman, 312–33. San Francisco, CA: Jossey Bass, 1994.

Deer, Sarah. *The Beginning and End of Rape: Confronting Sexual Violence in Native America.* Minneapolis: University of Minnesota Press, 2015.

———. "Decolonizing Rape Law: A Native Feminist Synthesis of Safety and Sovereignty." *Wicazo Sa Review* 24, no. 2 (Fall 2009): 149–67.

Demers, Patricia. "Location, Dislocation, Relocation: Shooting Back with Cameras." In *Indigenous Women and Feminism: Politics, Activism, Culture,* edited by Cheryl Suzack, Shari M. Huhndorf, Jeanne Perreault, and Jean Barman, 298–314. Vancouver: UBC Press, 2010.

Denetdale, Jennifer Nez. "Chairmen, Presidents, and Princesses: The Navajo Nation, Gender, and the Politics of Tradition." *Wicazo Sa Review* 21, no. 1 (2006): 9–28.

———. "Securing Navajo National Boundaries: War, Patriotism, Tradition, and the Dine Marriage Act of 2005." *Wicazo Sa Review* 24, no. 2 (2009): 131–48.

Denzin, Norman K., Yvonne S. Lincoln, and Linda Tuhiwai Smith. *Handbook of Critical and Indigenous Methodologies.* Los Angeles: Sage, 2008.

Devereux, Cecily. "Finding Indian Maidens on eBay: Tales of the Alternative Archive (and More Tales of White Commodity Culture)." In *Basements and Attics, Closets and Cyberspace: Explorations in Canadian Women's Archives*, edited by Linda M. Morra and Jessica Schagerl, 36–59. Waterloo: Wilfrid Laurier University Press, 2012.

Devine, Heather. *The People Who Own Themselves: Aboriginal Ethnogenesis in a Canadian Family, 1660–1900.* Calgary: University of Calgary Press, 2004.

Dhruvarajan, Vanaja, and Jill Vickers, eds. *Gender, Race, and Nation: A Global Perspective.* Toronto: University of Toronto Press, 2002.

Dibbelt, Dan. "Nations Gather to Protest Glenbow's Spirit Sings Display." *Windspeaker* 5, no. 23 (1998): 2.

Dorion, Leah. "Opikinawasowin: The Life-Long Process of Growing Cree and Métis Childern." Master's thesis, Athabasca University, 2010.

Driskill, Qwo-Li. *Asegi Stories: Cherokee Queer and Two-Spirit Memory.* Tucson: University of Arizona Press, 2016.

———. "Doubleweaving Two-Spirit Critiques: Building Alliances between Native and Queer Studies. *GLQ: A Journal of Lesbian and Gay Studies* 16, no. 1/2 (2010): 69–92.

———. *Walking with Ghosts.* Cambridge: Salt, 2005.

Driskill, Qwo-Li, Chris Finley, Brian Joseph Gilley, and Scott Lauria Morgensen, eds. *Queer Indigenous Studies: Critical Interventions in Theory, Politics, and Literature.* Tucson: University of Arizona Press, 2011.

———. "The Revolution Is for Everyone: Imagining an Emancipatory Future through Queer Indigenous Critical Theories." In Driskill, Finley, Gilley, and Morgensen, *Queer Indigenous Studies*, 211–21.

Driskill, Qwo-Li, Daniel Heath Justice, Deborah Miranda, and Lisa Tatonetti. "Introduction: Writing in the Present." In *Sovereign Erotics: A Collection of Two-Spirit Literature*, edited by Qwo-Li Driskill, Daniel Heath Justice, Deborah Miranda, and Lisa Tatonetti, 1–17. Tucson: University of Arizona Press, 2011.

Duff, Wilson. *The Upper Stalo Indians of the Fraser Valley, British Columbia.* Anthropology in British Columbia Memoir 1. Victoria, BC: British Columbia Provincial Museum, 1952.

Duran, Eduardo, Bonnie Duran, Maria Yellow Horse Brave Heart, and Susan Yellow Horse-Davis. "Healing the American Indian Soul Wound." In *International Handbook of Multigenerational Legacies of Trauma*, edited by Yael Danieli, 341–54. New York: Plenum Press, 1998.

Eberts, Mary. "Being an Indigenous Woman Is a 'High-Risk Lifestyle.'" In Green, *Making Space for Indigenous Feminism*, 2nd ed., 69–102.

Egale Canada. "Just Society Report—Grossly Indecent: Confronting the Legacy of State Sponsorted Discrimination against Canada's LGBTQ2SI Communities." Last modified 10 June 2016. http://egale.ca/wpcontent/uploads/2016/06/FINAL_REPORT_EGALE.pdf.

Eggen, Øyvind. "Troens Bekjennere: Kontinuitet og endring i en læstadiansk menighet." Thesis, second degree level, University of Tromsø, 1998.

Eikjok, Jorunn. "Gender, Essentialism, and Feminism in Sámiland." In Green, *Making Space for Indigenous Feminism*, 1st ed., 108–23.

———. "Indigenous Women in the North: The Struggle for Rights and Feminism." *Indigenous Affairs* 3 (2000): 38–41.

Eisler, Riane. *The Chalice and the Blade: Our History, Our Future.* New York: HarperCollins, 1995.

Ekhoe, Naqi, and Uqsuralik Ottokie. *Childrearing Practices.* Vol. 3 of *Interviewing Inuit Elders.* Iqaluit, NU: Language and Culture Program of Nunavut Arctic College, 2000.

Ellingson, Ter. *The Myth of the Noble Savage.* Berkeley: University of California Press, 2001.

Enloe, Cynthia. *The Curious Feminist: Searching for Women in a New Age of Empire.* Berkeley: University of California Press, 2004.

Enos, Tony. "8 Things You Should Know About Two Spirit People." *Indian Country Today*, 28 March 2017.

Eriksen, Astrid M., Ketil Lenert Hansen, Cecille Javo, and Berit Shei. "Emotional, Physical and Sexual Violence among Sámi and Non-Sámi Populations in Norway: The SÁMINOR 2 Questionanaire Study." *Scandinavian Journal of Public Health* 43, no. 6 (2015): 588–96.

Evans-Campell, Tessa. "Historical Trauma in American Indian/Native Alaska Communities: A Multilevel Framework for Exploring Impacts on Individuals, Families, and Communities." *Journal of Interpersonal Violence* 23, no. 3 (2008): 316–38.

Evans-Campbell, Tessa, Taryn Lindhorst, Bu Huang, and Karina L. Walters. "Interpersonal Violence in the Lives of Urban American Indian and Alaska Native Women: Implications for Health, Mental Health, and Help-Seeking." *American Journal of Public Health* 96, no. 8 (2006): 1416–22.

Evans-Campbell, Tessa, and Karina L. Walters. "Catching Our Breath: A Decolonizing Framework for Healing Indigenous Peoples." In *Intersecting Child Welfare, Substance Abuse, and Family Violence: Culturally Competent Approaches,* edited by R. Fong, R. McRoy, and C.O. Hendricks, 91–110. Alexandria, VA: Council on Social Work Education Press, 2006.

Fahrenthold, David. "Trump Recorded Having Extremely Lewd Conversation about Women in 2005." *Washington Post,* 8 October 2016. https://www.washingtonpost.com/politics/trump-recorded-having-extremely-lewd-conversation-about-women-in-2005/2016/10/07/3b9ce776-8cb4-11e6-bf8a-3d26847eeed4_story.html?utm_term=.beb54e2b2e8f.

Felix, Dolly. *The Mosquito Story.* Sardis, BC: Stó:lō Sitel Curriculum and the Coqualeetza Education Training Centre, 1979. Stó:lō Archives Reference Collection, Sardis, British Columbia.

Fieland, Karen C., Karin L. Walters, and Jane M. Simoni. "Determinants of Health among Two-Spirit American Indians and Alaska Natives." In *The Health of Sexual Minorities: Public Health Perspectives on Lesbian, Gay, Bisexual and Transgender Populations,* edited by Ilan H. Meyer and Mary E. Northridge, 268–300. New York: Springer, 2007.

Finley, Chris. "Decolonizing the Queer Native Body (and Recovering the Native Bull-Dyke): Bringing 'Sexy' Back and Out of a Native Studies' Closet." In Driskill, Finley, Gilley, and Morgensen, *Queer Indigenous Studies,* 31–42. Tuscon: University of Arizona Press, 2011.

Fiola, Chantal. *Rekindling the Sacred Fire: Métis Ancestry and Anishinaabe Spirituality.* Winnipeg: University of Manitoba Press, 2015.

Fiske, Jo-anne. "Colonization and the Decline of Women's Status: The Tsimshian Case." *Feminist Studies* 17, no. 3 (Fall 1991): 509–35.

Francis, Daniel. *The Imaginary Indian: The Image of the Indian in Canadian Culture.* Vancouver: Arsenal Pulp Press, 2012.

Fraser, Simon. *The Letters and Journals of Simon Fraser, 1806–1808.* Edited by W. Kaye Lamb. Toronto: Dundurn Press, 2007.

Friedman, Marilyn. "Liberating Care." In *What Are Friends For? Feminist Perspectives on Personal Relationships and Moral Theory,* 142–83. Ithaca, NY: Cornell University Press, 1993.

Fung, Amy. "The Past, The Present, and The Same: Deanna Bowen Interviewed." *C Magazine* 135 (Autumn 2017): 8–13.

Galka, Sophie. "Father Lacombe, OMI: The West Was His Parish." *Indian Record* (published by the Oblate Fathers of Canada), October/November 1969, 8–12. http://archives.algomau.ca/main/sites/default/files/2012-33_001_032_pdf6_0.pdf.

Galloway, Brent. *Dictionary of Upriver Halkomelem*. Vol. 1. Berkeley: University of California Press, 2009.

Gardner, Ethel B. (Stelórrethet). "Tset Híkwstexw Te Sqwélteltset, We Hold Our Language High: The Meaning of Halq'eméylem Language Renewal in the Everyday Lives of Stó:lō People." PhD Diss., Simon Fraser University, 2002.

Garneau, David. "Imaginary Spaces of Conciliation and Reconciliation." *West Coast Line* 24, no. 3 (Summer 2012): 28–39.

———. Presentation at the 2nd Annual Symposium on the Future Imaginary. Institute for Indigenous Futurisms, Kelowna, BC, 5 August 2016. http://abtec.org/iif/wp-content/uploads/2016/06/Future-Imaginary-Symposium-Kelowna-David-Garneau-1.pdf.

Gilligan, Carol. "Resisting Injustice: A Feminist Ethic of Care." In *Joining the Resistance*, 164–80. Cambridge: Polity Press, 2011.

Gjessing, G. "Sjamanistisk og Læstadiansk ekstase hos samene." In *Studia Septentrionalia V*, edited by Nils Lid, 91–102. Oslo: Aschehoug, 1953.

Goeman, Mishuana. "Indigenous Interventions and Feminist Methods." In Andersen and O'Brien, *Sources and Methods in Indigenous Studies*, 185–94.

———. *Mark My Words: Native Women Mapping Our Nations*. Minneapolis: University of Minnesota Press, 2013.

Goeman, Mishuana, and Jennifer Nez Denetdale. "Native Feminisms: Legacies, Interventions, and Indigenous Sovereignties." *Wicazo Sa Review* 24, no. 2 (Fall 2009): 9–13.

Green, Joyce. "Cultural and Ethnic Fundamentalism: Identity, Liberation and Oppression." In *Contesting Fundamentalisms*, edited by C. Schick, J. Jaffe, and A. M. Watkinson, 19–34. Halifax: Fernwood Publishing, 2004.

———, ed. *Making Space for Indigenous Feminism*. 1st ed. Halifax: Fernwood Publishing, 2007.

———, ed. *Making Space for Indigenous Feminism*. 2nd ed. Halifax: Fernwood Publishing, 2017.

———. "Taking Account of Aboriginal Feminism." In *Making Space for Indigenous Feminism*, 1st ed., 20–33.

Halfe, Louise. *Burning in This Midnight Dream*. Regina: Coteau Books, 2016.

Hall, Lynda. "Writing Selves Home at the Crossroads: Anzaldúa and Chrystos (Re) Configure Lesbian Bodies." *ARIEL: A Review of International English Literature* 30, no. 2 (1999): 99–117.

Halsaa, Beatrice. "Mobilisering av svart og Sámiske feminism." In *Krysningspunkter: Likestillingspolitikk i et flerkulturelt Norge*, edited by Beret Bråten and Cecilie Thun, 209–49. Oslo: Akademika forlag, 2013.

Hardt, Michael, and Antonia Negri. "De Singularitate 1: Of Love Possessed." In *Commonwealth*, 179–88. Cambridge: Belknap Press, 2011.

Harmon, Alexandra. *Rich Indians: Native People and the Problem of Wealth in American History*. Chapel Hill: University of North Carolina Press, 2010.

Harris, Aroha, and Mary Jane Logan McCallum. "'Assaulting the Ears of Government': The Indian Homemakers' Clubs and the Maori Women's Welfare League in Their

Formative Years." In *Indigenous Women and Work: From Labor to Activism*, edited by Carol Williams, 225–39. Urbana: University of Illinois Press, 2012.

Harris, Cole. "Voices of Smallpox around the Strait of Georgia." In *The Resettlement of British Columbia: Essays on Colonialism and Geographical Change*, 3–30. Vancouver: UBC Press, 1997.

Hill, Gabrielle, and Sophie McCall. *The Land We Are: Artists and Writers Unsettle the Politics of Reconciliation*. Winnipeg: ARP Books, 2015.

Hill-Tout, Charles. *The Mainland Halkomelem*. Vol. 3 of *The Salish People: The Local Contribution of Charles Hill-Tout*. Edited by Ralph Maud. Vancouver: Talonbooks, 1978.

Hokowhitu, Brendan. "Taxonomies of Indigeneity: Indigenous Heterosexual Patriarchal Masculinity." In *Indigenous Men and Masculinities: Legacies, Identities, Regeneration*, edited by Robert Alexander Innes and Kim Anderson, 80–95. Winnipeg: University of Manitoba Press, 2015.

hooks, bell. *Outlaw Culture*. Abingdon: Routledge, 2006.

Hopkins, Ruth. "On Skirt Shaming—Another Perspective." *Windspeaker* 31, August 2016. http://www.windspeaker.com/news/windspeaker-news/on-skirt-shaming-another-perspective-guest-column/.

Howard, Liz. *Infinite Citizen of the Shaking Tent*. Toronto: McClelland and Stewart, 2015.

Huhndorf, Shari M., and Cheryl Suzack. "Indigenous Feminism: Theorizing the Issues." In Suzack, Huhndorf, Perreault, and Barman, *Indigenous Women and Feminism*, 1–17.

Human Rights Watch. *Submission to the Government of Canada on Police Abuse of Indigenous Women in Saskatchewan and Failures to Protect Indigenous Women from Violence*. https://www.hrw.org/news/2017/06/19/submission-government-canada-police-abuse-indigenous-women-saskatchewan-and-failures.

Hunt, Sarah. "Embodying Self-Determination: Beyond the Gender Binary." In *Determinants of Indigenous Peoples' Health*, edited by Margo Greenwood et al., 104–19. Toronto: Canadian Scholars' Press, 2015.

———. "Ontologies of Indigeneity: The Politics of Embodying a Concept." *Cultural Geographies* 21, no. 1 (2014): 27–32.

———. "Representing Colonial Violence: Trafficking, Sex Work, and the Violence of Law." *Atlantis: Critical Studies in Gender, Culture, and Social Justice* 37, no. 1 (2015): 25–39.

———. "Witnessing the Colonialscape: Lighting the Intimate Fires of Indigenous Legal Pluralism." PhD dissertation, Simon Fraser University, 2014.

"Indian Women Want a Far Greater Role: Says S.I.W.A. President." *Saskatchewan Indian* 3, no. 5 (June 1973): 14.

Jacobs, Sue-Ellen, Wesley Thomas, and Sabine Lang, eds. *Two-Spirit People: Native American Gender Identity, Sexuality, and Spirituality*. Urbana and Chicago: University of Illinois Press, 1997.

Jaimes, M. Annette, with Theresa Halsey. "American Indian Women: At the Heart of Indigenous Resistance in Contemporary North America." In *The State of Native America*, 311–44. Boston: South End Press, 1992.

Jåma, Ellinor Marita. "Vi vet bare at de har en annerledes kultur, men vi lærer ikke å forstå den." Master's thesis, Department of Psychology, NTNU: Norwegian University of Science and Technology, 2008.

Jamieson, Amber, Simon Jeffery, and Nicole Puglise. "A Timeline of Donald Trump's Alleged Sexual Misconduct: Who, When and What." *Guardian*, 27 October 2016. https://www.theguardian.com/us-news/2016/oct/13/list-of-donald-trump-sexual-misconduct-allegations.

Kejonen, Olle, and Karen Eira, "Partiledarna: Vi är inte feminister." *SVT Sápmi*, 7 March 2014. http://sverigesradio.se/sida/artikel.aspx?programid=2327&artikel=5802180.

Kelm, Mary-Ellen. *Colonizing Bodies: Aboriginal Health and Healing in British Columbia, 1900–50*. Vancouver: UBC Press, 1998.

Knickerbocker, Madeline. "'We Want Our Land': A Stó:lō Land Claims Negotiations Comic." In *Finding/Trouvailles*. Champlain Society, 2019. https://champlain-society.utpjournals.press/findings-trouvailles/archive/1976-stolo-land-claims-negotiations-comic.

———. "'What We've Said Can Be Proven in the Ground': Stó:lō, Sovereignty, and Historical Narratives at X̱á:ytem, 1990–2006." *Journal of the Canadian Historical Association* 24, no. 1 (2013): 297–342.

Knickerbocker, Madeline Rose, and Sarah Nickel. "Negotiating Sovereignty: Indigenous Perspectives on the Patriation of a Settler Colonial Constitution, 1975–83." *BC Studies* 190 (Summer 2016): 67–88.

Knobblock, Ina, and Rauna Kuokkanen, "Decolonizing Feminism in the North: A Conversation with Rauna Kuokkanen." *NORA: Nordic Journal of Feminist and Gender Research* 23, no. 4 (2015): 275–81.

Kovach, Margaret. *Indigenous Methodologies: Characterstics, Conversations and Contexts*. Toronto: University of Toronto Press, 2009.

Krouse, Susan Applegate, and Heather A. Howard, eds. *Keeping the Campfires Going: Native Women's Activism in Urban Communities*. Lincoln: University of Nebraska Press, 2009.

Kuokkanen, Rauna. "Gendered Violence and Politics in Indigenous Communities." *International Feminist Journal of Politics* 17, no. 2 (2015): 271–88.

———. "Indigenous Women in Traditional Economies: The Case of Sámi Reindeer Herding. *Signs: Journal of Women in Culture and Society* 34, no. 3 (Spring 2009): 499–504.

———. "Myths and Realities of Sámi Women: A Post-Colonial Feminist Analysis for the Decolonization and Transformation of Sámi Society." In Green, *Making Space for Indigenous Feminism*, 1st ed., 72–92.

———. "Politics of Gendered Violence in Indigenous Communities." In Green, *Making Space for Indigenous Feminism*, 2nd ed., 103–21.

———. "Towards an 'Indigenous Paradigm' from a Sámi Perspective." *Canadian Journal of Native Studies* 20, no. 2 (2000): 411–36.

———. "Violence against Women, Indigenous Self-Determination and Autonomy in Sámi Society." In *L'Image du Sápmi* 2, edited by K. Anderson, 436–52. Örebro University Press, 2013.

Kurbegovic, Erna. "The Famous Five." Eugenics Archive. 13 September 2013. http://eugenicsarchive.ca/discover/connections/5233768a5c2ec500000.

Lang, Sabine. *Men as Women, Women as Men: Changing Gender in Native American Cultures*. Austin: University of Texas Press, 1998.

———. "Various Kinds of People: Gender Variance and Homosexuality in Native American Communities." In *Two-Spirit People: Native American Gender Identity, Sexuality, and Spirituality*, edited by Sue-Ellen Jacobs et al., 100–18. Urbana and Chicago: University of Illinois Press, 1997.

LaRocque, Emma. "Aboriginal Women." In *Aboriginal Justice Implementation Commission*, chap. 13. http://www.ajic.mb.ca/volume1/chapter13.html#0.

———. "The Colonization of a Native Woman Scholar." In *Women of the First Nations: Power, Wisdom, and Strength*, edited by Christine Miller, Patricia Chuchryk, with Marie Smallface Marule, Brenda Manyfingers, and Cheryl Deering, 11–18. Winnipeg: University of Manitoba Press, 1996.

———. "Métis and Feminist: Ethical Reflections on Feminism, Human Rights, and Decolonization." In Green, *Making Space for Indigenous Feminism*, 1st ed., 53–71.

———. "Re-examining Culturally Appropriate Models in Criminal Justice Applications." In *Aboriginal and Treaty Rights in Canada: Essays on Law, Equity and Respect for Difference*, edited by Michael Asch, 75–96. Vancouver: UBC Press, 2007.

Larsen, Dan Robert, and Nils H. Måsø. "Trakassering av kvinner: Dette tar vi internt i organisasjonen." *NRK Sápmi*, 2 June 2015. http://www.nrk.no/sapmi/trakassering-av-kvinner_-_-dette-tar-vi-internt-i-organisasjonen-1.12393786.

Larsson, Carl-Gøran, Mattis Wilhelmsen, Samuel Idivuoma, and Inga Elin Marakatt, "Etter trakasseringsavsløringene – flere kvinner bekjenner at de er sjikanert." *NRK Sápmi*, 3 June 2015. http://www.nrk.no/sapmi/sametingsrepresentant-vurderer-a-anmelde-trusler-1.12392670.

Lawrence, Bonita. *"Real" Indians and Others: Mixed-Blood Urban Native Peoples and Indigenous Nationhood*. Vancouver: UBC Press, 2004.

Lee, Erica Violet. "'Skirting the Issue': A Response and Call to Action." *Moontime Warrior* (blog). 19 June 2015. https://moontimewarrior.com/2015/06/19/skirting-the-issue/.

Leger-Anderson, Ann. *Women's Organizations in Saskatchewan: Report for Culture, Youth, and Recreation*. 31 March 2005. http://www.pcs.gov.sk.ca/Women%27sOrgs.

Lehavot, Keren, Karina L. Walters, and Jane M. Simoni. "Abuse, Mastery, and Health among Lesbian, Bisexual, and Two-spirit American Indian and Alaska Native Women." *Cultural Diversity and Ethnic Minority Psychology* 15, no. 3 (2009): 275–84.

Letmark, Peter. "För mig känns det bra att vara queer." *Dagens nyheter*, 26 July 2012. http://www.dn.se/insidan/for-mig-kanns-det-bra-att-vara-queer/.

Lewis, Oscar. "The Manly Hearted Women among the North Piegan." *American Anthropologist* (1941): 173–87.

Little Thunder, Beverly. *One Bead at a Time: A Memoir*. Toronto: Inanna Memoir Series, 2016.

Lund, Eliv, Marita Melhus, Ketil Lenert Hansen, Tove Nystad, Ann Ragnhild Broderstad, Randi Selmer, and Per G. Lund-Larsen. "Population Based Study of Health and Living Conditions in Areas with Both Sámi and Norwegian Populations—the SÁMINOR Study." *International Journal of Circumpolar Health* 66, no. 2 (2007): 113–28.

Lutz, John. *Makúk: A New History of Aboriginal-White Relations*. Vancouver: UBC Press, 2008.

Lyons, Richard Scott. *X-Marks: Native Signatures of Assent*. Minneapolis: Minnesota University Press, 2010.

MacDonald, Katya. "Making Histories and Narrating Things: Histories of Handmade Objects in Two Indigenous Communities." Doctoral dissertation, University of Saskatchewan, 2017.

Macdougall, Brenda. *One of the Family: Metis Culture in Nineteenth-Century Northwestern Saskatchewan*. Vancouver: UBC Press, 2010.

———. "Wahkootowin as Methodology: How Archival Records Reveal a Métis Kinscape." Presented at the Daniels Conference: In and Beyond the Law, Rupertsland Centre for Métis Research, University of Alberta, 28 January 2017.

Magee, Kathryn. "For Home and Country: Education, Activism, and Agency in Native Homemakers' Clubs, 1942–1970." *Native Studies Review* 18, no. 2 (2009): 27–49.

Maracle, Lee. *I Am Woman: A Native Perspective on Sociology and Feminism*. Vancouver: Press Gang Publishers, 1996.

Martin-Hill, Dawn. "She No Speaks and Other Colonial Constructs of 'the Traditional Woman.'" In *Strong Women Stories: Native Vision and Community Survival*, edited by Kim Anderson and Bonita Lawrence, 106–20. Toronto: Sumach Press, 2003.

Marubbio, M. Elise. *Killing the Indian Maiden: Images of Native American Women in Film*. Lexington: University Press of Kentucky, 2009.

Maskegon-Iskwew, Ahasiw. "Native Love: Subverting the Boundaries of the Heart." *FUSE* 19, no. 4 (Summer 1996): 24–33.

McCallum, Mary Jane Logan. *Indigenous Women, Work, and History, 1940–1980*. Winnipeg: University of Manitoba Press, 2014.

McDowell, Melissa. "This Is Stó:lō Indian Land: The Struggle for Control of Coqualeetza, 1968–1976." Ethnohistory field school report, 2002, Stó:lō Archives, Sardis, British Columbia.

McGuire, Patricia. "Wisaakodewikwe Anishinaabekwe Diabaajimotaw Nipigon Zaaga'igan: Lake Nipigon Ojibway Métis Stories about Women." *Canadian Woman Studies/Les Cahiers de la Femme* 26, no. 3/4 (2008): 217–22.

McHalsie, Albert (Sonny), David M. Schaepe, and Keith Thor Carlson. "Making the World Right." In Carlson, ed., *A Stó:lō-Coast Salish Historical Atlas*, 6–7.

McMahon, Thomas. "Canada's Legal System Hates Indigenous Women." June 2017. Available at SSRN: https://ssrn.com/abstract=2852544.

Medicine, Beatrice, and Patricia Albers. *The Hidden Half: Studies of Plains Indian Women*. Lanham, MD: University Press of America, 1983.

Midnight Sun. "Sex/Gender Systems in Native North America." In *Living the Spirit: A Gay American Indian Anthology*, edited by Will Roscoe, 32–47. New York: St. Martin's Press, 1988.

Millán, Márgara. "The Traveling of 'Gender' and Its Accompanying Baggage: Thoughts on the Translation of Feminism(s), the Globalization of Discourses, and Representational Divides." *European Journal of Women's Studies* 23, no. 1 (2016): 6–27.

Miller, J.R. *Shingwauk's Vision: A History of Native Residential Schools*. Toronto: University of Toronto Press, 1996.

Million, Dian. "Felt Theory." *American Quarterly* 60, no. 2 (2008): 267–72.

Milne, Jennifer. "Cultivating Domesticity—The Homemakers' Clubs of Saskatchewan, 1911 to 1961." Master's thesis, University of Saskatchewan, 2004.

Miranda, Deborah. "Dildos, Hummingbirds, and Driving Her Crazy: Searching for American Indian Women's Love Poetry and Erotics." *Frontiers: A Journal of Women Studies* 23, no. 2 (2002): 135–49.

Mohanty, Chandra Talpade. "Cartographies of Struggle: Third World Women and the Politics of Feminism." In *Third World Women and the Politics of Feminism*, ed. Chandra Mohanty, Ann Russo, and Lourdes Torres, 1–50. Bloomington: Indiana University Press, 1991.

———. "Under Western Eyes: Feminist Scholarship and Colonial Discourses." In *Third World Women and the Politics of Feminism*, edited by Chandra Mohanty, Ann Russo, and Lourdes Torres, 51–80. Bloomington: Indiana University Press, 1991.

Monture, Patricia A. "Ka-Nin-Geh-Heh-Gah-E-Sa-Nonh-Yah-Gah." In *Breaking Anonymity: The Chilly Climate for Women Faculty*, edited by The Chilly Collective, 265–78. Waterloo, ON: Wilfrid Laurier University Press, 1995.

Moraga, Cherríe. "Catching Fire: Preface to the Fourth Edition." In *This Bridge Called My Back: Writings by Radical Women of Color*, 4th ed., edited by Cherríe Moraga and Gloria Anzaldúa. Albany: SUNY Press, 2015.

Moran, Bridget. *Sai'k'uz Ts'eke Stoney Creek Woman: The Story of Mary John*. Vancouver: Arsenal Pulp Press, 1999.

Morgensen, Scott L. "Cutting to the Roots of Colonial Masculinity." In Innes and Anderson, eds., *Indigenous Men and Masculinities*, 38–61.

———. *Spaces between Us: Queer Settler Colonialism and Indigenous Decolonization*. Minneapolis: University of Minnesota Press, 2011.

Mosby, Ian. "Administering Colonial Science: Nutrition Research and Human Biomedical Experimentation in Aboriginal Communities and Residential Schools, 1942–1952." *Histoire Sociale/Social History* 46, no. 1 (2013): 145–72.

Muñoz, José Esteban. "Introduction: Feeling Utopia." In *Cruising Utopia: The Then and There of Queer Futurity*, 1–18. New York: New York University Press, 2009.

Muñoz, José Esteban, Jinthana Haritaworn, Myra Hird, Zakiyyah Iman Jackson, Jasbir K. Puar, Eileen Joy, Uri McMillan, Susan Stryker, Kim TallBear, Jami Weinstein, and Jack Halberstam. "Theorizing Queer Inhumanisms." *GLQ: A Journal of Lesbian and Gay Studies* 21, no. 2 (2005): 209–48.

Myrvoll, M. "'Bare gudsordet duger': Om kontinuitet og brudd i samisk virkelighetsforståelse." PhD thesis, University of Tromsø, 2010.

Napoleon, Val. "Aboriginal Discourse: Gender, Identity, and Community." In *Indigenous Peoples and the Law: Comparative and Critical Perspectives*, edited by Benjamin J. Richardson, Shin Imai, and Kent McNeil, 233–55. Oxford: Hart, 2009.

National Aboriginal Health Organization (NAHO). *Suicide Prevention and Two-Spirited People*. 8 May 2012. http://www.naho.ca/documents/fnc/english/2012_04_%20Guidebook_Suicide_Prevention.pdf.

Nergård, J.I. *Den levende erfaring: en studie i samisk kunnskapstradisjon*. Oslo: Cappelen akademisk, 2006.

———. "Læstadianismen—kristendom i et samisk kulturlandskap." In *Vekkelse og vitenskap: Lars Leve Læstadius 200 års*, edited by Ø. Norderval og S. Nesset, 207–24. Tromsø: UiT. Ravnetrykk, 2000.

Nickel, Sarah. *Assembling Unity: Indigenous Politics, Gender, and the Union of BC Indian Chiefs*. Vancouver: UBC Press, 2019.

———. "'A Genuine Revolution': Transracial Gendered Relationships during International Women's Year, 1975." *Shekon Neechie*, 21 March 2019. https://shekonneechie.ca/2019/03/21/a-genuine-revolution-transracial-gendered-relationships-during-international-womens-year-1975/.

———. "'I Am Not a Women's Libber Although Sometimes I Sound Like One': Indigenous Feminism and Politicized Motherhood." *American Indian Quarterly* 41, no. 4 (Fall 2017): 299–335.

———. "Sewing the Threads of Resilience: Twentieth-Century Indian Homemakers' Clubs in Western Canada." In *From Suffragette to Homesteader: Exploring British and Canadian Colonial Histories and Women's Politics through Memoir*, 157–74. Halifax: Fernwood Publishing, 2018.

———. "'You'll Probably Tell Me That Your Grandmother Was an Indian Princess': Identity, Community, and Politics in the Oral History of the Union of British Columbia Indian Chiefs, 1969–1980." *Oral History Forum* 34 (2014): 1–19.

Nickel, Sarah, and Emily Snyder. "Indigenous Feminisms in Canada." *The Canadian Encyclopedia*, 15 January 2019. https://www.thecanadianencyclopedia.ca/en/article/indigenous-feminisms-in-canada.

Nixon, Lindsay. "Making Space in Indigenous Art for Bull Dykes and Gender Weirdos." *Canadian Art Online*, April 20, 2017. http://canadianart.ca/features/making-space-in-indigenous-art-for-bull-dykes-and-gender-weirdos/.

———. "My Pronouns Are Kiy/Kin." *Red Rising Magazine*, 13 May 2016. http://redrisingmagazine.ca/my-pronouns-are-kiy-kin/.

Norbakken, Ellen. "Når ord mangler: Om seksuelle overgrep i luthersk-læstadianske miljøer." Master's thesis, Diakonhjemmet University College, 2012.

Olsen, Torjer Andreas. "Kall, skaperordning og mak: En analyse av kjønn i lyngenlæstadianismen." PhD thesis, University of Tromsø, 2008.

———. "Læstadianisme og seksualitet—en pietistisk diskurs i endring." In *Kampen om kroppen. Kulturanalytiske blikk på kropp, helse, kjønn og seksualitet*, edited by J. Børtnes, S.E. Kraft og L. Mikaelsson. Kristiansand: HøgskoleForlaget, 125–36. Oslo: Cappelen Damm Høyskoleforlaget, 2004.

———. "This Word Is (Not?) Very Exciting: Considering Intersectionality in Indigenous Studies." *NORA: Nordic Journal of Feminist and Gender Research* 26, no. 3 (2018): 182–96. doi: 10.1080/08038740.2018.1493534.

Olshefsky, Alexandra. "Revisionist History: St Paul des Métis." *McGill Human Rights Interns* (blog). 24 June 2013. http://blogs.mcgill.ca/humanrightsinterns/2013/06/24/revistionist-history-st-paul-des-metis/.

Ouelette, Grace Josephine Mildred Wuttunee. *The Fourth World: An Indigenous Perspective on Feminism and Aboriginal Women's Activism*. Halifax: Fernwood Publishing, 2002.

Palmberg, Mai. "The Nordic Colonial Mind." In *Complying with Colonialism: Gender, Race and Ethnicity in the Nordic Region*, edited by Suvi Keskinen, Salla Tuori, Sari Irni, and Diana Mulinari, 35–50. Farnham, UK: Ashgate, 2009.

Passante, Lisa. "Aboriginal Two-Spirit and LGBTQ Mobility: Meanings of Home, Community and Belonging in a Secondary Analysis of Qualitative Interviews." Master's thesis, University of Manitoba, 2012.

Paul, Alexandra. "Pipe Ceremony Dress Code 'Uncalled For.'" *Winnipeg Free Press*, 17 June 2015. http://www.winnipegfreepress.com/local/Joanne-Boucher308003471.html.

Paxton, Katrina A. "Learning Gender: Female Students at the Sherman Institutue, 1907–1925." In *Boarding School Blues: Revisiting American Indian Educational Experiences*, edited by Clifford E. Trafzer, Jean E. Keller, and Lorene Sisquoc, 174–86. Lincoln: University of Nebraska Press, 2006.

Pennier, Henry. *Call Me Hank: A Stó:lō Man's Reflections on Logging, Living, and Growing Old*. 2nd ed. Toronto: University of Toronto Press, 2006.

Perry, Adele. "The Autocracy of Love and the Legitimacy of Empire: Intimacy, Power and Scandal in Nineteenth-Century Metlakahtlah." *Gender and History* 16, no. 2 (2004): 261–88.

Pesantubbee, Michelene E. *Choctaw Women in a Chaotic World: The Clash of Cultures in the Colonial Southwest*. Albuquerque: University of New Mexico Press, 2005.

Pettipas, Katherine. *Severing the Ties That Bind: Government Repression of Indigenous Religious Ceremonies on the Prairies*. Winnipeg: University of Manitoba Press, 1994.

Point, Gwendolyn Rose. "Intergenerational Experiences in Aboriginal Education: My Family Story." PhD Diss., Simon Fraser University, 2015.

Pulk, Åse, and Maret Inga Smuk. "Har opplevd trusler og ryktespredning som leder i NRL." *NRK Sápmi*, 2 June 2015. http://www.nrk.no/sapmi/har-opplevd-trusler-og-ryktespredning-som-leder-i-nrl-1.12390459.

Quist, Christina. "Etterforsker 31 overgrepssaker i Tysfjord." *VG*, 15 September 2016. http://www.vg.no/nyheter/innenriks/tysfjord-saken/etterforsker-31-overgrepssaker-i-tysfjord/a/23794237/.

Razack, Sherene H. *Looking White People in the Eye: Gender, Race, and Culture in Courtrooms and Classrooms*. Toronto: University of Toronto Press, 2001.

———, ed. *Race, Space, and the Law: Unmapping a White Settler Society*. Toronto: Between the Lines, 2002.

Recollet, Karyn, and Emily Johnson. "Kin-dling and Other Radical Relationalities." *Movement Research* 52/53 (2019): Article 18.

Redbird, Elsie B. "Honouring Native Women: The Backbone of Native Sovereignty." In *Popular Justice and Community Regeneration: Pathways of Indigenous Reform*, edited by Kayleen M. Hazlehurst, 121–42. Westport, CT: Praeger, 1995.

Rickard, Jolene. "Considering Traditional Practices of 'Seeing' as Future." Presentation at the Initiative for 1st Annual Symposium for the Future Imaginary, Toronto, Ontario, 16 October 2015.

Rifkin, Mark. *The Erotics of Sovereignty: Queer Native Writing in the Era of Self-Determination*. Minneapolis: University of Minnesota Press, 2012.

Ristock, Janice. "Aboriginal Two-Spirit and LGBTQ Migration, Mobility, and Health Research Project." Winnipeg Final Report. 2010. http://www.2spirits.com/PDFolder/MMHReport.pdf.

Roscoe, Will. *Changing Ones: Third and Fourth Genders in Native North America*. New York: St. Martin's Griffin, 1998.

———. *The Zuni Man-Woman*. Albuquerque: University of New Mexico Press, 1992.

Ross, Luana. "From the 'F' Word to Indigenous/Feminisms." *Wicazo Sa Review* 24, no. 2 (Fall 2009): 39–52.

Royal Commission on Aboriginal Peoples (RCAP). *Final Report*. 1996. https://www.bac-lac.gc.ca/eng/discover/aboriginal-heritage/royal-commission-aboriginal-peoples/Pages/final-report.aspx.

Sangster, Joan. "Criminalizing the Colonized: Ontario Native Women Confront the Criminal Justice System 1920–1960." *Canadian Historical Review* 80, no. 1 (March 1999): 32–60.

"The Saskatchewan Indian Women's Association." *Saskatchewan Indian* 3, no. 1 (January 1972): 9.

Silko, Leslie Marmon. *Almanac of the Dead*. New York: Simon and Schuster, 1991.

———. *Laguna Women: Poems*. Greenfield Center, NY: Greenfield Review Press, 1974.

———. *Storyteller*. New York: Seaver Books, 1981.

Simoni, Jane M., K.L. Walters, Kimberly F. Balsam, and Seth B. Meyers, "Victimization Substance Use, and HIV Risk Behaviors Among Gay/Bisexual/Two-Spirit and Heterosexual American Indian Men in New York City." *American Journal of Public Health* 96, no. 12 (2006): 2240–45.

Simpson, Audra. "Consent's Revenge." *Cultural Anthropology* 31, no. 3 (2016): 326–33. https://doi.org/10.14506/ca31.3.02.

———. "From White into Red: Captivity Narratives as Alchemies of Race and Citizenship." *American Quarterly* 60, no. 2 (2008): 251–57.

———. "Making Native Love." Catalogue text, *Native Love* exhibition. Nation to Nation arts collective, 1995. http://cyberpowwow.net/nation2nation/love.htm.

———. *Mohawk Interruptus: Political Life across the Borders of Settler States*. Durham, NC: Duke University Press, 2014.

Simpson, Audra, and Andrea Smith. Introduction to *Theorizing Native Studies*, edited by Audra Simpson and Andrea Smith, 1–30. Durham, NC: Duke University Press, 2014.

Simpson, Leanne. *As We Have Always Done*. Minneapolis: University of Minnesota, 2017.

———. *Dancing on Our Turtle's Back: Stories of Nishnaabeg Re-Creation, Resurgence, and a New Emergence*. Winnipeg: ARP Books, 2012.

———. *Islands of Decolonial Love*. Winnipeg: ARP Books, 2013.

———, ed. *Lighting the Eighth Fire: The Liberation, Resurgence, and Protection of Indigenous Nations*. Winnipeg: Arbeiter Ring Publishing, 2008.

Smith, Andrea. *Conquest: Sexual Violence and the American Indian Genocide.* Cambridge, MA: South End Press, 2005.

———. "Heteropatriarchy and the Three Pillars of White Supremacy: Rethinking Women of Color Organizing." In *Color of Violence: the Incite! Anthology*, edited by Beth Ritchie, Julia Sudbury and Janelle White, 70–76. Cambridge, MA: South End Press, 2006).

———. "Native American Feminism, Sovereignty, and Social Change." *Feminist Studies* 31, no. 1 (2005): 116–32.

Smith, Andrea, and J. Kēhaulani Kauanui, eds. "Forum: Native Feminisms without Apology." *American Quarterly* 60, no. 2 (June 2008).

———. "Native Feminisms Engage American Studies." *American Quarterly* 60, 2 (2008): 241–49.

Smith, Linda Tuhiwai. *Decolonizing Methodologies: Research and Indigenous Peoples.* New York: Zed Books, 1999.

———. *Decolonizing Methodologies: Research and Indigenous Peoples* 2nd ed. London: Zed Books, 2012.

Snyder, Emily. "Indigenous Feminist Legal Theory." *Canadian Journal of Women and the Law* no. 26 (2014): 365–401.

Snyder, Emily, Val Napoleon, and John Borrows. "Gender and Violence: Drawing on Indigenous Legal Resources." *University of British Columbia Law Review* 48, no. 2 (2015): 593–654.

Solem, Erik. *Lappiske rettstudier.* Oslo: Universitetsforlaget, 1970.

Spears, Jim. "Troops Were 'Away' When Invaders Came." *Province*, 19 March 1976.

Spivak, Gayatri Chakravorty. *Other Worlds: Essays in Cultural Politics.* New York and London: Routledge, 1987.

Stanbrook, Barb. "Indians Frustrated by Negotiations for Coqualeetza Complex." *Chilliwack Progress*, 14 January 1976.

Stanbrook, Barb, and Mike Doyle. "Seventeen Natives Charged in Coqualeetza Clash." *Chilliwack Progress*, 5 May 1976.

St. Denis, Verna. "Feminism Is for Everybody: Aboriginal Women, Feminism, and Diversity." In Green, *Making Space for Indigenous Feminism*, 1st ed., 33–52.

Stone, Merlin. *When God Was a Woman.* New York: Marboro Books, 1990.

Stote, Karen. *An Act of Genocide: Colonialism and the Sterilization of Aboriginal Women.* Black Point, NS: Fernwood Publishing, 2015.

———. "The Coercive Sterilization of Aboriginal Women in Canada." *American Indian Culture and Research Journal* 36, no. 3 (2012): 117–50.

Sunseri, Lina. "Moving beyond the Feminism versus Nationalism Dichotomy: An Anti-Colonial Feminist Perspective on Indigenous Liberation Struggles." *Canadian Woman Studies/Les Cahiers de la Femme* 20, no. 2 (2000): 143–48.

Suttles, Wayne. "Private Knowledge, Morality, and Social Classes among the Coast Salish." In *Coast Salish Essays*, 3–14. Vancouver, Seattle, and London: Talonbooks and University of Washington Press, 1987.

Suzack, Cheryl. "Emotion before the Law." In Suzack, Huhndorf, Perreault, and Barman, eds., *Indigenous Women and Feminism*, 126–51.

———. "Transitional Justice, Termination Policies, and the Politics of Literary Affect in Chrystos' *Not Vanishing*." *Canadian Review of American Studies* 47, no. 1 (2017): 1–25.

Suzack, Cheryl, Shari H. Huhndorf, Jeanne Perreault, and Jean Barman, eds. *Indigenous Women and Feminism: Politics, Activism, Culture*. Vancouver: UBC Press, 2010.

TallBear, Kim. "Standing with and Speaking as Faith: A Feminist-Indigenous Approach to Inquiry." In Andersen and O'Brien, *Sources and Methods in Indigenous Studies*, 78–85.

TallBear, Kim, Kim Anderson, and Audra Simpson. "Indigenous Feminism Power Panel." Station 20 West, Saskatoon, SK, 15 March 2016. https://www.youtube.com/watch?v=-HnEvaVXoto.

Task Force Report on Museums and First Peoples. *Turning the Page: Forging New Partnerships Between Museums and First Peoples*. 3rd ed. Assembly of First Nations and Canadian Museums Association. Ottawa, 1994, https://museums.in1touch.org/uploaded/web/docs/Task_Force_Report_1994.pdf.

Taylor, Drew Hayden. "The Shame of Skirt Shaming." *Windspeaker* 34, no. 6 (2016). https://ammsa.com/publications/windspeaker/shame-skirt-shaming-column.

Teengs, Doris O'Brien, and Robb Travers. "'River of Life, Rapids of Change': Understanding HIV Vulnerability among Two-Spirit Youth Who Migrate to Toronto." *Canadian Journal of Aboriginal Community-Based HIV/AIDS Research* 1 (2006): 17–28.

Thomas, Wesley. "Navajo Cultural Constructions of Gender and Sexuality." In *Two-Spirit People: Native American Gender Identity, Sexuality, and Spirituality*, edited by Sue-Ellen Jacobs, Wesley Thomas, and Sabine Lang, 156–73. Urbana and Chicago: University of Illinois Press, 1997.

Tinker, George E. *Missionary Conquest: The Gospel and Native American Cultural Genocide*. Minneapolis: Fortress Press, 1993.

Torpy, Sally J. "Native American Women and Coerced Sterilizations: On the Trail of Tears in the 1970s." *American Indian Cultures and Research Journal* 24, no. 2 (2000): 1–22.

"Transcript: Donald Trump's Taped Comments About Women." *New York Times* online, 8 October 2016. https://www.nytimes.com/2016/10/08/us/donald-trump-tape-transcript.html.

Trinidad, A.M. " Toward Kuleana (Responsibility): A Case Study of a Contextually Grounded Intervention for Native Hawaiian Youth and Young Adults." *Aggression and Violent Behavior* 14, no. 6 (2009): 488–98.

Truth and Reconciliation Commission of Canada (TRC). *Calls to Action*. 2015. http://www.trc.ca/assets/pdf/Calls_to_Action_English2.pdf.

Tsosie, Rebecca. "Native Women and Leadership: An Ethics of Culture and Relationship." In Suzack, Huhndorf, Perrealut, and Barman, eds., *Indigenous Women and Feminism*, 29–42.

Tuck, Eve., and K. Wayne Yang. "Decolonization Is Not a Metaphor." *Decolonization: Indigeneity, Education and Society* 1, no. 1 (2012): 1–40.

T'xwelátse, Stone, et al. *Man Turned to Stone: T'xwelátse*. Chilliwack, BC: Stó:lō Nation, 2012.

United Nations General Assembly. Declaration on the Rights of Indigenous Peoples (UNDRIP). Resolution Adopted by the General Assembly, September 2007. United Nations, 2008. http://www.un.org/esa/socdev/unpfii/documents/DRIPS_en.pdf.

Verran, Helen. "A Postcolonial Moment in Science Studies: Alternative Firing Regimes of Environmental Scientists and Aboriginal Landowners." *Social Studies of Science* 32, no. 5/6 (2002): 729–62.

Victor, Qwí:qwélstom/Wenona. "'Searching for the Bone Needle': The Sto:lo Nation's Continuing Quest for Justice." MA Thesis, Simon Fraser University, 2001.

———. "X̲ex̲á:ls and the Power of Transformation: The Stó:lō, Good Governance and Self-Determination." PhD Diss., Simon Fraser University, 2012.

Vowel, Chelsea. "Language, Culture, and Two-Spirit Identity." *Âpihtawikosisân*, 29 March 2012. http://apihtawikosisan.com/2012/03/language-culture-and-two-spirit-identity/.

Walters, Karina L., Ramona Beltrán, T. Evans-Campbell, and J. M. Simoni. "Keeping Our Hearts from Touching the Ground: HIV/AIDS in American Indian and Alaska Native Women." *Women's Health Issues* 21, no. 6 (2011): 261–65.

Walters, Karina L., Teresa Evans-Campbell, Jane M. Simoni, Theresa Ronquillo, and Rupaleem Bhuyan. "'My Spirit in My Heart': Identity Experiences and Challenges among American Indian Two-Spirit Women." *Journal of Lesbian Studies* 10, no. 1/2 (2006): 125–49.

Walters, Karina L., Pamela F. Horwath, and Jane M. Simoni. "Sexual Orientation Bias Experiences and Service Needs of Gay, Lesbian, Bisexual, Transgendered, and Two-Spirited American Indians." *Journal of Gay and Lesbian Social Services* 13, no. 1/2 (2001): 133–49.

Walters, Karina L., and J.M. Simoni. "Reconceptualizing Native Women's Health: An 'Indigenist' Stress-Coping Model." *American Journal of Public Health* 92, no. 4 (2002): 520–24.

Wells, Oliver. *Salish Weaving: Primitive and Modern, as Practised by the Salish Indians of South West British Columbia*. Sardis, BC, 1969.

Wesley, Saylesh. "Twin-Spirited Women: Sts'iyóye Smestíyexw Slhá:li." *Transgender Studies Quarterly* 1, no. 3 (August 2014): 338–51.

Whitbeck, L.B., D.R. Hoyt, J.D. Stubben, and T. LaFamboise. "Traditional Culture and Academic Success Among American Indian Children in the Upper Midwest." *Journal of American Indian Education* 40, no. 2 (2001): 48–60.

Wilson, Alex. "N'tacimowin inna nah': Our Coming In Stories." *Canadian Woman Studies/Les Cahiers de la Femme* 26, no. 3/4 (2008): 193–99.

———. "Two-Spirit People, Body Sovereignty, and Gender Self-Determination." *Red Rising Magazine*, 21 September 2015. http://redrisingmagazine.ca/two-spirit-people-body-sovereignty-and-gender-self-determination/.

Wilson, Shawn. *Research Is Ceremony: Indigenous Research Methods*. Black Point, NS: Fernwood Publishing, 2008.

Woods, Jody R. "Coqualeetza: Legacies of Land Use." In Carlson, ed., *A Stó:lō-Coast Salish Historical Atlas*, 74–75.

Wunker, Erin. *Notes from a Feminist Killjoy: Essays on Everyday Life*. Toronto: BookThug, 2016.

Yep, Gust A. "The Violence of Heteronormativity in Communication Studies: Notes on Injury, Healing, and Queer World-Making." *Journal of Homosexuality* 45, no. 2/3/4 (2003): 11–59.

Zimmerman, M., J. Ramirez, K. Wahienko, B. Walter, and S. Dyer. "The Enculturation Hypothesis: Exploring Direct and Protective Effects Among Native American Youth." In *Resiliency in Ethnic Minority Families*, Vol. 1, *Native and Immigrant American Families*, edited by H. McCubbin, E. Thompson, and A. Thompson, 199–220. Madison: University of Wisconsin, 1994.

Contributors

Antonia R.G. Alvarez, LMSW, PhD, is a queer mestiza Pinay-American scholar and mother and assistant professor at Portland State University School of Social Work. Antonia is committed to liberatory research and community-engaged practice with LGBTQI/Two-Spirit/Mahu communities of colour. Using arts and culture-based interventions, her work emphasizes healing and protection from suicidality. Antonia received her MSW from the University of Michigan School of Social Work and is a licensed social worker in Hawai'i.

Joi T. Arcand is a photo-based artist from Muskeg Lake Cree Nation and based in Ottawa, Ontario. She received her Bachelor of Fine Arts degree from the University of Saskatchewan in 2005. Arcand was a co-founder and editor of *kimiwan* zine, a quarterly Indigenous arts publication showcasing Indigenous art and literature from across North America. Her work has been exhibited at Gallery 101 in Ottawa, York Quay Gallery in Toronto, PAVED Arts in Saskatoon, grunt gallery in Vancouver, and published in *BlackFlash Magazine*.

Ramona Beltrán (Yaqui/Mexica), MSW, PhD, is a Xicana of Yaqui and Mexica descent and a dancer/activist/scholar. As an associate professor at the University of Denver Graduate School of Social Work, her scholarship is committed to interrupting legacies of historical trauma that affect Indigenous and Latinx communities. She focuses on disrupting the problem-focused approach to understanding Indigenous/Latinx health that dominates main-stream research. She does this through centring culture, resistance, healing, storytelling, and arts-based research methods in knowledge production with and for Indigenous/Latinx communities.

Astri Dankertsen (Sámi/Norwegian), PhD, is an associate professor in sociology at the Faculty for Social Sciences at Nord University, where she is a member of the research group for environmental studies, international relations, northern studies, and social security. Dankertsen is also the leader of ELSA, Nord University's network for ethnicity, gender equality, and equity, named after the Sámi activist and politician Elsa Laula Renberg. She has worked with issues such as Sámi urbanization, Sámi melancholia, Sámi identities, decolonization, Sámi youth organizations, Sámi feminism, Indigenous perspectives, and gender equality in academia. She is a deputy member of the board of the Norwegian Sámi Association, and is also board member of Sálto sámesiebrre/Salten Sámi organization. She is also an active politician and is city council member in Bodø, Norway.

Amanda Fehr is a white settler scholar from Saskatoon, Saskatchewan, Treaty 6 Territory and the Homeland of the Métis. Her scholarship has focused on community-engaged oral history work with Indigenous and Immigrant / Refugee communities. She holds a PhD in history from the University of Saskatchewan and currently works as a Public Engagement Consultant for the City of Saskatoon.

Chantal Fiola is Michif (Red River Métis), with family from St. Laurent and Ste. Geneviève, Manitoba. She is the author of *Rekindling the Sacred Fire: Métis Ancestry and Anishinaabe Spirituality*, which won the John Hirsch Award for Most Promising Manitoba Writer and the Beatrice Mosionier Aboriginal Writer of the Year Award. Dr. Fiola is an assistant professor in the Urban and Inner-City Studies Department at the University of Winnipeg. She is undertaking a study funded by the Social Sciences and Humanities Research Council (SSHRC) exploring Métis relationships with ceremony in Manitoba Métis communities, and developing a Métis-specific research design and methodology. Chantal is Two-Spirit, Midewiwin, a Sundancer, and lives in Winnipeg with her wife Nicki.

Louise Bernice Halfe – Sky Dancer was raised on Saddle Lake Reserve and attended Blue Quills Residential School. Louise is married and has two adult children and three grandsons. She graduated with a Bachelor of Social

Work from the University of Regina. She also completed two years of Nechi Training in St. Albert's Nechi Institute where she also facilitated the program. She served as Saskatchewan's Poet Laureate for two years and has travelled extensively. She has served as keynote speaker at numerous conferences. Her books, *Bear Bones and Feathers, Blue Marrow, The Crooked Good*, and *Burning In This Midnight Dream* published by Coteau Publishers have all received numerous accolades and awards. Louise was awarded honorary degrees from Wilfrid Laurier University and the University of Saskatchewan.

Aubrey Jean Hanson is a mama, a queer woman, a bookworm, an educator, and partner, sister, daughter, and cousin in a prairie family with widespread Métis and European roots. She grew up in Calgary and is a member of the Métis Nation of Alberta. She holds degrees from the University of Victoria (BA Hons in English), from the Ontario Institute for Studies in Education of the University of Toronto (BEd, MEd in sociology and equity studies, and women's and gender studies), and the University of Calgary (PhD in education). Pursuing questions that bring Indigenous literary arts and notions of gender into conversation with curriculum studies, Aubrey's research spans both education and literature. Having joined the Werklund School of Education at the University of Calgary in 2015 as an assistant professor, Aubrey teaches in the areas of Indigenous and social justice education.

Tasha Hubbard is a filmmaker and an associate professor at the Faculty of Native Studies at the University of Alberta. Her documentaries have won awards across Canada, including a Gemini and a Director's Guild of Canada award. As part of her academic career, Tasha researches the ongoing return of the buffalo to the land and Indigenous peoples' media.

Madeline Rose Knickerbocker is a white settler of English, Irish, Scottish, German, and Dutch heritage, and she is part of the third generation of her family to live on the traditional, unceded territories of the Musqueam, Squamish, and Tsleil-Waututh nations. Her research uses community-engaged archival and oral history methods to study Indigenous sovereignty, cultural heritage, gender, and settler colonialism in British Columbia. She holds a PhD in history from Simon Fraser University, where she is currently a lecturer in First Nations Studies.

Darian Lonechild comes from the White Bear First Nation in Treaty 4 territory. She has worked internationally as a model, with experience in acting as well. Darian is working toward a bachelor's degree in Indigenous studies and political science at the University of Saskatchewan. Darian is passionate about advocating for treaty rights and encouraging Indigenous youth to reclaim their nationhood. Darian plans on entering into law and pursuing politics.

Anina Major is a visual artist from The Bahamas whose work investigates the relationships between self and place in efforts to cultivate a sense of belonging. Major studied at the College of The Bahamas before earning her BS in Graphic Design from Drexel University and her MFA from the Rhode Island School of Design. She is the recipient of numerous awards and residencies, including the St. Botolph Club Foundation Emerging Artist Award for sculpture, MassMoCA Studio Artist Program and Provincetown Fine Arts Work Center Fellowship. Her work has been exhibited in The Bahamas, across the United States, and Europe.

Elaine McArthur is an award-winning poet from Ocean Man First Nation in South East Saskatchewan. She has a degree in Indigenous Education from First Nations University of Canada.

Sarah Nickel is a Tk'emlúpsemc (Kamloops Secwépemc), Ukrainian, and French Canadian assistant professor of Indigenous Studies at the University of Saskatchewan. She received her PhD in history from Simon Fraser University in 2015, and brings her historical training to the field of Indigenous studies. Her work focuses on the multiple ways in which Indigenous peoples are political, remaining especially attuned to how gender operates in these settings. Her research has appeared in several journals including *American Indian Quarterly, BC Studies,* and the *Canadian Historical Review,* and her first book, *Assembling Unity: Pan-Indigenous Politics, Gender, and the Union of BC Indian Chiefs,* was released by UBC Press in 2019. Her next project explores Indigenous women's political work in the twentieth-century west.

Lindsay Nixon is a Cree-Métis-Saulteaux curator, editor, writer, SSHRC doctoral scholarship recipient and McGill art history PhD student. Nixon won the prestigious 2019 Dayne Ogilive Prize and has been nominated for a Lambda Literary Award, an Indigenous Voices Literary Award, and several National Magazine Awards. They currently hold the position of

Editor-at-Large for Canadian Art and previously edited *mâmawi-âcimowak*, an independent Indigenous art, art criticism, and literature journal. Their writing has appeared in *Malahat Review*, *Room*, *GUTS*, *Mice*, *esse*, *The Inuit Art Quarterly*, *Teen Vogue*, and other publications. Nixon's first book, *nîtisânak*, is out now through Metonymy Press. Born and raised in the prairies, they currently live in Tio'tia:ke/Mooniyaang—unceded Haudenosaunee and Anishinabe territories (Montreal, QC).

Miriam Madrid Puga is a two-spirit Indigenous queer facilitator and organizer in violence prevention in LGBTQ youth communities in Denver, Colorado.

Kai Pyle is a Two-Spirit Métis and Sault Ste. Marie Nishnaabe writer originally from Green Bay, Wisconsin. Currently a PhD candidate in American Studies at the University of Minnesota – Twin Cities, they are working on a history of Two-Spirit Anishinaabe kinship and memory-making practices. In addition, they are active in numerous Ojibwe and Michif language revitalization efforts in the western Great Lakes and northern plains.

Zoey Roy is an activist, spoken word poet, hip-hop artist, and social entrepreneur. With roots in the Black Lake Denesuline Nation and Cormorant Lake, Manitoba, Zoey grew up in rural, remote, and urban regions all over Canada. Her greatest passion is building social infrastructure with youth in community, and she believes the arts are an inclusive way to make that happen. Zoey has completed a Bachelor of Education degree through the SUNTEP program at the University of Saskatchewan.

Marie Sanderson is a Woodland Cree from Lac La Ronge, Saskatchewan, who currently studies nursing in Saskatoon. She has a Bachelor of Arts degree in psychology from the University of Regina and plans on returning home to work in the healthcare field. Marie hopes the experiences she shares shed some light on what it is like to be an Indigenous woman living in an urban setting.

waaseyaa'sin christine sy is Ojibway bear clan and Scottish-Irish-Canadian from bawating Sault Ste. Marie, Ontario, area and obiishkikaang Lac Seul First Nation. She is a poet and big fan of the natural, supernatural, and spiritual world. She and her girl live in Lekwungen and WSÁNEĆ territories where she is assistant professor in Gender Studies at the University of Victoria.

Aja Sy a doting human to her cat, loves physics and math, and plays volleyball competitively. Hitting the road with the windows down and the music up is one of her favorite things to do.

Zoe Todd (Métis/otipemisiw) is from Amiskwaciwâskahikan (Edmonton), Alberta, Canada. She is an associate professor in the Department of Sociology and Anthropology at Carleton University. She writes about fish, art, Métis legal traditions, the Anthropocene, extinction, and decolonization in urban and prairie contexts. She also studies human-animal relations, colonialism and environmental change in north/western Canada.